SOURCE BOOK IN
ANCIENT PHILOSOPHY

SOURCE BOOK IN
ANCIENT PHILOSOPHY

BY

CHARLES M. BAKEWELL

REVISED EDITION

GORDIAN PRESS
NEW YORK
1973

PREFACE TO THE REVISED EDITION

Besides corrections of errors, and a few minor additions to the text, the most important changes in this edition are the substitution of the translation by R. D. Hicks for that by Yonge of the passages quoted from Diogenes Laertius in Chapters XI, XVII and XVIII, and the inclusion of a chapter on the Sceptics. In this chapter I have attempted to bring together enough of the more important references to give a fair picture, (1) of the thoroughgoing scepticism of the Early Pyrrhonists, which was developed primarily from the ethical motive, as a preparation for the life of imperturbability (and have included here The Ten Tropes of Pyrrhonism as later classified by Ænesidemus); (2) of the positive contribution made by Carneades in his theory of knowledge constructed on the background of scepticism, his "probabilism," which strikingly anticipates the standpoint of modern science; and (3) of the searching criticism of the concept of cause made by Ænesidemus, the Hume of the ancient world.

The arguments of the Later Pyrrhonists, as well as those of the Sceptics in the Academy, were directed mainly against the Stoics, and I have included a section in which I have brought together a number of passages, taken from the work of Sextus Empiricus, which give the substance of their criticisms of the Stoic theory of demonstration and proof, not only for their intrinsic interest, as illustrating the dialectic of Later Pyrrhonism, but also for the light they throw on the Stoic theory of knowledge.

All of the quotations which are not taken from Diogenes are from Sextus Empiricus, the last of the great Sceptics of antiquity, and the painstaking historian of the whole movement, and the translation is by Rev. R. G. Bury.

The quotations from Diogenes Laertius and Sextus Empiricus are made from volumes in the Loeb Classical Library by the kind permission of the President and Fellows of Harvard College, the proprietors of the Library.

C.M.B.

PREFACE

EVERY one who has attempted to introduce students
to the study of Philosophy by way of its history must
have felt the need of having in compact form the most
significant documents upon which the interpretations
of that history are based, in order that it may be possible
from the first to bring the student into direct contact
with the sources, so far at least as that may be done
through the medium of translations. The primary aim
of this book is to supply this need. It is intended to
serve either as a companion volume to any History of
Philosophy that may be adopted as a text-book, or as a
substitute for such a history where the instructor may
prefer through his own lectures to give his own interpretation of this philosophical movement. It is hoped
that the book may also, as a reference work, prove of
value to students of philosophy generally, as well as
to all who are interested in the development of ancient
thought.

No attempt has been made to make an exhaustive
Source Book. I have simply brought together the more
significant passages from the earlier philosophers, beginning with Thales and reaching as far as Plotinus. The
book includes most of the fragments of the earliest
philosophers, together with the passages from the secondary sources which are most important in throwing light
upon these fragments. In the case of the other philosophers it includes a number of brief extracts which may

serve as texts to hang discussions on, and also some more
extended passages selected with the view of bringing one
directly into the spirit and method of the several philosophers represented. More space has been given to
Plotinus than his relative importance would warrant.
This, however, needs no apology. Plotinus is perhaps
more frequently misrepresented in historical discussions
than any other Greek philosopher. Here especially is
it necessary to let the philosopher speak for himself.
And, besides, Plotinus's works are comparatively inaccessible to English readers, whereas the extracts from
Plato and Aristotle, from Lucretius and the later Stoics
can be supplemented at will.

While most of these sources are already accessible in
translation they are scattered through so many volumes,
and are mixed with so much material that is chiefly of
value to the advanced student whose historical interests
have become highly specialized, as to be practically
unavailable for use in connection with introductory
courses.

My obligations to others are so numerous that it would
be impossible to mention them all. In making the
translations I have in each case had before me all of the
translations already in the field, whether in English,
German, French, or Latin, upon which I could lay my
hands; and I have borrowed freely from most of them.
In especial, however, I should like to acknowledge my
indebtedness to Professors Diels, Burnet, and Fairbanks;
and in the selection of passages I have taken many
suggestions from the works of Ritter and Preller,
Wallace, Jackson, and Adam.

I wish also to express my gratitude to Prof. G. H.
Palmer for many valuable suggestions, and for the con-

tribution of his translation of the Hymn of Cleanthes; and to Dr. B. A. G. Fuller for the selection and translation of the passages from Plotinus, and the passages from Plutarch in criticism of the Stoic theodicy.

My thanks are also due to Mr. T. W. Higginson for permission to quote from his translation of Epictetus, to Dr. W. T. Harris for permission to reprint from *The Journal of Speculative Philosophy* the translation of the fragments of Parmenides, made by the late Thomas Davidson, and to the Cambridge University Press, the Oxford University Press, Messrs. George Bell & Sons, The Macmillan Company, and Little, Brown & Company, for permission to use translations published by them. Special acknowledgments of borrowed translations are made in foot-notes. The only case where confusion is likely to arise is in the extracts from Plato. I assume responsibility myself for the translation of the Apology; the selections from the Republic are from the translation of Davies and Vaughan, and all the remaining Plato selections are from the latest edition of Jowett's work.

CONTENTS

PAGE

I.—THE MILESIAN SCHOOL 1
   Thales: General standpoint of the early philosophers, and
   the opinions of Thales, 1. *Anaximander:* The "boundless" as first principle, 3. Scientific speculations, 5.
   Anaximenes: His opinions, 7.

II.—THE ELEATIC SCHOOL 8
   Xenophanes: The fragments, 8. An illustration of Xenophanes's scientific reasoning, 10. *Parmenides:* The fragments of his poem "On Nature," 11. Plato and Aristotle
   on Eleatic philosophy, 20. *Zeno:* The puzzles of composition and division, 22. Space not a real thing, 23. The
   puzzles of motion, 24. The purpose of Zeno's arguments
   as reported by Plato, 25.

III.—HERACLITUS 28
   The fragments, 28.

IV.—THE PYTHAGOREAN PHILOSOPHY 36
   The number philosophy of the Pythagoreans, 36. The
   Pythagorean "Golden Words," 40.

V.—EMPEDOCLES 43
   The fragments, 43. Secondary sources, 46.

VI.—ANAXAGORAS 49
   The fragments, 49. Secondary sources, 53. Some of
   Aristotle's comments on Anaxagoras, 55.

VII.—THE ATOMISTS 57
   Leucippus, 57. Leucippus and Democritus, 58. *Democ-
   ritus:* The fragments, 59. The "Golden Sayings" of
   Democritus, 60. The atomists on the soul according to
   Aristotle, 65.

xi

PAGE

VIII.—The Sophists 67

Two sayings of *Protagoras*, 67. A saying of *Gorgias*, 67. An account of the calling and profession of the Sophist from the writings of Plato, 68. Aristotle on the Sophists, 69. The Sophists and the Athenian youth, 69. The Protagorean doctrine of relativity as Plato interprets it in the *Theœtetus*, 78. Gorgias as a rhetorician, 85.

IX.—Socrates 86

Aristotle on Socrates's achievement, 86. Xenophon's tribute to Socrates, 86. The sort of questions Socrates was concerned with, 90. Socrates on the Good and the Beautiful, 91. Socrates's method, 95. A bit of his biography, as reported by Plato, 96. An illustration of his method of showing up ignorance, 101.

X.—Socrates's Defence of Himself as Reported by Plato in the *APOLOGY* 104

XI.—The Lesser Socratics 142

The Cyrenaics. *Aristippus*, 142. The Cynics. *Antisthenes* and *Diogenes*, 145.

XII.—Plato 148

Plato's relation to his predecessors according to Aristotle, 148. From the *Phœdrus:* Dialectic *vs.* rhetoric, 149. From the *Symposium:* On love, 152. From the *Philebus:* Pleasure and the other goods, 157. From the *Timœus:* The creation of the world, 160. Why it is necessary to assume the existence of the Ideas, 167. From the *Parmenides:* Puzzles presented by the theory of ideas, 168.

XIII.—Plato—*Continued* 180

From the *Republic:* The nature of virtue, 180. The four cardinal virtues, 182. The higher education leading up to the Idea of the Good, 186. The Idea of the Good as the source of truth and of reality, 192. Reality and appearance; knowledge and opinion, 199. The allegory of the den; shadows and realities, 203. Dialectic the coping stone of the sciences, 213.

PAGE

XIV.—ARISTOTLE 217

Origin and nature of philosophy, 217. Aristotle's criticism of the theory of ideas, 220. Aristotle's own view regarding the universal, 223. The four causes, 225. Aristotle's conception of God: Necessity of assuming a first cause or prime mover, 227. Divine reason as the prime mover, 230. Divine reason and its object, 233.

XV.—ARISTOTLE ON PSYCHOLOGY 236

The nature of the soul, 236. The animate and the inanimate, 240. Nourishment the fundamental function, touch the fundamental sense, 242. Sense-perception, 243. Cognition, 244. Creative reason, 246. Reason and judgment, 247. Reason and its object, 248. The springs of action, 249.

XVI.—ARISTOTLE ON ETHICS 251

The summum bonum, 251. To find it we ask what is man's function, 253. How virtue is acquired, 257. Virtue and vice alike voluntary, 259. On friendship, 261. Highest happiness found in the vision of truth, 264. How the end is to be realized, 266.

XVII.—THE STOICS 269

The parts of philosophy and the criterion of truth, 269. Ethics: Following nature, 272. The Hymn of Cleanthes, 277. Plutarch's refutation of the Stoic theodicy, 278.

XVIII.—EPICURUS 290

Theory of knowledge, 290. Physical speculations, 292. The practical philosophy of Epicurus, 296. Some maxims of Epicurus, 302.

XIX.—LUCRETIUS 305

The wages of philosophy, 305. The course of the atoms, 307. The unconcerned gods, 309. The nature of mind and soul, 309. Dispelling the dread of death, 313. No designer of nature, 316.

PAGE

XX.—EPICTETUS 317
Things which are in our power, 317. The essence of good, 320. As Socrates would have done, 322. In harmony with God and His universe, 324.

XXI.—MARCUS AURELIUS 326
Follow nature, 326. The harmony of the universe, 331. Man's insignificance and his grandeur, 336.

XXII.—THE SCEPTICS 340
Pyrrho and the Pyrrhonists, 340. The ten modes of doubt, 343. The five modes of doubt according to Agrippa, 347. Pyrrhonism in Practice, 348. Scepticism in the Academy, 351. Later Pyrrhonism, 358. Ænesidemus—on cause, 364.

XXIII.—PLOTINUS 370
The Soul, 370. The intellect, 383. The One, 393. The process of emanation, 401.

XXIV.—PLOTINUS—*Continued* 405
Matter, 405. Sin and salvation, 414.

THE MILESIAN SCHOOL

I

THE MILESIAN SCHOOL

THALES

[Flourished 585 B.C.]

MOST[1] of the early philosophers were content to seek
a material first principle as the cause of all things. For
that of which all things consist, from which they arise,
into which they pass away, the substance remaining
the same through all its changing states—that, I say,
is what they mean by the element, or the first principle,
of the things that are. And this is why they hold that,
strictly speaking, nothing comes into being or perishes,
since the primal nature remains ever the same. For
instance, when Socrates becomes handsome or cultured
we do not just say he comes into being; nor, when he
loses these characteristics, do we say that Socrates is
no more. Socrates, the subject, remains the same
throughout these changes. And it is the same with all
things. There must be some natural body (φύσις),
one or many, from which all things arise, but which
itself remains the same.

But of what sort this first principle is, and how many
such there are, this is a point upon which they are not
agreed. Thales, the originator of this kind of philosophy,

[1] Aristotle, *Met.* I. 3, 983 b 6 (R. P. 9 A).

1

declares it to be water. (And this is why he said that the earth floats on water.) Possibly he was led to this opinion by observing that the nourishment of all things is moist, and that heat itself is generated and kept alive by moisture. And that from which all things are generated is just what we mean by their first principle. This may be where he got his idea, and also from observing that the germs of all things are moist, and that moist things have water as the first principle of their nature.

Some indeed hold that those who lived ages ago, long before the present generation, and who were the first to reason about the gods, held a similar view about nature, since they sang of Oceanus and Tethys as the parents of creation, and since the oath by which their gods swore was water, or, as the poets themselves called it, Styx. Now that which is most held in esteem is the object by which men swear; and that which is most ancient is that which is most esteemed. Whether there be any such ancient and primitive opinion about nature is doubtless an obscure question. However, Thales is said to have expressed the opinion above set forth concerning the first cause.

***

And [2] some hold that the soul † is diffused through the universe. Perhaps this is what led Thales to say that all things are full of gods.

[2] Aristotle, *Psychology*, I. 5, 411 a 7 (R. P. 10 A).

† One must beware of reading later meanings into the word 'soul.' To 'have soul' ($\psi\upsilon\chi\dot{\eta}\nu$ $\check{\epsilon}\chi\epsilon\iota\nu$) means little more than 'to be alive.' 'Vital principle' would perhaps express the meaning better, were it not for the fact that that expression implies a greater degree of abstraction than we can properly attribute to these early thinkers.

Judging [3] from what is reported of him, Thales appears to have viewed the soul as something having the capacity to set up movement, if it is true that he said that the loadstone has a soul because it moves iron.

ANAXIMANDER

[Flourished about 570 B.C.]

THE "BOUNDLESS" AS FIRST PRINCIPLE

Among [4] those who say that the first principle is one and mobile and boundless is to be reckoned Anaximander of Miletus, the son of Praxiades, the successor and follower of Thales. He said that "the boundless" (τὸ ἄπειρον) was the first principle and element of the things that are, being the first to make use of this term in describing the first principle. He says it is neither water nor any of the other elements now recognized, but some other and different natural body which is boundless; and from it arise all the heavens and all the worlds which they contain.

That from which things take their origin, into that again they pass away, as destiny orders; for they are punished and give satisfaction to one another for their injustice in the ordering of time, as he puts it in rather poetical language.

It is evident that, observing the way in which the four elements are transformed into one another, he thought fit to take for the substratum, not some one

---

[3] Aristotle, 405 a 17 (R. P. 10 B).

[4] Theophr. Fr. 2 ap. Simplic. *Phys.*, 24 (Dox. 476; R. P. 12). [I use throughout the customary abbreviations,—"Dox." for Diels' *Doxographi Græci*, and "R. P." for Ritter and Preller, *Historia Philosophiæ Græcæ*.]

of them, but rather something else over and above them all. And he did not attribute creation (γένεσις) to any change in this element, but rather to the separating of the opposites occasioned by the eternal movement. This is why Aristotle compares his view with that of Anaxagoras.   ***

And [5] he says that this principle, which encompasses all worlds, is eternal and ageless.—And besides this, there is eternal movement in which there results the creation of the heavens.

***

And [6] there is another point of view from which one does not make the cause any change of matter, nor ascribe creation to any transformation of the substratum, but rather to separation. Anaximander says that the opposites inhering in the substratum, which is a boundless body, are separated out,—he being the first to name the substratum as first principle. And the "opposites" are, hot and cold, moist and dry, etc.

***

Everything [7] either is a first principle or arises from a first principle; but of the boundless there is no first principle, for to find a first principle for it would be to give it bounds. Further, it (the boundless) is unbegotten and indestructible, being a first principle. That which is created perishes, and there is a limit to all destruction. Therefore there is no first principle of the boundless, but it is rather the first principle of other things. And it encompasses all things and rules all things, in the opinion of those who do not assume, in

[5] Hipp. *Ref.* I. 6 (Dox. 559; R. P. 13).

[6] Simpl. *Phys.* 150, 29 D (R. P. 14 A).

[7] Aristotle, *Phys.* III. 4, 203 b 6 (R. P. 13).

addition to the boundless, some other cause such as "reason," or "love." And this is the divine, for it is deathless and indestructible, as Anaximander holds in agreement with most of the physical philosophers.

*_**

But [8] it is not possible that there should be an infinite body which is one and simple; either, as some hold, something over and above the elements and from which they arise, or as one of the elements themselves. For there are some who hold that this (i. e., the something other than the elements) is the boundless, and not air or water, in order that other things may not be destroyed by the boundless. For these (elements themselves) are opposed to one another; air is cold, water moist, fire hot. If one of them were boundless, the rest would have perished ere this. So they say that the boundless is something other than the elements and that from it they arise.

SCIENTIFIC SPECULATIONS

The [9] earth hangs free, supported by nothing. It keeps its place because it is in the centre (lit. is equally distant from all things). It is convex and round, like a stone pillar.† There are two surfaces opposite one another, on one of which we are.

The stars are circles of fire, separated from the fire which surrounds the world and covered all around with air. But there are breathing holes, certain tube-like openings, through which the stars appear. When these holes close there is an eclipse; and the moon appears now

[8] Aristotle, *Phys.* III. 5, 204 b 22 (R. P. 12 B).
[9] Hipp. *Ref.* I. 6 (Dox. 559–60; R. P. 14 c).

† So Diels, Dox. 218, and after him Burnet, p. 72, note. The 'convex' is then taken as referring to the surface of the earth.

to wax and now to wane through the opening and closing of these holes. . . . The sun is highest of all the heavenly bodies and lowest are the circles of the fixed stars. . . . Rain comes from the vapor drawn up from the earth by the sun.

*_**

From [10] the eternal principle was separated at the creation of the world something generative of hot and cold; and from this a sphere of flame grew around the air which surrounds the earth, as the bark grows around the tree. And when the sphere was broken up, and cut into distinct rings, the sun and the moon and the stars came into being.

*_**

Living [11] things sprang from (the moist element †) evaporated by the sun. Man sprang from a different animal, in fact from a fish, which at first he resembled.

*_**

(Anaximander)[12] says that at first man sprang from a different kind of animal, his reason being that whereas all the other animals are speedily able to find nourishment for themselves, man alone requires a long period of suckling; and if he had been at the beginning such as he is now, he would not have survived.

*_**

The [13] first living things were generated in moisture, and were covered with a hard skin. When they were old enough they came up on the dry banks, and after a while the skin cracked off, and they lived on.

[10] Ps. Plut. *Strom.* 2 (R. P. 14 B; Dox. 579).
[11] Hipp. *Ref.* I. 6 (R. P. 16; Dox. 560).
[12] Ps. Plut. *Strom.* 2 (R. P. 16; Dox. 579) .
[13] Aet. *Plac.* V, 19 (R. P. 16; Dox. 430).

† Cf. Diels, Dox., 560, note.

ANAXIMENES

[Flourished about 550 B.C.]

THE OPINIONS OF ANAXIMENES

Anaximenes [14] said air was the first principle.

* * *

Anaximenes of Miletus,[15] son of Eurystratos, an associate of Anaximander, agreed with him in holding that the substance of nature was one and boundless; but he did not agree with him in holding that it was indeterminate, for he said it was air. But it differs in rarity and density with different things. When it is very attenuated fire arises; when it is condensed wind, then cloud, then, when more condensed, water, earth, stones; and other things come from these. He too holds the movement eternal by which the changes arise.

* * *

Just [16] as our soul which is air holds us together, so it is breath and air that encompasses the whole world.

* * *

All [17] things are generated by a sort of rarefaction and condensation of air.   * * *

The [18] earth is flat like a table top.

* * *

The [19] earth is flat and floats on the air.

* * *

The [20] stars are fixed like nails in the crystalline vault.

[14] Arist. *Met.* I 3, 984 a 5.
[15] Theophr. Fr. 2, ap. Simplic. *Phys.*, 24 (R. P. 19 B; Dox. 476).
[16] Aet. *Plac.* I. 3, 4 (Dox. 278; R. P. 18).
[17] Ps. Plut. *Strom.* Fr. 3 (R. P. 19 A; Dox. 579).
[18] Aet. *Plac.* III. 10, 3 (Dox. 377).
[19] Hipp. *Ref.* I, 7 (R. P. 21; Dox. 560).
[20] Aet. 14, 3 (Dox. 344).

II

THE ELEATIC SCHOOL

XENOPHANES

[Flourished about 530 B.C.]

THE FRAGMENTS

1.† THERE is one god, supreme among gods and men; resembling mortals neither in form nor in mind.

2. The whole of him sees, the whole of him thinks, the whole of him hears.

3. Without toil he rules all things by the power of his mind.

4. And he stays always in the same place, nor moves at all, for it is not seemly that he wander about now here, now there.

5. But mortals fancy gods are born, and wear clothes, and have voice and form like themselves.

6. Yet if oxen and lions had hands, and could paint with their hands, and fashion images, as men do, they would make the pictures and images of their gods in their own likeness; horses would make them like horses, oxen like oxen.

(D. 16) Æthiopians †† make their gods black and snub-nosed; Thracians give theirs blue eyes and red hair.

34. Xenophanes [1] said it was just as impious to say

---

[1] Aristotle, *Rhet.* II. 23. 1399 B 6.

† The numbers given the fragments are those of Karsten.

†† R. P. 83. Fr. 16 in Diels' arrangement in his *Die Fragmente der Vorsokratiker*, a work hereafter referred to as "Diels."

that the gods are born as to say that they die. For it follows from either view that at some time or other they do not exist.

7. Homer and Hesiod have ascribed to the gods all deeds that are a shame and a disgrace among men: thieving, adultery, fraud.

16. The gods did not reveal all things to men at the start; but, as time goes on, by searching, they discover more and more.

14. There never was, nor ever will be, any man who knows with certainty the things about the gods and about all things which I tell of. For even if he does happen to get most things right, still he himself does not know it. But mere opinions all may have.

15. Let these opinions of mine pass for semblances of truths.
                                        **

37. (Upon [2] Empedocles remarking to him (Xenophanes) that it was impossible to find a wise man he replied: Very likely; it takes a wise man to know a wise man when he finds one.)

8. From earth to earth,—the beginning and end of all things.

9. We all sprang from earth and water.

10. All things that come into being and grow are earth and water.

12. The upper limit of the earth we see at our feet, where it strikes against the air; but below it reaches down without limit.

13. The (rainbow) which men call Iris is also by nature a cloud, of aspect purple and red and green.

19. Let one but win a race through fleetness of foot, or be victorious in the pentathlon, there where lies the

[2] Diog. Laert. IX. 20.

sacred field of Zeus, in Olympia, hard by the river of Pisas; or let him be victorious in wrestling, or in a bloody boxing match, or in the terrible contest called the pancration,—in the eyes of the citizens he will be resplendent with glory; he will gain a conspicuous seat of honor in the public assemblies, there will be feasting for him at the public expense, and a gift from his city for a token. Yes, if he should win a chariot race, all these things would fall to his lot, though not so deserving as I am. For our wisdom is better than the strength of men or of horses. This is in truth a most heedless custom; nor is it right thus to prefer strength to precious wisdom.

What if there be among the people a good boxer, or one who excels in the pentathlon, or in wrestling, or in fleetness of foot,—which is more highly honored than strength in the contests at the games! The city is not on that account one whit better governed. Small profit does the city get out of it, when one is victorious in contests by the banks of the Pisas. That does not enrich the innermost parts of the state.

20. Having learned from the Lydians useless luxuries, what time they were free from hateful servitude, they used to come swaggering into the place of assembly by the thousand, wearing loose mantles all purple-dyed, glorying in their flowing comely hair, and reeking with the odor of curiously compounded perfumes.

AN ILLUSTRATION OF XENOPHANES' SCIENTIFIC REASONING

Xenophanes [3] thought that a mixture of land and sea came into being, and that in course of time this was resolved into its parts under the influence of the moist

[3] Hipp., *Ref.* I. 14 (R. P. 86 A; Dox. 565).

element. And he adduces such proofs as these: Fossils are found in the midst of the land and on mountains; and in the quarries of Syracuse the imprints of a fish and of seals have been found; and at Paros the imprint of a sardine deep in stone; and at Malta traces of all sorts of things of the sea. And he says that these were made when, long ago, all things were mud, and the imprint was dried in the mud. And when the earth, having sunk in the sea, becomes mud once more, all men will disappear. Then a new creation will begin. And this change happens to all worlds.

PARMENIDES

[Flourished about 495 B.C.]

THE FRAGMENTS OF PARMENIDES' POEM "ON NATURE" †

I. Introduction

Soon as the coursers that bear me and drew me as far as
    extendeth
Impulse, guided me and threw me aloft in the glorious
    pathway,
Up to the Goddess that guideth through all things man
    that is conscious,
There was I carried along, for there did the coursers
    sagacious,
Drawing the chariot, bear me, and virgins preceded to
    guide them—
Daughters of Helios leaving behind them the mansions of
    darkness—

† The translation of Parmenides' poem *On Nature* that is here given was made by Thomas Davidson, and published in Vol. IV of the *Journal of Speculative Philosophy*.

Into the light, with their strong hands forcing asunder
the night-shrouds,
While in its socket the axle emitted the sound of a syrinx,
Glowing, for still it was urged by a couple of wheels well-
rounded,
One upon this side, one upon that, when it hastened its
motion.
There were the gates of the paths of the Night and the
paths of the Day-time.
Under the gates is a threshold of stone and above is a
lintel.
These too are closed in the ether with great doors guarded
by Justice—
Justice the mighty avenger, that keepeth the keys of
requital.
Her did the virgins address, and with soft words deftly
persuaded,
Swiftly for them to withdraw from the gates the bolt
and its fastener.
Opening wide, they uncovered the yawning expanse of
the portal,
Backward rolling successive the hinges of brass in their
sockets,—
Hinges constructed with nails and with clasps; then onward the virgins
Straightway guided their steeds and their chariot over
the highway.
Then did the goddess receive me with gladness, and
taking my right hand
Into her own, thus uttered a word and kindly bespake
me:
Youth that art mated with charioteers and companions
immortal,

Coming to us on the coursers that bear thee, to visit our
    mansion,
Hail! for it is not an evil Award that hath guided thee
    hither,
Into this path—for, I ween, it is far from the pathway of
    mortals—
Nay, it is Justice and Right. Thou needs must have
    knowledge of all things,
First of the Truth's unwavering heart that is fraught
    with conviction,
Then of the notions of mortals, where no true conviction
    abideth;
But thou shalt surely be taught this too, that every
    opinion
Needs must pass through the ALL, and vanquish the
    test with approval.

II. On Truth

Listen, and I will instruct thee—and thou, when thou
    hearest, shalt ponder—
What are the sole two paths of research that are open to
    thinking.
One path is: That Being doth be, and Non-Being is not:
This is the way of Conviction, for Truth follows hard in
    her footsteps.
Th' other path is: That Being is not, and Non-Being must
    be;
This one, I tell thee in truth, is an all-incredible pathway.
For thou never canst know what is not (for none can
    conceive it),
Nor canst thou give it expression, for one thing are
    Thinking and Being.

    .   .   .   .   .

. . . And to me 'tis indifferent
Whence I begin, for thither again thou shalt find me
    returning.

        .   .   .   .   .

Speaking and thinking must needs be existent, for IS
    is of being.
Nothing must needs not be; these things I enjoin thee to
    ponder.
Foremost of all withdraw thy mind from this path of
    inquiry,
Then likewise from that other, wherein men, empty of
    knowledge,
Wander forever uncertain, while Doubt and Perplexity
    guide them—
Guide in their bosoms the wandering mind; and onward
    they hurry,
Deaf and dumb and blind and stupid, unreasoning cattle—
Herds that are wont to think Being and Non-Being one
    and the self-same,
Yet not one and the same; and that all things move in a
    circle.

        .   .   .   .   .

Never I ween shalt thou learn that Being can be of what
    is not;
Wherefore do thou withdraw thy mind from this path of
    inquiry,
Neither let habit compel thee, while treading this path-
    way of knowledge,
Still to employ a visionless eye or an ear full of ringing,
Yea, or a clamorous tongue; but prove this vexed dem-
    onstration
Uttered by me, by reason.   And now there remains for
    discussion

One path only: That Being doth be—and on *it* there are
    tokens

Many and many to show that what is is birthless and
    deathless,

Whole and only-begotten, and moveless and ever-
    enduring:

Never it was or shall be; but the ALL simultaneously
    now is,

One continuous one; for of it what birth shalt thou
    search for?

How and whence it hath sprung? I shall not permit
    thee to tell me,

Neither to think: 'Of what is not,' for none can say or
    imagine

How Not-Is becomes Is; or else what need should have
    stirred it,

After or yet before its beginning, to issue from nothing?

Thus either wholly Being must be or wholly must not be.

Never from that which is will the force of Intelligence
    suffer

Aught to become beyond itself. Thence neither pro-
    duction

Neither destruction doth Justice permit, ne'er slacken-
    ing her fetters;

But she forbids. And herein is contained the decision
    of these things;

Either there is or is not; but Judgment declares, as it
    needs must,

One of these paths to be uncomprehended and utterly
    nameless,

No true pathway at all, but the other to be and be real.

How can that which is now be hereafter, or how can it
    have been?

For if it hath been before, or shall be hereafter, it is
not:

Thus generation is quenched and decay surpasseth
believing.

Nor is there aught of distinct; for the All is self-similar
alway.

Nor is there anywhere more to debar it from being unbroken;

Nor is there anywhere less, for the All is sated with
Being;

Wherefore the All is unbroken, and Being approacheth
to Being.

Moveless, moreover, and bounded by great chains'
limits it lieth,

Void of beginning, without any ceasing, since birth and
destruction

Both have wandered afar, driven forth by the truth of
conviction.

Same in the same and abiding, and self through itself it
reposes.

Steadfast thus it endureth, for mighty Necessity holds
it—

Holds it within the chains of her bounds and round doth
secure it.

Wherefore that that which IS should be infinite is not
permitted;

For it is lacking in naught, or else it were lacking in all
things.

. . . . .

Steadfastly yet in thy spirit regard things absent as
present;

Surely thou shalt not separate Being from clinging to
Being,

Nor shalt thou find it scattered at all through the All
    of the Cosmos,
Nor yet gathered together.

    .   .   .   .   .

One and the same are thought and that whereby there is
    thinking;
Never apart from existence, wherein it receiveth ex-
    pression,
Shalt thou discover the action of thinking; for naught
    is or shall be
Other besides or beyond the Existent; for Fate hath
    determined
That to be lonely and moveless, which all things are but
    a name for—
Things that men have set up for themselves, believing
    as real
Birth and decay, becoming and ceasing, to be and to
    not-be,
Movement from place to place, and change from color
    to color.
But since the uttermost limit of Being is ended and
    perfect,
Then it is like to the bulk of a sphere well-rounded on all
    sides,
Everywhere distant alike from the centre; for never there
    can be
Anything greater or anything less, on this side or that
    side;
Yea, there is neither a non-existent to bar it from coming
Into equality, neither can Being be different from Being,
More of it here, less there, for the All is inviolate ever.
Therefore, I ween, it lies equally stretched in its limits
    on all sides.

And with this I will finish the faithful discourse and the
    thinking
Touching the truth; and now thou shalt learn the notions
    of mortals.
Learn and list to the treach'rous array of the words I
    shall utter.

III. On Opinion

Men have set up for themselves twin shapes to be named
    by Opinion
(One they cannot set up, and herein do they wander in
    error),
And they have made them distinct in their nature, and
    marked them with tokens,
Opposite each unto each—the one, flame's fire of the ether,
Gentle, exceedingly thin, and everywhere one and the
    self-same,
But not the same with the other; the other, self-similar
    likewise,
Standing opposed, by itself: brute night, dense nature
    and heavy.
All the apparent system of these will I open before thee,
So that not any opinion of mortals shall ever elude thee.

.   .   .   .   .

All things now being marked with the names of light and
    of darkness,
Yea, set apart by the various powers of the one or the
    other,
Surely the All is at once full of light and invisible darkness,
Both being equal, and naught being common to one
    with the other.

.   .   .   .   .

For out of the formless fire are woven the narrower circlets,
Those over these out of night; but a portion of flame
    shooteth through them.
And in the centre of all is the Goddess that governeth
    all things:
She unto all is the author of loathsome birth and coition,
Causing the female to mix with the male, and by mutual
    impulse
Likewise the male with the female.

      .   .   .   .   .

Foremost of gods, she gave birth unto Love; yea, fore-
    most of all gods.

      .   .   .   .   .

Then thou shalt know the ethereal nature and each of
    its tokens—
Each of the signs in the ether, and all the invisible
    workings
Wrought by the blemishless sun's pure lamp, and
    whence they have risen.
Then thou shalt hear of the orb-eyed moon's circumambi-
    ent workings,
And of her nature, and likewise discern the heaven that
    surrounds them,
Whence it arose, and how by her sway Necessity bound it
Firm, to encircle the bounds of the stars.

      .   .   .   .   .

. . . How the earth, and the sun, and the moon, and
    the ether
Common to all, and the milk of the sky, and the peak of
    Olympus,
Yea, and the fervent might of the stars, were impelled
    into being.

      .   .   .   .   .

Circling the earth, with its wanderings, a borrowed, a
    night-gleaming splendor.

      .   .   .   .   .

Wistfully watching forever, with gaze turned toward
    the sunlight.

      .   .   .   .

Even as in each one of men is a union of limbs many-
    jointed,
So there is also in each one a mind; for one and the same
    are
That which is wise and the nature generic of members
    in mortals,
Yea, unto each and to all; for that which prevaileth is
    thinking.

      .   .   .   .   .

Here on the right hand the youths, and there on the
    left hand the maidens.

      .   .   .   .   .

Thus by the strength of opinion were these created and
    now are,
Yea, and will perish hereafter, as soon as they grow unto
    ripeness;
Men have imposed upon each one of these a name as a
    token.

      .   .   .   .   .

PLATO AND ARISTOTLE ON ELEATIC PHILOSOPHY

And [4] our Eleatic tribe of philosophers, beginning
with Xenophanes—yes and earlier, embodied this truth
in a tale, that "all things," so-called, are really one.

*_**

Some [5] have put forth the opinion that the All is a
single natural body (μιᾶς οὔσης φύσεως). But they have

    [4] Plato, *Soph.* 242 D.   [5] Aristotle, *Met.* I. 5, 986 b 11.

not all expressed this opinion in the same way: they differ in excellence of statement, and also as to what that natural body is. The account of them lies quite outside our present inquiry into causes; for they do not, like some of the physical philosophers, first assume that that which is (τὸ ὄν) is a single body, and then produce things from this single body as from a material cause. They speak in a different fashion. The former add motion, in explaining the origin of the universe; whereas these say that it (the first principle) is immovable. Nevertheless, so much at least is germane to our present inquiry: Parmenides seems to have grasped the unity as formal cause (κατὰ τὸν λόγον), Melissus as material cause (κατὰ τὴν ὕλην). Accordingly the former holds it to be bounded, the latter to be boundless.

Xenophanes, the first of these men to assert this unity, Parmenides being generally spoken of as his disciple, made nothing very clear, and does not seem to have reached either of the above views of nature; but, gazing up into the broad heavens, he simply declared: The One is god.

And so, as we said, these men we may pass over in our present inquiry, two of them without a further word, as being rather too crude, Xenophanes and Melissus; but Parmenides seems to speak at times with keener vision.

For, holding as he does that over and above being there is no such thing as non-being, of necessity he holds that being is One, and that there is nothing else existent. (This subject we have discussed more clearly in our work on nature.) Still, compelled to follow where the plain facts led, he supposes that whereas according to reason things are one, for sense-perception they are more than one; and he falls back on the assumption that there are two causes and two principles, heat and cold, to wit, fire and earth; and of these the one, the hot, he classes with being, the other (the cold) with non-being.

ZENO

[Flourished about 465 B.C.]

THE PUZZLES OF COMPOSITION AND DIVISION

If [6] that which is, had no magnitude it could not even be. Everything that truly is must needs have magnitude and thickness, and one part of it must be separated from another by a certain interval. And the same may be said of the next smaller part; it too will have magnitude, and a next smaller part. As well say this once for all as keep repeating it forever. For there will be no such part that could serve as a limit. And there will never be one part save in reference to another part. Thus, if the many have being, they must be both large and small—so small as to have no size at all, and so large as to be infinite.

***

That [7] which has neither magnitude, thickness, nor bulk could not *be* at all. "For," says Zeno, "were it added to anything else that is it would not make it one whit larger, for it is impossible to increase the magnitude of anything by adding that which has no magnitude. And this itself would be enough to show that what was added was nothing. . . . † If when it is taken away from

[6] Simpl. 140, 34.   (R. P. 105 C.   Fr. 2 in Diels' arrangement.)
[7] Simpl. 139, 9.   (R. P. 105 A.   Fr. 1 Diels.)

† Assuming with Zeller and Burnet that there is a lacuna here.

another thing that other will be no less, and when it is added to another thing that other will be no larger, it is clear that what was added and what was taken away was nothing at all."

$*_*^*$

If [8] the absolute unit is indivisible it would be, according to Zeno's axiom, nothing at all. For that which neither makes anything larger by its addition, nor makes anything smaller by its subtraction, is not one of the things that are, since it is clear that what *is* must be a magnitude, and, if a magnitude, corporeal, for the corporeal has being in all dimensions. Other things, such as the surface and the line, when added in one way make things larger, when added in another way do not; but the point and the unit do not make things larger however added.

$*_*^*$

If [9] things are a many, there must of necessity be just so many as there actually are, neither more nor less. If, however, there are just so many as there actually are, then would they be finite in number. (On the other hand) If things are a many, then the things that are are infinite in number; for, between the things that are are always other things, and between them again still other things. And thus the things that are are infinite in number.

SPACE NOT A REAL THING

If [10] space *is*, it will be in something; for everything that *is* is in something; and to be in something is to be in space. Space then will be in space, and so on *ad infinitum*. Therefore space does not exist.

[8] Arist. *Met.* II. 4, 1001 b 7.   [9] Simpl. 140, 27 (R. P. 105 B).
[10] Simpl. 130^v. 562, 3 D (R. P. 106).

(1.) You † cannot traverse an infinite number of points in a finite time. You must traverse the half of any given distance before you traverse the whole, and the half of that again before you can traverse it. This goes on *ad infinitum*, so that (*if space is made up of points*) there are an infinite number in any given space, and it cannot be traversed in a finite time.

(2.) The second argument is the famous puzzle of Achilles and the tortoise. Achilles must first reach the place from which the tortoise started. By that time the tortoise will have got on a little way. Achilles must then traverse that, and still the tortoise will be ahead. He is always coming nearer, but he never makes up to it.

(3.) The third argument against the possibility of motion *through a space made up of points* is that, on this hypothesis, an arrow in any given moment of its flight must be at rest in some particular point.[11]

---

[11] Burnet adds: " Aristotle observes quite rightly that this argument depends upon the assumption that time is made up of ' nows,' that is, of indivisible instants. This no doubt, was the Pythagorean view."

With the third argument as given above, compare the following saying of Zeno reported by Diogenes Laertius, IX, 72: "That which moves can neither move in the place where it is, nor yet in the place where it is not."

† Zeno's arguments have been preserved by Aristotle, *Phys.* VI. 9, 230 b. They are, however, given in a much condensed form, being referred to as matters of common information, and are introduced in order to give Aristotle an opportunity to criticise them. In place of giving this passage I have, therefore, reproduced the arguments in the expanded form given them by Burnet, which is a free paraphrase of Aristotle's statements, with a few interpolations introduced for the benefit of the modern reader, far from the heat of the controversy, which are amply justified by Aristotle's discussions in the *Physics*. If any doubt should

(4.) Suppose three parallel rows of points in juxtaposition:

Fig. 1   Fig. 2

A . . . . . . | A . . . . .
B . . . . . . | B . . . . . .
C . . . . . . | C . . . . . .

One of these (B) is immovable, while A and C move in opposite directions with equal velocity so as to come into the position represented in Fig. 2. The movement of C relatively to A will be double its movement relatively to B, or, in other words, any given point in C has passed twice as many points in A as it has in B. It cannot, therefore, be the case that an instant of time corresponds to the passage from one point to another.

THE PURPOSE OF ZENO'S ARGUMENTS AS REPORTED BY PLATO

[In the *Parmenides* Zeno is represented as reading his work to Socrates and a few others. Before the conclusion of the reading Parmenides enters. After Zeno has finished reading a discussion ensues, part of which I quote.[12] Socrates is speaking:]

"In all that you say, Zeno, have you any other purpose except to disprove the being of the many? and is not each division of your treatise intended to furnish a separate proof of this, there being in all as many proofs of the not-being of the many as you have composed arguments? Is that your meaning, or have I misunderstood you?"

be raised on this score it could only be with regard to the fourth argument, but it seems to me that Burnet and Tannery have made good their case here. See Burnet, *Early Greek Philosophy*, pp. 331 ff.; Tannery, *Science Hellene*, p. 257.

[12] Parmenides, 127 D. Jowett's translation.

"No," said Zeno; "you have correctly understood my general purpose."

"I see, Parmenides," said Socrates, "that Zeno would like to be not only one with you in friendship but your second self in his writings too; he puts what you say in another way, and would fain make believe that he is telling us something which is new. For you, in your poems, say, The All is one, and of this you adduce excellent proofs; and he on the other hand says, There is no many; and on behalf of this he offers overwhelming evidence. You affirm unity, he denies plurality. And so you deceive the world into believing that you are saying different things when really you are saying much the same. This is a strain of art beyond the reach of most of us."

"Yes, Socrates," said Zeno. "But although you are as keen as a Spartan hound in pursuing the track, you do not fully apprehend the true motive of the composition, which is not really such an artificial work as you imagine; for what you speak of was an accident; there was no pretence of a great purpose; nor any serious intention of deceiving the world. The truth is, that these arguments of mine were meant to protect the arguments of Parmenides against those who make fun of him and seek to show the many ridiculous and contradictory results which they suppose to follow from the affirmation of the one. My answer is addressed to the partisans of the many, whose attack I return with interest by retorting upon them that their hypothesis of the being of the many, if carried out, appears to be still more ridiculous than the hypothesis of the being of the one. Zeal for my master led me to write the book in the days of my youth, but some one stole the copy; and therefore I had no choice whether it should be published or not; the motive, however, of writing, was not the ambition of an elder man, but the pugnacity of a young one. This you do not seem to see, Socrates; though in other respects, as I was saying, your notion is a very just one."

III

HERACLITUS

[Flourished about 505 B.C.]

THE FRAGMENTS

1.† THIS Word (λόγος)†† is everlasting, but men are unable to comprehend it before they have heard it or even after they have heard it for the first time. Although everything happens in accordance with this Word, they behave like inexperienced men whenever they make trial of words and deeds such as I declare as I analyze each thing according to its nature and show what it is. But other men have no idea what they are doing when awake, just as they forget what they do when they are asleep.

2. One ought to follow the lead of that which is common to all men. But although the Word (λόγος) is common to all, yet most men live as if each had a private wisdom of his own.

† The numbering of the fragments is that of Diels, and I follow his text except where otherwise noted.

†† Burnet follows Zeller and translates λόγος as "discourse," rendering the first clause: "Though this discourse is true evermore." λόγος, it is held, did not mean "reason" in the time of Heraclitus. See Burnet, p. 133, *n.* 13; Zeller, I. p. 572, *n.* 2. *Cf.* Teichmüller, *Neue Studien,* I. pp. 170 ff. Burnet's position is not free from objections, and, in order not to enter into the controversy, I have thought it best to follow Diels in rendering λόγος "Word," and, where I have departed from that rendering, to give the Greek term also

17. Most men have no comprehension even of such things as they meet with, nor do they understand what they experience though they themselves think they do.

18. If you do not expect the unexpected you will never find it, for it is hard to find and inaccessible.

4. If happiness consisted in the pleasures of the body, we should call cattle happy when they find grass to eat.

5. Men seek in vain to purify themselves from blood-guiltiness by defiling themselves with blood; as if, when one has stepped into the mud, he should try to wash himself with mud. And I should deem him mad who should pay heed to any man who does such things. And, forsooth, they offer prayers to these statues here! It is as if one should try to converse with houses. They know nothing of the real nature of gods and heroes.

15. Were it not in honor of **Dionysus that they made** a procession and sang the Phallus-song, it were a most shameless thing to do. Is Hades then the same thing as **Dionysus** that they should go mad in his honor with their bacchanalian revels?

22. They who seek after gold dig up a lot of earth, and find a little.

23. Were there no injustice men would never have known the name of justice.

24. Gods and men alike honor those who fall in battle.

25. Greater deaths receive greater rewards.

(77 Bywater.) Man is kindled and put out like a light in the night time.

27. There await men after death things they do not expect nor dream of.

28. Even he who is most highly esteemed knows and cherishes nothing but opinions. And yet justice shall surely overcome forgers of lies and false witnesses.

29. There is one thing that the best men prize above all—eternal glory above all perishable things. Most men, however, stuff themselves with food like cattle.

30. This universe, the same for all, no one, either god or man, has made; but it always was, and is, and ever shall be an ever-living fire, fixed measures kindling and fixed measures dying out.

31. The transformations of fire are, first of all, sea; and one-half of the sea is earth and half the stormy wind. . . The sea is dispersed and keeps its measure according to the same Word that prevailed before it became earth.

32. Wisdom is one and one only. It is both willing and unwilling to be called by the name of Zeus.

33. Law also means to obey the counsel of one.

34. Fools even when they hear the truth are like deaf men. Of them the proverb holds true, 'being present they are absent.'

35. Right many things must men know who are lovers of wisdom.

36. For souls it is death to become water, for water it is death to become earth. From the earth water springs, and from water soul.

37. Swine like to wash in the mire; barnyard fowls in dust and ashes.

40. Much learning does not teach wisdom, else would it have taught Hesiod and Pythagoras, Xenophanes, too, and Hecatæus.

41. Wisdom is one thing. It is to know the thought by which all things through all are guided.

42. Homer ought to be thrown out of the lists and whipped, and Archilochus too.

43. It is more necessary to extinguish wantonness than a conflagration.

44. The people ought to fight in defence of the law as they do of their city wall.

45. You could not discover the boundaries of the soul though you tried every path, so deep does its reason (λόγος) reach down.

47. Let us not make random conjectures about the weightiest matters.

48. The bow is called life,† but its work is death.

49. One to me is as good as ten thousand if he be but the best.

50. It is wise to hearken not to me, but to the Word, and to confess that all things are one.

8. Opposition brings men together, and out of discord comes the fairest harmony, and all things have their birth in strife.

51. Men do not understand how that which is torn in different directions comes into accord with itself,— harmony in contrariety, as in the case of the bow and the lyre.

52. Time is like a child playing at draughts; the kingdom is a child's.

53. War is the father of all and the king of all, and some he has made gods and some men, some bond and some free.

54. The hidden harmony is better than that which is obvious.

57. Hesiod is most men's teacher; they are convinced that he knew nearly everything,—a man who didn't even know night and day! For they are one.

59. The straight and crooked path of the fuller's comb is one and the same.

60. The way up and the way down is one and the same.

† A play on the words βίος, life, and βιός, bow.

61. The sea is the purest and the impurest water; fishes drink it and it keeps them alive, men find it unfit to drink and even deadly.

62. The immortal are mortal, the mortal immortal, each living in the other's death and dying in the other's life.

67. God is day and night, winter and summer, war and peace, satiety and hunger.   But he assumes various forms, just as fire when it is mingled with different kinds of incense is named according to the savor of each.

72. From reason (λόγος), the guide of all things, with which they are most continually associated they are become estranged; and things they meet with every day appear to them unfamiliar.

73. We ought not to act and speak like men asleep.

76. Fire lives the death of air, and air the death of fire; water lives the death of earth, and earth the death of water.

(72 Bywater.)   Souls delight to get wet.

78. The customs of men possess no wisdom, those of the gods do.

79. Man is called a child by god, as a boy is by man.

80. We ought to know that war is the common lot, and that justice is strife, and that all things arise through strife and necessity.

82. The most beautiful ape is ugly as compared with the human race.

83. The wisest man compared with god is like an ape in wisdom, in beauty, and in everything else.

84. In change one finds rest; and it is weariness to be always toiling at the same things and always beginning afresh.

85. It is hard to contend against the heart; for it is ready to sell the soul to purchase its desires.

86. For the most part the knowledge of things divine escapes us because of our unbelief.

87. The stupid man is wont to be struck dumb at every word.

88.† One and the same thing are the living and the dead, the waking and the sleeping, the young and the old; the former change and are the latter, the latter change in turn and are the former.

89. Those who are awake have one world in common; those who are asleep retire every one to a private world of his own.

90. All things are exchanged for fire and fire for all things, just as wares are exchanged for gold and gold for wares.

0.†† All things flow; nothing abides.

91. One cannot step twice into the same river.

(81 Bywater.) Into the same rivers we step and we do not step; we are and we are not.

94. The sun will not overstep his measures, else would the Erinnyes, the handmaids of justice, find him out.

92. The sibyl with raving lips uttering things solemn, unadorned and rude, reaches with her voice over a thousand years because of the god that inspires her.

93. The lord whose oracle is in Delphi neither reveals nor conceals but indicates.

95. It is best to hide one's folly, but it is hard when relaxed over the wine cups.

† Following the text of Bywater here.

†† Though this cannot be proved to be a quotation from Heraclitus, nothing is more certainly Heraclitean than the view it expresses. It is repeatedly referred to both by Plato and by Aristotle.

97. Dogs bark at every one whom they do not know.

101. I have sought to understand myself.

102. To god all things are beautiful and good and right; men deem some things wrong and some right.

103. In the circumference of a circle beginning and end coincide.

104. What wisdom, what understanding is theirs? They put their trust in bards and take the mob for their teacher, not knowing that many are bad and few good.

106. One day is like another.

107. Eyes and ears are bad witnesses to men who have not an understanding heart.

108. No one of all the men whose words I have heard has arrived at the knowledge that wisdom is something apart from all other things.

110. It were not good for men that all their wishes should be fulfilled.

111. It is disease that makes health pleasant; evil, good; hunger, plenty; weariness, rest.

112. Wisdom is the foremost virtue, and wisdom consists in speaking the truth, and in lending an ear to nature and acting according to her.

113–14. Wisdom is common to all. . . . They who would speak with intelligence must hold fast to the [wisdom that is] common to all, as a city holds fast to its law, and even more strongly. For all human laws are fed by one divine law, which prevaileth as far as it listeth and suffices for all things and excels all things.

116. It is in the power of all men to know themselves and to practise temperance.

117. A man when he is drunk is led about by a beardless boy; he reels along paying no heed where he goes, for his soul is wet.

118. A dry soul is the wisest and the best.

119. Man's character is his fate.

121. The Ephesians would do well to hang themselves, every man of them, and to leave the city to beardless boys. For they banished Hermodorus, the best man of them all, declaring: We will have no best man among us; if there be any such let him be so elsewhere and amongst other men.

123. Nature loves to hide.

126. It is the cold things that become warm, the warm that become cold, the moist that become dry, and the dry that become moist.

129. Pythagoras the son of Mnesarchus pursued his investigations further than all other men, . . . he made himself a wisdom of his own,—much learning, bad science.

IV

THE PYTHAGOREAN PHILOSOPHY †

THE NUMBER PHILOSOPHY OF THE PYTHAGOREANS

AT [1] this time and even earlier †† the so-called Pythagoreans applied themselves to mathematics and were the first to advance this branch of knowledge, and spending all their time in these pursuits they came to think that the first principles of mathematics were the first principles of all things that exist. And inasmuch as numbers are what is naturally first in this field, and since they thought they discovered in numbers a great many more similarities with things that exist and that arise in the processes of nature than one could find in fire or earth or water, they thought, for example, that such and such a property of numbers was justice, another the soul and reason, another opportunity, and in the same way of practically everything else; and inasmuch as they saw in numbers the properties and proportions of the different kinds of harmonies, and since all other things so far as their entire nature is concerned were modelled upon numbers, whereas numbers are prior to anything else in nature,—from all this they inferred that the first

[1] Arist. *Met.* I. 5, 985 b 23.

† Pythagoras flourished about 530 B.C.; Philolaus about 440. The number philosophy of the Pythagoreans seems to have been fully developed by the time of Philolaus.

†† Aristotle has just been speaking of Empedocles, Leucippus and Democritus.

elements of numbers were the first elements of all things that exist, and that the whole heaven was a harmony and a number. And so all the analogies they could point to between numbers and harmonies on the one hand, and the properties and divisions and the whole arrangement of the heavens on the other hand, these they would collect and piece together, and if any gap appeared anywhere they would greedily seek after something to fill it, in order that their entire system might be coherent. For example, since they thought that the number ten was a perfect thing and included all other numbers they affirmed that the heavenly bodies must also be ten in number, but inasmuch as only nine are visible they invented a tenth, which they called the counter-earth.

These philosophers evidently regarded number as the first principle, both as being the material cause of things that exist and as describing their qualities and states as well. And the elements of number they described as the odd and the even, the former being limited and the latter unlimited; and the number one they thought was composed of both of these elements (for it is both even and odd) and from the number one all other numbers spring, and the whole heavens are simply numbers.

Others of the same school assume ten first principles which they arrange in parallel rows:

limit	unlimited	at rest	in motion
odd	even	straight	crooked
one	many	light	darkness
right	left	good	evil
masculine	feminine	square	oblong

Alcmæon of Croton seems also to have shared this view, and indeed either he got this theory from them or they from him, which latter is possible for Alcmæon was a younger contemporary of Pythagoras, and he expressed views very much like those of the Pythagoreans, for he said that most human affairs are two-phased; but he did not clearly define the opposites, as they did, but took them just as they came—white, black; sweet, bitter; good, evil; large, small. With regard to the rest he vaguely threw out a few random opinions; the Pythagoreans on the other hand tell us just how many and what the opposites are.

So much at least we can gather from both of these schools, that the opposites are the principles of things that are; and from one of them we can learn how many and what these opposites are. But how it is possible to bring their view back to the causes which we have ourselves laid down is a matter that has not been clearly and definitely stated by them. Apparently they put their elements under the head of material cause; for they say that it is from these elements as already existent that substance arises and that it is composed of them.

***

The [2] so-called Pythagoreans employ first principles and elements more unusual than those of the physical philosophers, the reason being that they do not derive them from objects of sense: for the realities with which mathematics deals, if we except those of astronomy, do not partake of motion. None the less they discuss and elaborate views about nature in all its aspects; they account for the origin of the heavens, and with regard to its parts and its attributes and its activities, closely observing what happens, they apply their first principles

[2] Arist. *Met.* I. 8, 989 b 29.

and causes to the explanation of these things, just as
if they were in entire accord with the physical philosophers in holding that existence belongs only to that
which can be perceived by sense and which is comprised
within what we call the heavens. But, as we have said,
they introduce causes and first principles which are
adapted to lead them to a higher order of realities, and
indeed are more suitable for that purpose than for the
explanation of nature. But from what sort of a cause
movement arises, the limit and the unlimited, the odd
and the even being their only presuppositions,—they
say nothing of this, nor do they tell us how it is possible
that, apart from motion and change, there should be
generation and destruction or the revolutions of the
heavenly bodies.

Moreover, if we grant them their contention that size
arises from these elements, if we assume they have made
this out, still the question remains how it happens that
some bodies should be heavy and others light, for according to the principles which they presuppose, and
from what they say about them, they are no less applicable to the things of sense than they are to the objects with which mathematics is concerned. And this
is how it happens that they have said nothing about
fire or earth or bodies of that sort, not having, as I
suppose, anything to say that was specially applicable
to things of sense. Further, how is it possible to assume
that the cause of everything that exists under the
heavens and all that has come into being from the
beginning down to the present day is simply the properties of number and number itself, if at the same time
there is no other kind of number except precisely that
out of which the heavens are composed? For when in

such and such a part of the number series they have
found 'opinion,' or, possibly, 'opportunity,' and again
a little higher up or a little lower down, 'injustice,' or
'judgment,' or 'mixture,' and when they have given
us their proofs that every one of these things is a number, . . . the question arises whether the number which
we are to suppose each one of these things to be is
identical with the number which is found in the heavens,
or whether it is some other kind of a number over and
above this.

THE PYTHAGOREAN GOLDEN WORDS †

The gods immortal, as by law disposed,
First venerate, and reverence the oath:
Then to the noble heroes, and the powers
Beneath the earth, do homage with just rites.

Thy parents honor and thy nearest kin,
And from the rest choose friends on virtue's scale.
To gentle words and kindly deeds give way,
Nor hate thy friend for any slight offence.
Bear all thou canst; for Can dwells nigh to Must.
These things thus know.

What follow learn to rule:
The belly first, then sleep and lust and wrath.

† A word of caution. In inserting the "Golden Words" at this
point I do not mean to imply that they date from the time of
the early Pythagoreans. It is now generally recognized that they
have a much later origin. The earliest explicit mention of them is
found in the third century B.C. But before the time of Plato the
"Pythagorean Way of Life" had become proverbial, and I insert
the "Golden Words" here as giving a clear picture of what in later
times at least the Pythagorean Way of Life had come to represent.
The translation is that of Thomas Davidson, published in his
Aristotle and Ancient Educational Ideals.

Do nothing base with others or alone:
But most of all thyself in reverence hold.

Then practise justice both in deed and word,
Nor let thyself wax thoughtless about aught:
But know that death's the common lot of all.

Be not untimely wasteful of thy wealth,
Like vulgar men, nor yet illiberal.
In all things moderation answers best.

Do things that profit thee: think ere thou act.

Let never sleep thy drowsy eyelids greet,
Till thou hast pondered each act of the day:
' Wherein have I transgressed?   What have I done?
What duty shunned? '—beginning from the first,
Unto the last.   Then grieve and fear for what
Was basely done; but in the good rejoice.

These things perform; these meditate; these love.
These in the path of godlike excellence
Will place thee, yea, by Him who gave our souls
The number Four, perennial nature's spring!
But, ere thou act, crave from the gods success.

These precepts having mastered, thou shalt know
The system of the never-dying gods
And dying men, and how from all the rest
Each thing is sundered, and how held in one:
And thou shalt know, as it is right thou shouldst,
That nature everywhere is uniform,
And so shalt neither hope for things that lie
Beyond all hope, nor fail of any truth.

But from such food abstain as we have named,
And, while thou seek'st to purge and free thy soul,
Use judgment, and reflect on everything,
Setting o'er all best Thought as charioteer.

Be glad to gather goods, nor less to lose.

Of human ills that spring from spirit-powers
Endure thy part nor peevishly complain.
Cure what thou canst: 'tis well, and then reflect:
"Fate never lays too much upon the good."

Words many, brave and base, assail men's ears.
Let these not disconcert or trammel thee;
But when untruth is spoken, meekly yield.

What next I say in every act observe:
Let none by word or deed prevail on thee
To do or say what were not best for thee.
Think ere thou act, lest foolish things be done;—
For thoughtless deeds and words the caitiff mark;—
But strongly do what will not bring regret.
Do naught thou dost not know; but duly learn.
So shall thy life with happiness o'erflow.

Be not neglectful of thy body's health;
But measure use in drink, food, exercise—
I mean by "measure" what brings no distress.

Follow a cleanly, simple mode of life,
And guard against such acts as envy breed.
Then, if, when thou the body leav'st, thou mount
To the free ether, deathless shalt thou be,
A god immortal,—mortal never more!

V

EMPEDOCLES

[Flourished about 455 B.C.]

4.† . . . But come, use all the hands of sense in grasping each thing in the way that it is clear. Do not put greater confidence in what thou seest than in what thou hearest, nor trust a loud noise more than the things that the tongue makes clear; and do not withhold thy confidence in any of the other hands which open a way to knowledge; but know each thing in the way it is clear.

6. Hear first the four roots of all things: brightly shining Zeus, life-bringing Hera, Aidoneus, and Nestis who bedews with her tears the well-spring of mortals.

8. And another thing I shall tell thee: of no one of all the things that perish is there any birth, nor any end in baneful death. There is only a mingling and a separation of what has been mingled. But "birth" is the name men use for this.

11. Fools! Short is the reach of their thinking who suppose that what before was not comes into being, or that anything perishes and is utterly destroyed.

12. For it is inconceivable that anything should arise from that which in no way exists, and it is impossible, and a thing unheard of, that what exists should perish, for it will always be wherever one in every case puts it.

† I follow the text of Diels except where otherwise noted, and give his numbering of the fragments.

17. . . . Come hearken to my words, for learning adds strength to thy mind. As I said before, when I unfolded the chief points of my discourse, twofold is the truth I shall disclose. At one time things grew to be one alone out of many; and then again [this] fell asunder so that there were many from the one,—fire and water and earth and the endless height of the air; and, apart from these, baneful Strife, with equal weight throughout, and in their midst Love, equally distributed in length and breadth. Let thy mind's gaze rest upon her, nor sit with dazed eyes. It is she that is held to be implanted in the parts of mortals; it is she who awakens thoughts of love and fulfils the works of peace. They call her by the name of Delight and Aphrodite. No mortal man has searched her out as she swirls around in [the elements]. But do thou hearken to the guileless course of my argument. For all these [elements] are equal and of like age. Each one has a different office, each has its own character, but as time runs on they win in turn the upper hand. And besides them nothing is added, nothing taken away. For were they being continually destroyed they would no longer exist. But what could increase this All, and whence could it come? And whither could these elements pass away, since there is no place bereft of them? No, they are the same, but as they penetrate each other, sometimes one thing arises, sometimes another, and continuously and to all eternity they are the same.

35. . . . When Strife had fallen to the lowest depth of the vortex, and Love had come to be in the centre of the whirl, all things came together in Love so as to be one only,—not all at once, but coming together at their pleasure, one from this quarter, one from that. And

as they came together Strife retired to the outermost
boundary.† But many things unmixed remained,
alternating with the things that were mixed, as many
as Strife, still remaining on high, retained in its grasp;
for it had not yet blamelessly retired altogether to the
outermost boundaries of the circle. Partly it still
remained within, and partly it had separated from the
elements. But just in proportion as it was continuously
rushing out a gracious and divine impulse of blameless
Love kept ever coming in. And straightway things grew
mortal that were wont to be immortal before, and things
before unmixed were mixed, changing their ways of life.
And from these as they were mingled the countless tribes
of mortal creatures poured forth, fashioned in all manner
of forms, a wonder to behold.

82. Hair and leaves and the thick feathers of birds and
the scales that grow on tough limbs are the same thing.

100. In this wise do all breathe in and out. All have
bloodless tubes of flesh stretched over the surface of the
body, and at their mouths is the outermost surface of
the skin pierced with pores closely packed so that the
blood is kept in, while an easy way is cut for the air
through the openings. Then, whenever the smooth
blood rushes back, the blustering air rushes in with a
furious surge, and when the blood springs back, the air
is breathed out again. As when a girl playing with a
klepsydra of shining brass, as long as she holds the
mouth of the pipe pressed against her comely hand
and dips it in the smooth mass of silvery water, the
water does not flow into the vessel, but the weight of the
air inside as it presses on the closely packed pores keeps

† Following Stein's arrangement instead of repeating, as Diels
and Carsten do, a line given below.

it back, until she uncovers the compressed stream [of air].   Then, however, as the air escapes, a corresponding mass of water flows in.   And so in the same way when water fills the hollow of the brazen vessel, and the neck or opening is stopped by the human hand, the air outside which strives to get in holds back the water at the gates of the narrow gurgling passage, holding possession of the end, until she lets go with her hand.   Then, on the contrary, the opposite of what happened before takes place, and as the air rushes in a corresponding mass of water rushes out.   Just so, when the smooth blood that courses through the limbs turns backward and rushes into the interior, straightway the stream of air comes surging in, and when the blood crowds back the air breathes out again, retracing its steps.

109. For with earth we perceive earth, with water, water, with air, the air divine, and with fire, the devouring fire, and love we perceive by means of love, hate by means of dismal hate.

133. We cannot bring God near so as to reach him with our eyes or lay hold of him with our hands—the [two ways] along which the chief highway of persuasion leads into the mind of man.

134. For he has no human head attached to bodily members, nor do two branching arms dangle from his shoulders; he has neither feet nor swift knees nor any hairy parts. No, he is only mind, sacred and ineffable mind, flashing through the whole universe with swift thoughts.

SECONDARY SOURCES

He [Empedocles] [1] makes the material elements four in number; fire, air, earth, and water.   These are eternal,

---

[1] Theophrastus, *Phys. Opin.* 3 (Dox. 478).

but they change in size—are large or small—through
composition and separation. But, accurately speaking,
he makes the first principles love and strife, for by them
the others are set in motion. For the elements must
continually be set in motion by each of the two in its
turn, now being united by love, and anon separated by
strife. Consequently there are according to him six
first principles.

Empedocles speaks in the same way of all the senses,
and says that we perceive through [effluences] fitting
into the pores of each sense. And that is why one sense
cannot pick out the objects of another, for the pores of
some are too wide and of others too narrow with reference
to the object of sense, so that the [effluences] either go
through untouched or are unable to enter at all.

He tries, too, to explain the nature of the eye. He
says that its interior is fire [and water]. This is surrounded by earth and watery vapor through which the
fire passes like the light in lanterns. The pores of fire
and water are arranged alternately. And we perceive
light objects by means of the pores of fire, dark objects
by means of those of water. The objects in each case
fit the corresponding pores, and the colors are carried
into the eye by effluences.

. . . Hearing, he says, is caused by sounds outside.
For when [the air] is set in motion by the voice there is
a sound in the ear, for hearing is like a bell sounding in
the ear which he calls a "fleshy nodule." And the air
when set in motion strikes on the solid parts and makes
a sound.

Smell comes from breathing, and that is why those
whose respiratory movement is most violent have the
keenest sense of smell, and why light and subtle bodies

exhale the strongest odors. As for taste and touch he does not explain how or by what means they arise, except to give the general explanation that sensation is due to [effluences] fitting into the pores.

Pleasure is produced by what is like, in the parts of the body and in the mixtures, pain by what is unlike.

**

And [2] he gives a similar account of knowledge and ignorance. Thinking, he says, is caused by what is like, being ignorant, by what is unlike, speaking as if thinking were the same as sensation, or very much like it.

**

Moreover [3] Anaxagoras and Empedocles say that [plants] are set in motion by desire, and that they perceive, and feel pleasure and pain.

**

. . . Anaxagoras,[4] Democritus and Empedocles say that [plants] have mind and intelligence.

**

Empedocles [5] was of the opinion that sex had been mixed in them.

**

Again [6] Empedocles says that plants come into being in an inferior world that is not perfect in its completion, and when it is completed the animal comes into being.

**

And [7] so Empedocles was wrong when he said that animals have many characteristics because it just happens so in their genesis, as, for example, that they have such a vertebrated spine because it fell to their lot to be descended from one that bent around.

[2] Theophrast. *De Sens.* (Dox. 500).
[3] Pseudo-Arist. *De Plant.* 815 a 15.
[4] Ib. 815 b 16.   [6] Ib. 817 b 35 (cf. D. 173).
[5] Ib. 815 a 20.   [7] Arist. *De Part. An.* 640 a 19.

VI

ANAXAGORAS

[Flourished about 460 B.C.]

THE FRAGMENTS

1.† ALL things were together, in number and in smallness without limit, for the small, too, was without limit. And as long as all things were together no one of them could be clearly distinguished, because of their smallness. Yes, and air and ether, both being infinite, dominated all things, for they are the biggest things in the universe both in quantity and in size.

4. And this being so one must suppose that many things and of all sorts coexist in all [the worlds] that are brought together—seeds of all things, having all sorts of forms and colors and savors. And (in all these worlds) men have been put together, and all animals that have life; and these men possess inhabited cities and tilled fields, as we do; and they have a sun and moon and other heavenly bodies, as we have; and their earth brings forth many plants and of all sorts, the most serviceable of which they garner and use for their sustenance. This then is the view that I have put forward with regard to the differentiation [of the primal mixture],—that it takes place not with us alone but also elsewhere.

---

† I follow the text as given by Diels, with a few exceptions which are noted, and have given his numbering of the fragments.

Before these things were differentiated, when all things were still together, there was not even any color clearly distinguishable, for the mixture of all things prevented it,—of the moist and the dry, the warm and the cold, the bright and the dark.   (And there was much earth too in the mixture †) and an endless multitude of seeds, no one like another.

5. We must know that when these things are separated one from another the whole is neither more nor less [than it was before], for it is impossible that there should be more than the whole, but the whole is always equal to itself.

17. We Greeks are wrong in using the expressions " to come into being" and " to be destroyed," for no thing comes into being or is destroyed.   Rather, a thing is mixed with or separated from already existing things. And so it would be more accurate to say, instead of origin, commingling; instead of destruction, dissolution.

6. And since the parts of the great and of the small are equal in number, this is another reason for holding that all things are in everything.   Nor is it possible for one of the parts to exist in isolation from the rest, but everything includes a portion of everything.   Since it is impossible that there should be any least part no portion can be isolated, or come to be by itself, but as at the beginning, so now, all things are together.   And in everything that has been differentiated, in what is largest as in what is smallest, many things are contained, and an equal number.

8. Nor are the things that exist in one and the same world isolated, or chopped off from one another as with

† This clause does not seem to belong in this context.   The text is possibly corrupt.   See Burnet, p. 285, note.

a hatchet—the warm from the cold or the cold from the warm.

10. For how could hair come from what is not hair, flesh from what is not flesh?

9. . . . while these things are thus swirling around and becoming differentiated by force and velocity. And the velocity gives the force. But their velocity is not to be compared to the velocity of anything in our present world. It is in every way many times as swift.

15. The dense and the moist, the cold and the dark, crowded together where the earth now is; the rare, the warm, the dry, and the bright,† travelled out into the far-off ether.

16. And from these as they were differentiated the earth was fashioned. For from the clouds water is separated off, from the water, earth; and from the earth stones are solidified by the influence of the cold, and they travel out still farther from the water.

11. In everything there is a portion of everything except mind. There are some things in which there is mind also.

12. All other things contain a portion of everything, but mind is infinite and self-ruled and is mixed with nothing. For if it did not exist by itself, but were mixed with anything else, it would contain a portion of all things. . . . For in everything there is a portion of everything, as I have said above. And in that case the things mixed with it would prevent it from having power over anything else such as it now has, being alone and by itself. For it is the thinnest of all things and the purest, and it possesses all knowledge and the greatest

† Following Schorn rather than Diels here, and adding καὶ τὸ λαμπρόν, after Hippolytus.

power. And whatsoever things are alive, the largest as well as the smallest, over all is mind the ruler. And over the whole revolving universe mind held sway, so that it caused it to revolve in the beginning. The revolution first began in a small area; now it extends over a larger space, and it will extend still farther. And mind knows all things, whether mixed together, or differentiated and separate. Mind also regulated all things,—what they were to be, what they were [but are not now], and what they are; and mind regulated the revolution in which revolve the stars, the sun and the moon, and the air and the ether that are differentiated [from the primal mixture]. And it is this revolution that caused the differentiation. The dense is differentiated from the rare, the warm from the cold, the light from the dark, the dry from the moist; and there are many portions of many things. Nothing, however, is altogether differentiated and distinct from anything else, excepting only mind. And all mind, whether greater or smaller, is alike. Nothing else, however, is like anything else. But whatever portions are predominant in each individual thing, these it has always been taken to be, because they were the most conspicuous things.

13. And when mind began to set things in motion there was a differentiation of all that was in motion, and whatever mind set in motion was all separated; and when things were set in motion and separated the revolution caused them to be much more separated.

14. And mind, which is eternal, is most assuredly now also where all other things are,—in the surrounding mass, in the things that have been differentiated, and in the things that are being differentiated.

15. For there is no least of what is small: there is

always a still smaller. For it is impossible that that which is should cease to be by being divided. On the other hand there is always a still larger than the large. And [the large] is equal to the small in number [of portions]. In itself, however, each thing is both large and small.

7. And so we cannot know either by word or by deed † the number of the things that have been differentiated.

21. Because of the weakness of our senses we are unable to discern the truth.

SECONDARY SOURCES

Anaxagoras [1] of Clazomenæ, son of Hegesiboulus, asserted that the homoiomeries were the first principles of all that exists. How anything could arise from what is not, or pass away into nothingness, seemed to him to present insuperable difficulties. The fact is we take nourishment that is simple and uniform, such as bread and water, and from it hair, veins, arteries, flesh, nerves, bones, and other parts of the body are made to grow; and since these things come into being we must admit that in the food taken all the things that are exist, and that it is from the things that are that all things derive their increase. Consequently the food contains the parts that are generative of blood, nerves, bones, and other things,—parts which were visible only to the eye of

[1] Aet. I. 3, 5 (Diels 279).

† As we should say, by reason or by experience. From Aristotle's discussion it would appear that the ground for this assertion is the fact that all knowing is defining and setting limits, which cannot be done in the case of what is strictly limitless. But as Anaxagoras held that mind knows all things, he must, Aristotle thinks, have held that they were limited by thought. This Aristotle holds to be inconsistent. But it need not have appeared such from the standpoint of Anaxagoras.

reason.   For we must not reduce all things to objects
of sense.   Sense would indicate that it is bread and
water that make these things,† but the eye of reason
can detect these portions already in the bread and water.
From the fact that the portions contained in the food are
like the things generated by it he called them homoiomeries; and the first principles of existing things, so far as
their matter is concerned, he declared to be these
homoiomeries.   He began his work with these words:
"All things were together; and mind separated them and
put them in order."
                                    * * *

According [2] to Anaxagoras perception is by opposites;
for like is not affected by like.   He attempts to give the
details with regard to each sense separately.   Seeing,
for example, is occasioned by the image on the pupil of
the eye; but no image is cast on what is of the same
color, but only on what is of a different color.   With
most animals this difference of color occurs in the day-
time; with some, however, it occurs at night, and that
is why they are keen-sighted at that time.   Still, as a
rule, night rather than day is of the same color with the
eyes.   And it is in the daytime that the image is cast,
because light is a joint cause of the image; and the predominant color casts an image more readily on its
opposite.

In the same way touch and taste discriminate their
objects.   For what is just as hot or just as cold as we
are neither warms us nor cools us by its presence; nor
do we know sweet and sour by means of themselves.
By the warm we know the cold, by the brackish water

[2] Theophr. *De Sens.* 27 (Dox. 507–8).
† That is, blood, nerves, etc.

the fresh, by the sour the sweet—according to our deficiency in each case. For all these things exist in us from the first. And similarly we smell at the same time that we breathe; and we hear by means of the sound penetrating to the brain—for the surrounding bone on which the sound impinges is hollow.

Further, all sensation is accompanied by pain. This would seem to be the simple consequence of his presupposition; for the contact of unlike with unlike is in every case painful. This pain is conspicuous in the case of sensations long continued or very intense; for brilliant colors and loud noises cause pain, and one cannot stand the same sensations very long.

The larger animals are the more sensitive; and, in general, sensation is an affair of size. For animals that have large, clear, and bright eyes see large things and at a great distance, and the opposite is the case with small-eyed animals. The same holds of hearing. Big ears hear loud sounds and from afar, while fainter sounds pass unnoticed: small ears hear sounds that are faint and near. The same holds of smell too. . . . Roughly speaking, large noses do not perceive a thin smell, nor small noses a thick one.

SOME OF ARISTOTLE'S COMMENTS ON ANAXAGORAS

Anaxagoras [3] says that man is the wisest of animals because he has hands.

* * *

Anaxagoras, [4] older in years, younger in works (than Empedocles), makes the first principles of things limitless in number. Practically all things made up of like parts arise and perish, just as fire and water do, by

[3] Arist. *Part. An.* I. 10, 687 a 7 (R. P. 127 B).
[4] Arist. *Met.* I. 3, 984 a 11.

combination and separation. In no other sense do they
arise or perish. Rather, they last forever.

*_**

If [5] you follow up the theory of Anaxagoras, and
develop what he meant to say, you will very likely find
him speaking more like our modern philosophers. For
when as yet nothing was clearly differentiated, it is
obvious that one could say nothing true about that
[undifferentiated] substance. I mean, for example, it
was neither white nor black nor gray, nor of any other
color, but was necessarily colorless. Otherwise it would
have had some one of those colors. So, too, by the same
line of argument, it had no taste; nor any other like
quality. In fact, it could not have any quality at all,
or any quantity, nor could it be any definite thing. For
that would mean that it would have some definite form,
which is impossible, since all things were mixed together. That is [if it had any definite characteristic],
differentiation would already have taken place. But he
says explicitly, all things were mixed together, with the
exception of mind which alone was unmixed and pure.
The inference from all this is, that he took as his first
principles, Unity—for Unity is simple and unmixed—
and the Other, which we [Platonists?] call the indefinite
before it has been defined, and before it participates
in the ideas. So, while what he says is neither correct
nor clear, still he means something very much like that
which later philosophers, and thinkers now more in
vogue, affirm.

[5] Arist. Met. I. 8, 989 b 4.

VII

THE ATOMISTS

LEUCIPPUS

[Flourished about 440 B.C.]

NOTHING [1] comes into being without a reason, but everything arises from a specific ground and driven by necessity.

**

Leucippus,[2] the Eleate, or the Milesian (for he is described in both ways), at first agreed with the philosophical views of Parmenides. But he did not follow the same path as Parmenides and Xenophanes in his account of the things that are, but, apparently, just the opposite. For whereas they made the All one, immovable, uncreated and limited, and did not permit inquiry into that which is not (τὸ μὴ ὄν), he began by assuming an unlimited number of elements, the atoms, which were always in motion. And he supposed them to have an infinite variety of forms, because there was no reason why they should have one form rather than another, and because he observed that the process of birth and change was unceasing. He further believed that that which is (τὸ ὄν) does not more truly exist than that which is not (τὸ μὴ ὄν), and that both alike are causes of the things that come into being. For he

---

[1] Leucippus, Fr. 2, Diels.
[2] Theophr. Phys. Op. Fr. 8 (D. 359).

assumed that the substance of the atoms was solid and
full; and he called them "what is," and that they moved
in the void, and he called that "what is not," and he
said that it was no less real than that which is. And
very much in the same way his associate Democritus
of Abdera assumes as first principles the plenum and
the void.
                            ***

Leucippus [3] thought he had a theory which was in
accord with sense-perception, and which did not annul
coming into being, or passing away, or motion, or the
multiplicity of existent things. With regard to these
matters he spoke the language of experience; but he
agreed with the philosophers who set up the One, in
holding that there is no motion apart from empty space;
and he says further that empty space is non-being, and
that no part of being can be non-being. For, strictly
speaking, that which is, is a plenum. But, he added,
being which answers to this description is not one; rather
there is an infinite number of such beings, and they are
invisible on account of the smallness of their bulk. They
move in empty space (for there is empty space); and,
coming together, they cause coming-into-being; being
separated, they cause passing-away.

LEUCIPPUS AND DEMOCRITUS

In [4] the main Leucippus and Democritus explain all
things in the same way and by the same argument,
taking as their first principle what in the order of nature comes first. Some of the ancient philosophers had
thought that that which is (τὸ ὄν) must necessarily be
one and immovable, for [so ran their argument] it could

---

[3] Arist. *De Gen. et Corr.* 325 a 23 (D. 358).
[4] Arist. *De Gen. et Corr.* 324 b 35 (D. 358).

not possibly move unless there were empty space apart from it, whereas empty space is non-existent; and it could not be a many unless there were empty space to keep the many asunder.

DEMOCRITUS
[Flourished about 420 B.C.]
THE FRAGMENTS

6.† Man should know from this rule that he is cut off from truth.

7. This argument too shows that in truth we know nothing about anything, but every man shares the generally prevailing opinion.

8. And yet it will be obvious that it is difficult to really know of what sort each thing is.

10. Now, that we do not really know of what sort each thing is, or is not, has often been shown.

117. Verily we know nothing. Truth is buried deep.

9. In fact we do not know anything infallibly, but only that which changes according to the condition of our body and of the [influences] that reach and impinge upon it.

11. There are two forms of knowledge, one genuine, one obscure. To the obscure belong all of the following: sight, hearing, smell, taste, feeling. The other form is the genuine, and is quite distinct from this. (And then distinguishing the genuine from the obscure, he continues:) Whenever the obscure [way of knowing] has reached the *minimum sensibile* of hearing, smell, taste, and touch, and when the investigation must be carried

† The numbering of the fragments is that of Diels, and I follow his text.

farther into that which is still finer, then arises the genuine way of knowing, which has a finer organ of thought.
  ***

0. [Democritus] [5] says: By convention (νόμῳ) sweet is sweet, by convention bitter is bitter, by convention hot is hot, by convention cold is cold, by convention color is color. But in reality there are atoms and the void. That is, the objects of sense are supposed to be real and it is customary to regard them as such, but in truth they are not. Only the atoms and the void are real.

2. Of practical wisdom these are the three fruits: to deliberate well, to speak to the point, to do what is right.

3. He who intends to enjoy life should not be busy about many things, and in what he does should not undertake what exceeds his natural capacity. On the contrary, he should have himself so in hand that even when fortune comes his way, and is apparently ready to lead him on to higher things, he should put her aside and not o'erreach his powers. For a being of moderate size is safer than one that bulks too big.

THE GOLDEN SAYINGS OF DEMOCRITUS

35. If any one hearken with understanding to these sayings of mine many a deed worthy of a good man shall he perform and many a foolish deed be spared.

37. If one choose the goods of the soul, he chooses the diviner [portion]; if the goods of the body, the merely mortal.

38. 'Tis well to restrain the wicked, and in any case not to join him in his wrong-doing.

40. 'Tis not in strength of body nor in gold that men

[5] Sext. Emp. *Math.* VII. 135.

find happiness, but in uprightness and in fulness of understanding.

41. Not from fear but from a sense of duty (διὰ τὸ δεόν) refrain from your sins.

43. Repentance for one's evil deeds is the safeguard of life.

45. He who does wrong is more unhappy than he who suffers wrong.

49. 'Tis a grievous thing to be subject to an inferior.

53. Many who have not learned wisdom live wisely, and many who do the basest deeds can make most learned speeches.

54. Fools learn wisdom through misfortune.

55. One should emulate works and deeds of virtue, not arguments about it.

57. Strength of body is nobility in beasts of burden, strength of character is nobility in men.

58. The hopes of the right-minded may be realized, those of fools are impossible.

59. Neither art nor wisdom may be attained without learning.

60. It is better to correct your own faults than those of another.

61. Those who have a well-ordered character lead also a well-ordered life.

62. Good means not [merely] not to do wrong, but rather not to desire to do wrong.

64. There are many who know many things, yet are lacking in wisdom.

77. Fame and wealth without wisdom are unsafe possessions.

78. Making money is not without its value, but nothing is baser than to make it by wrong-doing.

68. You can tell the man who rings true from the man who rings false, not by his deeds alone, but also by his desires.

82. False men and shams talk big and do nothing.

89. My enemy is not the man who wrongs me, but the man who means to wrong me.

90. The enmity of one's kindred is far more bitter than the enmity of strangers.

98. The friendship of one wise man is better than the friendship of a host of fools.

99. No one deserves to live who has not at least one good-man-and-true for a friend.

108. Seek after the good, and with much toil shall ye find it; the evil turns up of itself without your seeking it.

111. For a man petticoat government is the limit of insolence.

118. (Democritus said he would rather discover a single demonstration than win the throne of Persia.)

119. Men have made an idol of luck as an excuse for their own thoughtlessness. Luck seldom measures swords with wisdom. Most things in life quick wit and sharp vision can set right.

154a. In the weightiest matters we must go to school to the animals, and learn spinning and weaving from the spider, building from the swallow, singing from the birds,—from the swan and the nightingale, imitating their art.

160. An evil and foolish and intemperate and irreligious life should not be called a bad life, but rather, dying long drawn out.

176. Fortune is lavish with her favors, but not to be depended on. Nature on the other hand is self-

sufficing, and therefore with her feebler but trust-worthy [resources] she wins the greater [meed] of hope.

174. The right-minded man, ever inclined to righteous and lawful deeds, is joyous day and night, and strong, and free from care. But if a man take no heed of the right, and leave undone the things he ought to do, then will the recollection of no one of all his transgressions bring him any joy, but only anxiety and self-reproaching.

175. Now as of old the gods give men all good things, excepting only those that are baneful and in-jurious and useless. These, now as of old, are not gifts of the gods: men stumble into them themselves because of their own blindness and folly.

178. Of all things the worst to teach the young is dal-liance, for it is this that is the parent of those pleasures from which wickedness springs.

231. A sensible man takes pleasure in what he has in-stead of pining for what he has not.

230. A life without a holiday is like a long journey without an inn to rest at.

232. The pleasures that give most joy are the ones that most rarely come.

233. Throw moderation to the winds, and the greatest pleasures bring the greatest pains.

234. Men in their prayers beg the gods for health, not knowing that this is a thing they have in their own power. Through their incontinence undermining it, they themselves become, because of their passions, the betrayers of their own health.

191. Men achieve tranquillity through moderation in pleasure and through the symmetry of life. Want and superfluity are apt to upset them and to cause great

perturbations in the soul. The souls that are rent by violent conflicts are neither stable nor tranquil. One should therefore set his mind upon the things that are within his power, and be content with his opportunities, nor let his memory dwell very long on the envied and admired of men, nor idly sit and dream of them. Rather, he should contemplate the lives of those who suffer hardship, and vividly bring to mind their sufferings, so that your own present situation may appear to you important and to be envied, and so that it may no longer be your portion to suffer torture in your soul by your longing for more. For he who admires those who have, and whom other men deem blest of fortune, and who spends all his time idly dreaming of them, will be forced to be always contriving some new device because of his [insatiable] desire, until he ends by doing some desperate deed forbidden by the laws. And therefore one ought not to desire other men's blessings, and one ought not to envy those who have more, but rather, comparing his life with that of those who fare worse, and laying to heart their sufferings, deem himself blest of fortune in that he lives and fares so much better than they. Holding fast to this saying you will pass your life in greater tranquillity and will avert not a few of the plagues of life—envy and jealousy and bitterness of mind.

235. All who delight in the pleasures of the belly, exceeding all measure in eating and drinking and love, find that the pleasures are brief and last but a short while—only so long as they are eating and drinking—but the pains that come after are many and endure. The longing for the same things keeps ever returning, and whenever the objects of one's desire are realized forthwith the pleasure vanishes, and one has no further use

for them. The pleasure is brief, and once more the need for the same things returns.

252. We ought to regard the interests of the state as of far greater moment than all else, in order that they may be administered well; and we ought not to engage in eager rivalry in despite of equity, nor arrogate to ourselves any power contrary to the common welfare. For a state well administered is our greatest safeguard. In this all is summed up: When the state is in a healthy condition all things prosper; when it is corrupt, all things go to ruin.

THE ATOMISTS ON THE SOUL, ACCORDING TO ARISTOTLE

There [6] are some who maintain that fundamentally and primarily the soul is the principle of movement. They reasoned that that which is not itself in motion cannot move anything else, and thus they regarded the soul as one of those objects which were in motion. Democritus, whose view agrees with that of Leucippus, consequently maintained soul to be a sort of fire and heat. For as the forms of the atoms are as the atoms themselves unlimited, he declares that those which are spherical in shape constitute fire and soul, these atoms being like the so-called motes which are seen in the sun-beams that enter through doorways, and it is in such a mixed heap of seeds that he finds the elements of the whole natural world. The reason why they maintain that the spherical atoms constitute the soul, is that atoms of such configuration are best able to penetrate through everything, and to set the other things in motion at the same time as they are moved themselves, the

[6] Arist. *De An.* I. 2, 403 b 30. The passages from Aristotle's *Psychology* are given in Wallace's translation.

assumption here being that the soul is that which supplies
animals with motion.   This same assumption led them
to regard respiration as the boundary with which life
was coterminous.   It was, they held, the tendency of
the encircling atmosphere to cause contraction in the
animal body and to expel those atomic forms, which,
from never being at rest themselves, supply animals
with movement.   This tendency, however, was counter-
acted by the reënforcement derived from the entrance
from outside in the act of respiration of new atoms of
a similar kind.   These last in fact—such was their
theory—as they united to repel the compressing and
solidifying forces prevented those atoms already existing
in animals from being expelled from them: and life, they
thought, continued so long as there was strength to
carry on this process.   ***

[Democritus held] [7] that the soul ($\psi v \chi \acute{\eta}$) and reason
($vo\hat{v}s$) were the same thing, and that this belonged to
the class of primary and indivisible bodies, and had the
capacity of motion because of the smallness of its parts
and because of its shape.   Now the most mobile shape
is the spherical, and such is the shape of reason and of
fire.

[7] Arist. *De An.* 405 a 8.

VIII

THE SOPHISTS

[440–400 B.C.] †

MAN [1] is a measure of all things, of things that are, that they are; and of things that are not, that they are not.

**

With [2] regard to the gods I know not whether they exist or not, or what they are like. Many things prevent our knowing; the subject is obscure and brief is the span of our mortal life.

A SAYING OF GORGIAS

In [3] his work "On Nature, or the Non-Existent," he (Gorgias) arranges his discussion under three heads: First, nothing exists; second, if anything did exist we could never know it; third, if perchance a man should come to know it, it would remain a secret, he would be unable to describe it to his fellow-men.

[1] Sext. Emp. *Pyrrh. h.* I. 216; cf. also Plato, *Cratyl.* 385 E.; *Theæt.* 151 E.

[2] Eus. *P. E.* XIV. 3, 7; cf. Plato, *Theæt.*

[3] Sext. Emp. *Adv. Math.* VII. 67.

† Protagoras of Abdera flourished 440 B.C.; Gorgias **of Leontini** about the same time, or possibly a few years later; Prodicus of Ceos about 430.

AN ACCOUNT OF THE CALLING AND PROFESSIONS OF THE SOPHIST
FROM THE WRITINGS OF PLATO, IN A DISCUSSION CARRIED
ON BY THE 'ELEATIC STRANGER' AND THEÆTETUS

Eleatic Stranger.—First [4] let us wait a moment and recover breath; and while we are resting we can reckon in how many forms he [the Sophist] has appeared. In the first place, he was discovered to be a paid hunter after wealth and youth. . . . In the second place, he was a merchant in the goods of the soul. . . . In the third place, he has turned out to be a retailer of the same sort of wares.

Theætetus.—Yes; and in the fourth place, he himself manufactured the learned wares which he sold.

E. S.—Quite right; I will try and remember the fifth myself. He belonged to the fighting class, and was further distinguished as a debater who professed the eristic art. . . . This point was doubtful; yet we at least agreed that he was a purger of souls, who cleaned away notions obstructive to knowledge. . . . Again, in private conversation when any universal assertion is made about generation and essence, we know that such persons are tremendous argufiers, and are able to impart their own skill to others. . . . In a word, is not the art of disputation the power of disputing about all things?

Theæt.—Certainly; there does not seem to be much that is left out.

E. S.—But oh! my dear youth, do you suppose this possible? For perhaps your young eyes may see things which to our duller sight do not appear.

Theæt.—To what are you alluding? I don't think I understand your present question.

[4] From Plato's *Sophist*, Jowett's translation, beginning p. 231 D.

E. S.—I asked whether anybody can understand all things.

ARISTOTLE ON THE SOPHISTS

Sophistic [5] is nothing but apparent wisdom in no wise real, and the Sophist is only eager to get rich off his apparent wisdom which is not the true. Evidently these fellows seek rather to appear wise than to be wise without so appearing.

**

Of [6] men some possess genuine health, others have the appearance only and are puffed up and deck themselves like victims for the altar. The former are fair in virtue of their own beauty; the latter look fair—when they have made their toilet.

**

The [7] Sophist is a speculator in sham wisdom.

THE SOPHISTS AND THE ATHENIAN YOUTH

[The following graphic passage from Plato's *Protagoras* is given to show the acclaim with which the Sophists were received by the Athenian youth; and also to give Protagoras (through Plato) an opportunity to describe his own profession.]

Last night,[8] or rather very early this morning, Hippocrates, the son of Apollodorus and the brother of Phason, gave a tremendous thump with his staff at my door; some one opened to him, and he came rushing in and bawled out: "Socrates, are you awake or asleep?"

I knew his voice and said: "Hippocrates, is that you? and do you bring any news?"

[5] Arist., *Soph. el.*, I. 1, 165.
[6] Arist., *Soph. el.*, I. 1, 164.
[7] Arist. *Met.* III. 2, 1004.
[8] From Plato's *Protagoras*, Jowett's translation, beginning at p. 310 A

"Good news," he said; "nothing but good."

"Delightful," I said; "but what is the news? and why have you come hither at this unearthly hour?"

He drew nearer to me and said: "Protagoras is come."

"Yes," I replied; "he came two days ago: have you only just heard of his arrival?"

"Yes, by the gods," he said; "but not until yesterday evening."

At the same time he felt for the truckle-bed, and sat down at my feet, and then he said: "Yesterday quite late in the evening, on my return from Oenoe whither I had gone in pursuit of my runaway slave Satyrus, as I meant to have told you, if some other matter had not come in the way;—on my return, when we had done supper and were about to retire to rest, my brother said to me: 'Protagoras is come.' I was going to you at once, and then I thought that the night was far spent. But the moment sleep left me after my fatigue, I got up and came hither direct."

I, who knew the very courageous madness of the man, said: "What is the matter? Has Protagoras robbed you of anything?"

He replied, laughing: "Yes, indeed he has, Socrates, of the wisdom which he keeps from me."

"But, surely," I said, "if you give him money, and make friends with him, he will make you as wise as he is himself."

"Would to heaven," he replied, "that this were the case! He might take all that I have, and all that my friends have, if he pleased. But that is why I have come to you now, in order that you may speak to him on my behalf; for I am young, and also I have never seen nor heard him (when he visited Athens before I was but a

child); and all men praise him, Socrates; he is reputed
to be the most accomplished of speakers. There is no
reason why we should not go to him at once, and then we
shall find him at home. He lodges, as I hear, with
Callias the son of Hipponicus: let us start."

I replied: "Not yet, my good friend; the hour is
too early. But let us rise and take a turn in the
court and wait about there until daybreak; when the
day breaks, then we will go. For Protagoras is generally at home, and we shall be sure to find him; never
fear."

Upon this we got up and walked about in the court,
and I thought that I would make trial of the strength
of his resolution. So I examined him and put questions
to him. "Tell me, Hippocrates," I said, "as you are going
to Protagoras, and will be paying your money to him,
what is he to whom you are going? and what will he
make of you? . . . "

"They call him a Sophist, Socrates," he replied.

"Then we are going to pay our money to him in the
character of a Sophist?"

"Certainly."

"But suppose a person were to ask this further
question: 'And how about yourself? What will Protagoras make of you, if you go to see him?' "

He answered, with a blush upon his face (for the
day was just beginning to dawn, so that I could
see him): "Unless this differs in some way from the
former instances, I suppose that he will make a Sophist
of me."

"By the gods," I said, "and are you not ashamed at
having to appear before the Hellenes in the character of
a Sophist?"

"Indeed, Socrates, to confess the truth, I am. . . ."

I said: "I wonder whether you know what you are doing?"

"And what am I doing?"

"You are going to commit your soul to the care of a man whom you call a Sophist. And yet I hardly think that you know what a Sophist is; and if not, then you do not even know to whom you are committing your soul and whether the thing to which you commit yourself be good or evil. . . .

"If you were going to commit your body to some one, who might do good or harm to it, would you not carefully consider and ask the opinion of your friends and kindred, and deliberate many days as to whether you should give him the care of your body? But when the soul is in question, which you hold to be of far more value than the body, and upon the good or evil of which depends the well-being of your all,—about this you never consulted either with your father or with your brother or with any one of us who are your companions. But no sooner does this foreigner appear, than you instantly commit your soul to his keeping. In the evening, as you say, you hear of him, and in the morning you go to him, never deliberating or taking the opinion of any one as to whether you ought to intrust yourself to him or not;— you have quite made up your mind that you will at all hazards be a pupil of Protagoras, and are prepared to expend all the property of yourself and of your friends in carrying out at any price this determination, although, as you admit, you do not know him, and have never spoken with him: and you call him a Sophist, but are manifestly ignorant of what a Sophist is; and yet you are going to commit yourself to his keeping."

When he heard me say this, he replied: "No other inference, Socrates, can be drawn from your words."

I proceeded: "Is not a Sophist, Hippocrates, one who deals wholesale and retail in the food of the soul? To me that appears to be his nature."

"And what, Socrates, is the food of the soul?"

"Surely," I said, "knowledge is the food of the soul; and we must take care, my friend, that the Sophist does not deceive us when he praises what he sells, like the dealers wholesale or retail, who sell the food of the body; for they praise indiscriminately all their goods, without knowing what are really beneficial or hurtful: neither do their customers know, with the exception of any trainer or physician who may happen to buy of them. In like manner those who carry about the wares of knowledge, and make the round of the cities, and sell or retail them to any customer who is in want of them, praise them all alike; though I should not wonder, O my friend, if many of them were really ignorant of their effect upon the soul; and their customers equally ignorant, unless he who buys of them happens to be a physician of the soul. If, therefore, you have understanding of what is good and evil, you may safely buy knowledge of Protagoras or of any one; but if not, then, O my friend, pause, and do not hazard your dearest interests at a game of chance. For there is far greater peril in buying knowledge than in buying meat and drink: the one you purchase of the wholesale or retail dealer, and carry them away in other vessels, and before you receive them into the body as food, you may deposit them at home and call in any experienced friend who knows what is good to be eaten or drunken, and what not, and how much, and when; and then the danger of purchasing them is not so great.

But you cannot buy the wares of knowledge and carry them away in another vessel; when you have paid for them you receive them into the soul and go your way, either greatly harmed or greatly benefited; and therefore we should deliberate and take counsel with our elders; for we are still young—too young to determine such a matter.   And now let us go, as we were intending, and hear Protagoras; and when we have heard what he has to say, we may take counsel of others; for not only is Protagoras at the house of Callias, but there is Hippias of Elis, and, if I am not mistaken, Prodicus of Ceos, and several other wise men."

To this we agreed, and proceeded on our way until we reached the vestibule of the house; and there we stopped in order to conclude a discussion which had arisen between us as we were going along; and we stood talking in the vestibule until we had finished and come to an understanding.   And I think that the door-keeper, who was a eunuch, and who was probably annoyed at the great inroad of the Sophists, must have heard us talking.   At any rate, when we knocked at the door, and he opened and saw us, he grumbled: "They are Sophists—he is not at home"; and instantly gave the door a hearty bang with both his hands.   Again we knocked, and he answered without opening: "Did you not hear me say that he is not at home, fellows?"

"But, my friend," I said, "you need not be alarmed; for we are not Sophists, and we are not come to see Callias, but we want to see Protagoras; and I must request you to announce us."   At last, after a good deal of difficulty, the man was persuaded to open the door.

When we entered, we found Protagoras taking a walk in the cloister; and next to him, on one side, were walking

Callias, the son of Hipponicus, and Paralus, the son of
Pericles, who, by the mother's side, is his half-brother,
and Charmides, the son of Glaucon. On the other side
of him were Xanthippus, the other son of Pericles,
Philippides, the son of Philomelus; also Antimœrus of
Mende, who of all the disciples of Protagoras is the most
famous, and intends to make sophistry his profession.
A train of listeners followed him; the greater part of
them appeared to be foreigners, whom Protagoras had
brought with him out of the various cities visited by
him in his journeys, he, like Orpheus, attracting them
by his voice, and they following. I should mention
also that there were some Athenians in the company.
Nothing delighted me more than the precision of their
movements: they never got into his way at all; but when
he and those who were with him turned back, then the
band of listeners parted regularly on either side; he was
always in front, and they wheeled round and took their
places behind him in perfect order.

After him, as Homer says, 'I lifted up my eyes and
saw' Hippias the Elean sitting in the opposite cloister
on a chair of state, and around him were seated on
benches Eryximachus, the son of Acumenus, and Phædrus
the Myrrhinusian, and Andron the son of Androtion, and
there were strangers whom he had brought with him from
his native city of Elis, and some others: they were putting
to Hippias certain physical and astronomical questions,
and he, *ex cathedrâ*, was determining their several questions to them, and discoursing of them.

Also, 'my eyes beheld Tantalus'; for Prodicus the
Cean was at Athens: he had been lodged in a room which,
in the days of Hipponicus, was a storehouse; but, as the
house was full, Callias had cleared this out and made

the room into a guest-chamber. Now Prodicus was still in bed, wrapped up in sheepskins and bedclothes, of which there seemed to be a great heap. . . . I was very anxious to hear what Prodicus was saying, for he seems to me to be an all-wise and inspired man; but I was not able to get into the inner circle, and his fine deep voice made an echo in the room which rendered his words inaudible. . . .

On entering we stopped a little, in order to look about us, and then walked up to Protagoras, and I said: "Protagoras, my friend Hippocrates and I have come to see you."

"Do you wish," he said, "to speak with me alone, or in the presence of the company?"

"Whichever you please," I said; "you shall determine when you have heard the purpose of our visit. . . ."

As I suspected that he would like to have a little display and glorification in the presence of Prodicus and Hippias, and would gladly show us to them in the light of his admirers, I said: "But why should we not summon Prodicus and Hippias and their friends to hear us?"

"Very good," he said.

"Suppose," said Callias, "that we hold a council in which you may sit and discuss." This was agreed upon, and great delight was felt at the prospect of hearing wise men talk; we ourselves took the chairs and benches, and arranged them by Hippias, where the other benches had been already placed. Meanwhile Callias and Alcibiades got Prodicus out of bed and brought in him and his companions.

When we were all seated, Protagoras said: "Now that the company are assembled, Socrates, tell me about the young man of whom you were just now speaking."

I replied: ". . . This is my friend Hippocrates, who is desirous of making your acquaintance; he would like to know what will happen to him if he associates with you. I have no more to say."

Protagoras answered: "Young man, if you associate with me, on the very first day you will return home a better man than you came, and better on the second day than on the first, and better every day than you were on the day before."

When I heard this, I said: ". . . When you say that on the first day on which he associates with you he will return home a better man, and on every day will grow in like manner,—in what, Protagoras, will he be better? and about what?"

When Protagoras heard me say this, he replied: "You ask questions fairly, and I like to answer a question which is fairly put. If Hippocrates comes to me he will not experience the sort of drudgery with which other Sophists are in the habit of insulting their pupils; who, when they have just escaped from the arts, are taken and driven back into them by these teachers, and made to learn calculation, and astronomy and geometry, and music" (he gave a look at Hippias as he said this); "but if he comes to me, he will learn that which he comes to learn. And this is prudence in affairs private as well as public; he will learn to order his own house in the best manner, and he will be able to speak and act for the best in the affairs of the state."

"Do I understand you," I said; "and is your meaning that you teach the art of politics, and that you promise to make men good citizens?"

"That, Socrates, is exactly the profession which I make."

"Then," I said, "you do indeed possess a noble art, if there is no mistake about this; for I will freely confess to you, Protagoras, that I have a doubt whether this art is capable of being taught, and yet I know not how to disbelieve your assertion. . . ."

THE PROTAGOREAN DOCTRINE OF RELATIVITY AS PLATO INTERPRETS IT IN THE THEÆTETUS

[The question that has been raised is: What is knowledge? Theætetus has hazarded the opinion that "Knowledge is sense-perception," whereupon Socrates proceeds as follows:]

Socrates.—Well,[9] you have delivered yourself of a very important doctrine about knowledge; it is indeed the opinion of Protagoras, who has another way of expressing it. Man, he says, is the measure of all things, of the existence of things that are, and of the non-existence of things that are not:—You have read him?

Theætetus.—Oh, yes, again and again.

Soc.—Does he not say that things are to you such as they appear to you, and to me such as they appear to me, and that you and I are men?

Theæt.—Yes, he says so.

Soc.—A wise man is not likely to talk nonsense. Let us try to understand him: the same wind is blowing, and yet one of us may be cold and the other not, or one may be slightly and the other very cold?

Theæt.—Quite true.

Soc.—Now is the wind, regarded not in relation to us, but absolutely, cold or not; or are we to say, with

[9] From Plato's *Theætetus*, beginning on p. 151 E., Jowett's translation.

Protagoras, that the wind is cold to him who is cold, and not to him who is not?

Theæt.—I suppose the last.

Soc.—Then it must appear so to each of them?

Theæt.—Yes.

Soc.—And 'appears to him' means the same as 'he perceives.'

Theæt.—True.

Soc.—Then, appearing and perceiving coincide in the case of hot and cold, and in similar instances; for things appear, or may be supposed to be, to each one such as he perceives them?

Theæt.—Yes.

Soc.—Then perception is always of existence, and being the same as knowledge is unerring?

Theæt.—Clearly.

Soc.—In the name of the Graces, what an almighty wise man Protagoras must have been! He spoke these things in a parable to the common herd, like you and me, but told the truth, 'his Truth,' in secret to his own disciples.

Theæt.—What do you mean, Socrates?

Soc.—I am about to speak of a high argument, in which all things are said to be relative; you cannot rightly call anything by any name, such as great or small, heavy or light, for the great will be small and the heavy light—there is no single thing or quality, but out of motion and change and admixture all things are becoming relatively to one another, which 'becoming' is by us incorrectly called being, but is really becoming, for nothing ever is, but all things are becoming. Summon all philosophers—Protagoras, Heracleitus, Empedocles, and the rest of them, one after another, and with the exception of Parmenides they will agree with you in this. Summon the great masters of either kind of poetry—Epicharmus, the prince of Comedy, and Homer of Tragedy; when the latter sings of

' Ocean whence sprang the gods, and mother Tethys,'

does he not mean that all things are the offspring of flux and motion? Then now apply his doctrine to perception, my good friend, and first of all to vision; that which you call white color is not in your eyes, and is not a distinct thing which exists out of them. And you must not assign any place to it: for if it had position it would be, and be at rest, and there would be no process of becoming.

Theæt.—Then what is color?

Soc.—Let us carry out the principle which has just been affirmed, that nothing is self-existent, and then we shall see that white, black, and every other color, arises out of the eye meeting the appropriate motion, and that what we call a color is in each case neither the active nor the passive element, but something which passes between them, and is peculiar to each percipient; are you quite certain that the several colors appear to a dog or to any animal whatever as they appear to you?

Theæt.—Far from it.

Soc.—Or that anything appears the same to you as to another man? Are you so profoundly convinced of this? Rather would it not be true that it never appears exactly the same to you, because you are never exactly the same?

Theæt.—The latter.

Soc.—And if that with which I compare myself in size, or which I apprehend by touch, were great or

white or hot, it could not become different by mere
contact with another unless it actually changed; nor
again, if the comparing or apprehending subject were
great or white or hot, could this, when unchanged from
within, become changed by any approximation or affection of any other thing. The fact is that in our ordinary
way of speaking we allow ourselves to be driven into
most ridiculous and wonderful contradictions, as Protagoras and all who take his line of argument would remark.
. . . I am charmed with his doctrine, that what appears
is to each one, but I wonder that he did not begin his
book on Truth with a declaration that a pig or a dog-
faced baboon, or some other yet stranger monster which
has sensation, is the measure of all things; then he might
have shown a magnificent contempt for our opinion of
him by informing us at the outset that while we were
reverencing him like a God for his wisdom he was no
better than a tadpole, not to speak of his fellow-men—
would not this have produced an overpowering effect?
For if truth is only sensation, and no man can discern
another's feelings better than he, or has any superior
right to determine whether his opinion is true or false,
but each, as we have several times repeated, is to himself
the sole judge, and everything that he judges is true and
right, why, my friend, should Protagoras be preferred
to the place of wisdom and instruction, and deserve to
be well paid, and we poor ignoramuses have to go to
him, if each one is the measure of his own wisdom?
Must he not be talking 'ad captandum' in all this? I
say nothing of the ridiculous predicament in which my
own midwifery and the whole art of dialectic is placed;
for the attempt to supervise or refute the notions or
opinions of others would be a tedious and enormous piece

of folly, if to each man his own are right; and this must be the case if Protagoras's Truth is the real truth, and the philosopher is not merely amusing himself by giving oracles out of the shrine of his book. . . .

Well, you ask, and how will Protagoras reënforce his position? Shall I answer for him?

Theæt.—By all means.

Soc.—. . . Oh, my good sir, he will say, Come to the argument in a more generous spirit; and either show, if you can, that our sensations are not relative and individual, or, if you admit them to be so, prove that this does not involve the consequence that the appearance becomes, or, if you will have the word, is, to the individual only. As to your talk about pigs and baboons, you are yourself behaving like a pig, and you teach your hearers to make sport of my writings in the same ignorant manner; but this is not to your credit. For I declare that the truth is as I have written, and that each of us is a measure of existence and of non-existence. Yet one man may be a thousand times better than another in proportion as different things are and appear to him. And I am far from saying that wisdom and the wise man have no existence; but I say that the wise man is he who makes the evils which appear and are to a man, into goods which are and appear to him. And I would beg you not to press my words in the letter, but to take the meaning of them as I will explain them. Remember what has been already said— that to the sick man his food appears to be and is bitter, and to the man in health the opposite of bitter. Now I cannot conceive that one of these men can be or ought to be made wiser than the other; nor can you assert that the sick man because he has one impression is foolish, and the healthy man because he has another is wise; but the one state requires to be changed into the other, the worse into the better. As in education, a change of state has to be effected, and the Sophist accomplishes by words the change which the physician works by the aid of drugs. Not that any one ever made another think truly, who previously thought falsely. For no one can think what is not, or think anything different from that which he feels; and this is always true. But as the inferior habit of mind has thoughts of a kindred nature, so I conceive that a good mind causes men to have good thoughts; and these which the inexperienced call true, I maintain to be only better, and not truer than others. And, O my dear Socrates, I do not call wise men tadpoles: far from it; I say that they are the physicians of the human body, and the husbandmen of plants—for the husbandmen also take away the evil and disordered sensations of plants, and infuse into them good and healthy sensations—aye, and true ones; and the wise and good rhetoricians make the good instead of the evil to seem just to states; for whatever appears to a state to be just and fair, so long as it is regarded as such, is just and fair to it; but the teacher of wisdom causes the good to take the place of the evil, both in appearance and in reality. And in like manner the Sophist who is able to train his pupils in this spirit is a wise man, and deserves to be well paid by them. And so one man is wiser than another; and no one thinks falsely, and you, whether you will or not, must endure to be a measure. On these foundations the argument stands firm, which you, Socrates, may, if you please, overthrow by an opposite argument, or if you like you may put questions to me—a method to which no intelligent person will object, quite the reverse. But I must beg you to put fair questions: for there is great inconsistency in saying that you have a zeal for virtue, and then always behaving unfairly in argument. The unfairness of which I complain is that you do not distinguish between mere disputation and dialectic: the disputer may trip up his opponent as often as he likes, and make fun; but the dialectician will be in earnest, and only correct his adversary when necessary, telling him the errors into which he has fallen through his own fault, or that of the company which he has previously kept. If you do so, your adversary will lay the blame of his own confusion and perplexity on himself, and not on you. He will follow and love you, and will hate himself, and escape from himself into philosophy, in order that he may become different from what he was. But the other mode of arguing, which is practised by the many, will have just the opposite effect upon him; and as he grows older, instead of turning philosopher, he will come to hate philosophy. I would recommend you, therefore, as I said before, not to encourage yourself in this polemical and controversial temper, but to find out, in a friendly and congenial spirit, what we really mean when we say that all things are in motion, and that to every individual and state what appears, is. In this manner you will consider whether knowledge and sensation are the same or different, but you will not argue, as you were just now doing, from the customary use of names and words, which the vulgar pervert in all sorts of ways, causing infinite perplexity to one another. Such, Theodorus, is the very slight help which I am able to offer to your old friend; had he been living, he would have helped himself in a far more gloriose style.

PLATO'S ACCOUNT OF GORGIAS AS A RHETORICIAN

O Meno,[10] there was a time when the Thessalians were famous among the other Hellenes only for their riches and their riding; but now, if I am not mistaken, they are equally famous for their wisdom, especially at Larissa, which is the native city of your friend Aristippus. And this is Gorgias's doing; for when he came there, the flower of the Aleuadæ, among them your admirer Aristippus, and the other chiefs of the Thessalians, fell in love with his wisdom. And he has taught you the habit of answering questions in a grand and bold style, which becomes those who know, and is the style in which he himself answers all comers; and any Hellene who likes may ask him anything.   ***

Chærephon.—Tell [11] me, Gorgias, is our friend Callicles right in saying that you undertake to answer any questions which you are asked?

Gorgias.—Quite right, Chærephon: I was saying as much only just now; and I may add, that many years have elapsed since any one has asked me a new one. . . .

Socrates.—Gorgias, . . . what are we to call you, and what is the art which you profess?

Gor.—Rhetoric, Socrates, is my art.

Soc.—Then I am to call you a rhetorician?

Gor.—Yes, Socrates, and a good one too, if you would call me that which, in Homeric language, "I boast myself to be." . . .

Soc.—[And] rhetoric, as would appear, is the artificer of a persuasion which creates belief about the just and unjust, but gives no instruction about them?

Gor.—True.

[10] From the *Meno* of Plato, p. 70 D., Jowett's translation.
[11] From the *Gorgias* of Plato, p. 447 E., Jowett's translation.

IX

SOCRATES

[469–399 B.C.]

ARISTOTLE ON SOCRATES'S ACHIEVEMENT

THERE [1] are two things that one would rightly attribute to Socrates: inductive reasoning and universal definition. And in fact these two things are the very foundations of knowledge. But Socrates did not give his universals, or his definitions, separate existence. Others, however, did, and called such reals 'ideas.'

XENOPHON'S TRIBUTE TO SOCRATES †

It [2] seems wonderful to me, that any should have been persuaded that Socrates corrupted the youth; Socrates, who, in addition to what has been said of him, was not only the most rigid of all men in the government of his passions and appetites, but also most able to withstand cold, heat, and every kind of labor; and, besides, so inured to frugality, that, though he possessed very little, he very easily made it a sufficiency. How, then, being of such a character himself, could he have rendered others impious, or lawless, or luxurious, or incontinent, or too effeminate to endure labor? On the contrary, he restrained many of them from such vices, leading them

---

[1] Arist. *Met.* 12, 4, 1078 b.

[2] Xenophon's *Memorabilia*, I. 2, 1.

† The passages from Xenophon's *Memorabilia* are given in Watson's translation

to love virtue, and giving them hopes, that if they would take care of themselves, they would become honorable and worthy characters. Not indeed that he ever professed to be an instructor in that way, but, by showing that he was himself such a character, he made those in his society hope that, by imitating him, they would become such as he was.

Of the body he was not neglectful, nor did he commend those who were. He did not approve that a person should eat to excess, and then use immoderate exercise, but recommended that he should work off, by a proper degree of exercise, as much as the appetite received with pleasure; for such a habit, he said, was peculiarly conducive to health, and did not prevent attention to the mind. He was not, however, fine or ostentatious in his clothes or sandals, or in any of his habits of life; yet he did not make those about him lovers of money, for he checked them in this as well as other passions, and asked no remuneration from those who desired his company. By refraining from such demand, he thought that he consulted his liberty, and called those who took money for their discourses their own enslavers, since they must of necessity hold discussions with those from whom they received pay. . . .

How then could a man of such a character corrupt the young, unless, indeed, the study of virtue be corruption?

**

[Socrates] [3] disciplined his mind and body by sucn a course of life, that he who should adopt a similar one, would, if no supernatural influence prevented, live in good spirits and uninterrupted health, nor would he ever

---

[a] Xenophon's *Memorabilia*, I. 3, 5.

be in want of the necessary expenses for it. So frugal was he that I do not know whether any one could earn so little by the labor of his hands, as not to procure sufficient to have satisfied Socrates. He took only so much food as he could eat with a keen relish; and, to this end, he came to his meals so disposed that the appetite for his meat was the sauce to it. Every kind of drink was agreeable to him, because he never drank unless he was thirsty. If he ever complied with an invitation to go to a feast, he very easily guarded, what is extremely difficult to most men, against loading his stomach to excess. Those who were unable to do so, he advised to be cautious of taking anything that would stimulate them to eat when they were not hungry, and to drink when they were not thirsty; for he said that those were the things that disordered the stomach, the head, and the mind; and he used to say, in jest, that he thought Circe transformed men into swine, by entertaining them with abundance of such luxuries, but that Ulysses, through the admonition of Mercury and through being himself temperate, and forbearing to partake of such delicacies to excess, was in consequence not changed into a swine.

***

Concerning [4] justice, too, he did not conceal what sentiments he entertained, but made them manifest even by his actions, for he conducted himself, in his private capacity, justly and beneficently towards all men, and, as a citizen, he obeyed the magistrates in all that the laws enjoined, both in the city and on military expeditions, so that he was distinguished above other men for his observance of order.   When he was president

[4] Xenophon's *Memorabilia*, IV. 4, 1.

in the public assembly, he would not permit the people to give a vote contrary to law, but opposed himself, in the defence of the laws, to such a storm of rage on the part of the populace as I think that no other man could have withstood. When the Thirty Tyrants commanded him to do anything contrary to the laws, he refused to obey them; for both when they forbade him to converse with the young, and when they ordered him, and some others of the citizens, to lead a certain person away to death, he alone did not obey, because the order was given contrary to the laws. When he was accused by Meletus, and others were accustomed, before the tribunal, to speak so as to gain the favor of the judges, and to flatter them, and to supplicate them, in violation of the laws, and many persons, by such practices, had often been acquitted by the judges, he refused, on his trial, to comply with any practices opposed to the laws, and though he might easily have been acquitted by his judges, if he had but in a slight degree adopted any of these customs, he chose rather to die abiding by the laws than to save his life by transgressing them.

To me, therefore, Socrates, being a man of such a character, appeared to be worthy of honor rather than of death; and any one, considering his case according to the laws, would find such to be the fact; for, by the laws, death is the punishment for a man if he be found stealing, or stripping people of their clothes, or cutting purses, or house-breaking, or kidnapping, or sacrilege, of which crimes Socrates was the most innocent of all men. Nor was he ever the cause of any war ending unfortunately for the state, or of any sedition or treachery; nor did he ever, in his private transactions, either deprive any man of what was for his good, or involve him in any evil; nor did he ever lie under suspicion of any of the crimes which I have mentioned.

***

How [5] then could he have been guilty of the charges brought against him? a man who, instead of not acknowledging the gods, as was stated in the indictment, evidently paid respect to the gods more than other men; and instead of corrupting the youth, as the accuser laid to his charge, plainly led such of his associates as had vicious inclinations to cease from indulging them, and exhorted them to cherish a love of that most honorable and excellent virtue, by which men successfully govern states and families.   How then, pursuing such a course of conduct, was he not deserving of great honor from the city?

THE SORT OF QUESTIONS SOCRATES WAS CONCERNED WITH

He [6] did not dispute about the nature of things as most other philosophers disputed, speculating how that which is called by the Sophists the world was produced, and by what necessary laws everything in the heavens is effected, but endeavored to show that those who chose such objects of contemplation were foolish; and used in the first place to inquire of them whether they thought that they already knew sufficient of human affairs, and therefore proceeded to such subjects of meditation, or whether, when they neglected human affairs entirely, and speculated on celestial matters, they thought that they were doing what became them.   He wondered, too, that it was not apparent to them that it is impossible for man to satisfy himself on such points, since even those who pride themselves most on discussing them, do not

[5] Xenophon's *Memorabilia*, I. 2, 64.   [6] Ib., I. 1, 16.

hold the same opinions one with another, but are, compared with each other, like madmen. . . .

*_**

He [7] would ask, also, concerning such philosophers, whether, as those who have learned arts practised by men expect that they will be able to carry into effect what they have learned, either for themselves, or for any one else whom they may wish, so those who inquire into celestial things imagine that, when they have discovered by what laws everything is effected, they will be able to produce, whenever they please, wind, rain, changes of the seasons, and whatever else of that sort they may desire, or whether they have no such expectation, but are content merely to know how everything of that nature is generated. Such were the observations which he made about those who busied themselves in such speculations; but for himself, he would hold discourse, from time to time, on what concerned mankind, considering what was pious, what impious; what was becoming, what unbecoming; what was just, what unjust; what was sanity, what insanity; what was fortitude, what cowardice; what a state was, and what the character of a statesman; what was the nature of government over men, and the qualities of one skilled in governing them; and touching on other subjects, with which he thought that those who were acquainted were men of worth and estimation, but that those who were ignorant of them might justly be deemed no better than slaves.

SOCRATES ON THE GOOD AND THE BEAUTIFUL

When [8] Aristippus attempted to confute Socrates, as he himself had previously been confuted by him, Socrates,

---

[7] Xenophon's *Memorabilia* I. 1, 15.   [8] Ib., III. 8, 1

wishing to benefit those who were with him, gave his
answers, not like those who are on their guard lest their
words be perverted, but like those who are persuaded
that they ought above all things to do what is right.
What Aristippus had asked him was, 'whether he knew
anything good,' in order that if he should say any such
thing as food, or drink, or money, or health, or strength,
or courage, he might prove that it was sometimes an
evil.   But Socrates, reflecting that if anything troubles
us we want something to relieve us from it, replied, as it
seemed best to do, "Do you ask me whether I know
anything good for a fever?"   "I do not."   "Anything
good for soreness of the eyes?"   "No."   "For hunger?"
"No, nor for hunger either."   "Well, then," concluded
Socrates, "if you ask me whether I know anything good
that is good for nothing, I neither know anything, nor
wish to know."

Aristippus again asking him if he knew anything
beautiful, he replied, "Many things."   "Are they then,"
inquired Aristippus, "all like each other?"   "Some of
them," answered Socrates, "are as unlike one another
as it is possible for them to be."   "How then," said he,
"can what is beautiful be unlike what is beautiful?"
"Because, assuredly," replied Socrates, "one man, who
is beautifully formed for wrestling, is unlike another
who is beautifully formed for running; and a shield, which
is beautifully formed for defence, is as unlike as possible
to a dart, which is beautifully formed for being forcibly
and swiftly hurled."   "You answer me," said Aristippus,
"in the same manner as when I asked you whether you
knew anything good."   "And do you imagine," said
Socrates, "that the good is one thing, and the beautiful
another?   Do you not know that with reference to the

same objects all things are both beautiful and good?
Virtue, for instance, is not good with regard to some
things and beautiful with regard to others; and persons,
in the same way, are called beautiful and good with
reference to the same objects; and human bodies, too,
with reference to the same objects, appear beautiful and
good; and in like manner all other things, whatever men
use, are considered beautiful and good with reference to
the objects for which they are serviceable."

***

When [9] some one asked him what object of study he
thought best for a man, he replied, "Good conduct."
When he asked him again whether he thought "good
fortune" an object of study, he answered, " 'Fortune'
and 'Conduct' I think entirely opposed; for, for a person
to light on anything that he wants without seeking it,
I consider to be 'good fortune,' but to achieve anything
successfully by learning and study, I regard as 'good
conduct'; and those who make this their object of study
appear to me to do well."

The best men, and those most beloved by the gods,
he observed, were those who, in agriculture, performed
their agricultural duties well, those who, in medicine,
performed their medical duties well, and those who, in
political offices, performed their public duties well;
but he who did nothing well, he said, was neither useful
for any purpose, nor acceptable to the gods.

***

"But [10] as to wisdom, Socrates, it is indisputably a good
thing; for what business will not one who is wise conduct
better than one who is untaught?" "Have you not
heard, then, of Dædalus," said Socrates, "how he was

[9] Xenophon's *Memorabilia*, III. 9, 14.　　[10] Ib., IV. 2, 33.

made prisoner by Minos and compelled to serve him as a slave; how he was cut off, at once, from his country and from liberty, and how, when he endeavored to escape with his son, he lost the child, and was unable to save himself, but was carried away among barbarians, and made a second time a slave?" "Such a story is told, indeed," said Euthydemus. "Have you not heard, too, of the sufferings of Palamedes? for everybody says that it was for his wisdom he was envied and put to death by Ulysses." "That, too, is said," replied Euthydemus. "And how many other men do you think have been carried off to the king on account of their wisdom, and made slaves there?"

"But as to happiness, Socrates," said Euthydemus, "that at least appears to be an indisputable good." "Yes, Euthydemus," replied Socrates, "if we make it consist in things that are indisputably good." "But what," said he, "among things constituting happiness can be a doubtful good?" "Nothing," answered Socrates, "unless we join with it beauty, or strength, or wealth, or glory, or any other such thing." "But we must assuredly join them with it," said Euthydemus; "for how can a person be happy without them?" "We shall then join with it, by Jupiter," said Socrates, "things from which many grievous calamities happen to mankind; for many, on account of their beauty, are ruined by those who are maddened with passion for their youthful attractions; many, through confidence in their strength, have entered upon undertakings too great for it, and involved themselves in no small disasters; many, in consequence of their wealth, have become enervated, been plotted against, and destroyed; and many, from the glory and power that they have acquired

in their country, have suffered the greatest calamities."
"Well, then," said Euthydemus, "if I do not say what
is right when I praise happiness, I confess that I do not
know what we ought to pray for to the gods."

*_**

You,[11] Antipho, seem to think that happiness consists
in luxury and extravagance; but I think that to want
nothing is to resemble the gods, and that to want as little
as possible is to make the nearest approach to the gods;
that the Divine nature is perfection, and that to be nearest to the Divine nature is to be nearest to perfection.

SOCRATES'S METHOD

And [12] he observed that the expression διαλέγεσθαι,
"to reason," had its origin in people's practice of meeting
together to reason on matters, and distinguishing them,
διαλέγοντες, according to their several kinds. It was
the duty of every one, therefore, he thought, to make
himself ready in this art, and to study it with the greatest
diligence; for that men, by the aid of it, became most
accomplished, most able to guide others, and most acute
in discussion.

*_**

Whenever [13] any person contradicted him on any point
who had nothing definite to say, and who perhaps asserted, without proof, that some person, whom he
mentioned, was wiser, or better skilled in political affairs,
or possessed of greater courage, or worthier in some such
respect [than some other whom Socrates had mentioned],
he would recall the whole argument, in some such way
as the following, to the primary proposition: "Do you
say that he whom you commend, is *a better citizen* than

[11] Xenophon's *Memorabilia*, I. 6, 10.
[12] Ib., IV. 5, 12.
[13] Ib., IV. 7, 13.

he whom I commend?" "I do say so." "Why should we not then consider, in the first place, what is the duty of *a good citizen*?" "Let us do so." "Would not he then be superior in the management of the public money who should make the state richer?" "Undoubtedly." "And he in war who should make it victorious over its enemies?" "Assuredly." "And in an embassy he who should make friends of foes?" "Doubtless." "And he in addressing the people who should check dissension and inspire them with unanimity?" "I think so." When the discussion was thus brought back to fundamental principles, the truth was made evident to those who had opposed him.

When he himself went through any subject in argument, he proceeded upon propositions of which the truth was generally acknowledged, thinking that a sure foundation was thus formed for his reasoning. Accordingly, whenever he spoke, he, of all men that I have known, most readily prevailed on his hearers to assent to his arguments; and he used to say that Homer had attributed to Ulysses the character of *a sure orator*, as being able to form his reasoning on points acknowledged by all mankind.

A BIT OF SOCRATES'S BIOGRAPHY REPORTED BY PLATO

[From Plato's *Phædo*. Socrates himself speaks:]

When [14] I was young, Cebes, I had a prodigious desire to know that department of philosophy which is called the investigation of nature; to know the causes of things, and why a thing is and is created or destroyed appeared to me to be a lofty profession; and I was always agitating myself with the consideration of questions such

[14] Plato, *Phædo*, beginning p. 96 A, Jowett's translation.

as these:—Is the growth of animals the result of some
decay which the hot and cold principle contracts, as
some have said? Is the blood the element with which
we think, or the air, or the fire? or perhaps nothing of the
kind—but the brain may be the originating power of the
perceptions of hearing and sight and smell, and memory
and opinion may come from them, and science may be
based on memory and opinion when they have attained
fixity. And then I went on to examine the corruption
of them, and then to the things of heaven and earth,
and at last I concluded myself to be utterly and absolutely incapable of these inquiries, as I will satisfactorily prove to you. For I was fascinated by them
to such a degree that my eyes grew blind to things which
I had seemed to myself, and also to others, to know quite
well; I forgot what I had before thought self-evident
truths; e. g., such a fact as that the growth of man is the
result of eating and drinking; for when by the digestion
of food flesh is added to flesh and bone to bone, and
whenever there is an aggregation of congenial elements,
the lesser bulk becomes larger and the small man great.
. . . I am not any longer satisfied that I understand
the reason why one or anything else is either generated
or destroyed or is at all, but I have in my mind some
confused notion of a new method, and can never admit
the other.

Then I heard some one reading, as he said, from a book
of Anaxagoras, that mind was the disposer and cause of
all, and I was delighted at this notion, which appeared
quite admirable, and I said to myself: If mind is the
disposer, mind wlil dispose all for the best, and put each
particular in the best place; and I argued that if any one
desired to find out the cause of the generation or de-

struction or existence of anything, he must find what state of being or doing or suffering was best for that thing, and therefore a man had only to consider the best for himself and others and then he would also know the worse, since the same science comprehended both. And I rejoiced to think that I had found in Anaxagoras a teacher of the causes of existence such as I desired, and I imagined that he would tell me first whether the earth is flat or round; and whichever was true, he would proceed to explain the cause and the necessity of this being so, and then he would teach me the nature of the best and show that this was best; and if he said that the earth was in the centre, he would further explain that this position was the best, and I should be satisfied with the explanation given, and not want any other sort of cause. And I thought that I would then go on and ask him about the sun and moon and stars, and that he would explain to me their comparative swiftness, and their returnings and various states, active and passive, and how all of them were for the best. For I could not imagine that when he spoke of mind as the disposer of them, he would give any other account of their being as they are, except that this was best; and I thought that when he had explained to me in detail the cause of each and the cause of all, he would go on to explain to me what was best for each and what was good for all. These hopes I would not have sold for a large sum of money, and I seized the books and read them as fast as I could in my eagerness to know the better and the worse.

What expectations I had formed, and how grievously was I disappointed! As I proceeded, I found my philosopher altogether forsaking mind or any other principle of order, but having recourse to air, and ether,

and water, and other eccentricities. I might compare
him to a person who began by maintaining generally
that mind is the cause of the actions of Socrates, but
who, when he endeavored to explain the causes of my
several actions in detail, went on to show that I sit here
because my body is made up of bones and muscles; and
the bones, as he would say, are hard and have joints
which divide them, and the muscles are elastic, and they
cover the bones, which have also a covering or environment of flesh and skin which contains them; and as the
bones are lifted at their joints by the contraction or
relaxation of the muscles, I am able to bend my limbs,
and this is why I am sitting here in a curved posture—
that is what he would say; and he would have a similar
explanation of my talking to you, which he would attribute to sound, and air, and hearing, and he would
assign ten thousand other causes of the same sort, forgetting to mention the true cause, which is, that the Athenians have thought fit to condemn me, and accordingly
I have thought it better and more right to remain here
and undergo my sentence; for I am inclined to think
that these muscles and bones of mine would have gone
off long ago to Megara or Bœotia—by the dog they
would, if they had been moved only by their own idea
of what was best, and if I had not chosen the better and
nobler part, instead of playing truant and running away,
of enduring any punishment which the state inflicts.
There is surely a strange confusion of causes and conditions in all this. It may be said, indeed, that without
bones and muscles and the other parts of the body I
cannot execute my purposes. But to say that I do as I
do because of them, and that this is the way in which
mind acts, and not from the choice of the best, is a very

careless and idle mode of speaking. I wonder that they cannot distinguish the cause from the condition, which the many, feeling about in the dark, are always mistaking and misnaming. And thus one man makes a vortex all round and steadies the earth by the heaven; another gives the air as a support to the earth, which is a sort of broad trough. Any power which in arranging them as they are arranges them for the best never enters into their minds; and instead of finding any superior strength in it, they rather expect to discover another Atlas of the world who is stronger and more everlasting and more containing than the good;—of the obligatory and containing power of the good they think nothing; and yet this is the principle which I would fain learn if any one would teach me. But as I have failed either to discover myself, or to learn of any one else, the nature of the best, I will exhibit to you, if you like, what I have found to be the second best mode of inquiring into the cause.

I should very much like to hear, he replied.

Socrates proceeded: I thought that as I had failed in the contemplation of true existence, I ought to be careful that I did not lose the eye of my soul; as people may injure their bodily eye by observing and gazing on the sun during an eclipse, unless they take the precaution of only looking at the image reflected in the water or in some similar medium. So in my own case, I was afraid that my soul might be blinded altogether if I looked at things with my eyes or tried to apprehend them by the help of the senses. And I thought that I had better have recourse to the world of mind and seek there the truth of existence. I dare say that the simile is not perfect—for I am very far from admitting that he who contemplates existences through the medium of thought, sees them only "through a glass darkly," any more than he who considers them in action and operation. However, this was the method which I adopted: I first assumed some principle which I judged to be the strongest, and then I affirmed as true whatever seemed to agree with this, whether relating to the cause or to anything else; and that which disagreed I regarded as untrue.

AN ILLUSTRATION OF SOCRATES'S METHOD OF SHOWING UP IGNORANCE [15]

[Socrates speaks:]

By the gods, Meno, be generous, and tell me what you say that virtue is; for I shall be truly delighted to find that I have been mistaken, and that you and Gorgias do really have this knowledge; although I have been just saying that I have never found anybody who had.

Meno—There will be no difficulty, Socrates, in answering your question. Let us take first the virtue of a man—he should know how to administer the state, and in the administration of it to benefit his friends and harm his enemies; and he must also be careful not to suffer harm himself. A woman's virtue, if you wish to know about that, may also be easily described: her duty is to order her house, and keep what is indoors, and obey her husband. Every age, every condition of life, young or old, male or female, bond or free, has a different virtue; there are virtues numberless, and no lack of definitions of them; for virtue is relative to the actions and ages of each of us in all that we do. And the same may be said of vice, Socrates.

[15] From the *Meno* of Plato, beginning on p. 71 D. **Jowett's** translation.

Soc.—How fortunate I am, Meno. When I ask you for one virtue, you present me with a swarm of them, which are in your keeping. Suppose that I carry on the figure of the swarm, and ask of you, What is the nature of the bee? and you answer that there are many kinds of bees, and I reply: But do bees differ as bees, because there are many and different kinds of them; or are they not rather to be distinguished by some other quality, as for example beauty, size, or shape? How would you answer me?

[After a little further questioning, Socrates succeeds in showing Meno that what is wanted is not an enumeration of different virtues, but a common definition of virtue.]

Men.—Will you have one definition of them all?

Soc.—That is what I am seeking.

Men.—If you want to have one definition of them all, I know not what to say, but that virtue is the power of governing mankind.

[Socrates then leads Meno to confess that this cannot describe the virtue of all, of children, e. g., and slaves, and, indeed, that it cannot describe any man's virtue, unless we add the words justly and not unjustly, which would introduce a vicious circle. Meno then enumerates the different recognized virtues, courage, temperance, etc. But this brings back the difficulty of his first answer. So he makes another attempt:]

Men.—Well, then, Socrates, virtue, as I take it, is when he, who desires the honorable, is able to provide it for himself; so the poet says, and I say too:

Virtue is the desire of things honorable and the power of attaining them.

[Socrates makes Meno admit that all men really desire

the honorable, so that nothing is left of his definition but "the power of attaining it"; and to make this virtue, we must again introduce the qualification, "of attaining it with justice," which once more lands us in a circle. In despair Meno exclaims:]

Men.—O Socrates, I used to be told, before I knew you, that you were always doubting yourself and making others doubt; and now you are casting your spells over me, and I am simply getting bewitched and enchanted, and am at my wits' end. And if I may venture to make a jest upon you, you seem to me both in your appearance and in your power over others to be very like the flat torpedo fish, who torpifies those who come near him and touch him, as you have now torpified me, I think. For my soul and my tongue are really torpid, and I do not know how to answer you; and though I have been delivered of an infinite variety of speeches about virtue before now, and to many persons—and very good ones they were, as I thought—at this moment I cannot even say what virtue is.

X

SOCRATES'S DEFENCE OF HIMSELF AS RE-PORTED BY PLATO IN THE *APOLOGY*

WHAT impression my accusers have made upon you, fellow-Athenians, I cannot say. For my part, I came near forgetting who I was; they spoke so plausibly. Yet there was scarcely a word of truth in what they said. But of the many lies they told there was one which astonished me most of all. I mean the one where they told you you would have to be on your guard lest I deceive you, because I am a clever speaker. They did indeed seem to me most brazen-faced, not to be ashamed to say that, when they were sure to be confuted by me the moment I opened my mouth and exhibited myself as anything but a clever speaker;—unless, indeed, they mean by "clever speaker" one who speaks the truth. If that is what they mean I am ready to confess that I am eloquent, though not after the fashion of their eloquence.

Well, as I was saying, my accusers have spoken scarcely a word of truth. From me, however, you shall hear the whole truth. But, Athenians, you will not hear a speech like theirs, carefully constructed, and decked out with fine words and phrases. Far from it. I shall speak without preparation, in the words that come first to my lips. For I am sure that my cause is just. Let no one expect any different course, for it would surely be unseemly that at my time of life I should

come before you forging arguments like a callow youth.
But there is one favor, Athenians, that I do most earnestly request of you.   If in defending myself I use the same
words I am accustomed to use in the market-place,
at the tables of the money changers, and elsewhere,
where many of you have heard me, do not be surprised,
and do not interrupt me for that.   The fact is, I am
seventy years old and this is the first time that I have
appeared in court, and so I am altogether a stranger to
your manner of speech.   Were I in truth a stranger you
would, I am sure, pardon me for speaking in my native
dialect and in the way that use had made familiar.   And
so now I beg that you will look upon me in that light,
and grant this request, which I think I have a right to
make: Pay no heed to my manner of speaking, which
may or may not be good; but look to this only, give your
undivided attention to this: Is what I say right, or is it
not?   That is what makes an excellent judge, as speaking the truth makes an excellent orator.

In the first place, fellow-Athenians, it is but right that
I should defend myself against my old, old accusers,
and answer their false charges.   After that I will take
up the charges of my present accusers.   For my accusers
are many, and now full many a year they have been
accusing me falsely to you.   It is these old accusers
that I fear, rather than Anytus and his accomplices,
formidable though they be.   But, my friends, the old
accusers are the more formidable, for they got hold of
most of you when you were mere boys and poured into
your ears their false charges against me, persuading you
that there is one Socrates, a wise man, who speculates
about the heavens above and pries into all the secrets
of the earth beneath, and who makes the worse appear

the better reason. The men who have been spreading that tale are, fellow-Athenians, the accusers whom I fear. For their hearers suppose that persons who pursue such investigations do not even believe in gods. Then, too, those accusers are many, and they have been at it a long while, and they got a hearing at a time when you would be most easily persuaded, for you were mere boys, some of you just crossing the threshold of youth. And the case went against me by default, for there was none to answer their charges. And the most absurd part of it is that I do not even know their names and cannot tell you who they are—except in the chance case of a writer of comedies. All these men who, through envy or malice, persuaded you,—and some of them quite likely sought to persuade others because they themselves had first been persuaded,—these are the accusers it is hardest to answer. For I cannot call any one of them into court to cross-examine him. I must defend myself exactly as if I were fighting shadows, and cross-examine where there is none to answer.

Assume with me, then, that my accusers are of two kinds, as I was saying: those who have brought the present charge, and my old time accusers whom I've just been describing. And by your leave I'll answer my old accusers first, for you heard them first, and much oftener than the rest. Well, I must make my defence, fellow-Athenians, and see if I can clear away in the short time at my disposal, the prejudice which you have had against me for many a year. Would that might be the result, if so it is best for you and for me; would I might succeed in my defence! However, let the issue be as God wills. In obedience to the law I must now make my defence.

Let us begin at the beginning then and ask, What is the charge that has created the prejudice against me which Meletus is relying on in bringing me to trial? Just what is the slander my enemies have been spreading? Let us word their affidavit, as if their charge had been brought before a court in regular form. It would read something like this: "Socrates is a wicked man. He is a meddlesome person who pries into the secrets of earth and of heaven, a man who makes the worse appear the better reason; and he teaches other men to do the same things." So it runs. It is what you yourselves have seen in the comedy of Aristophanes, where he represents a certain Socrates swinging about in a basket and declaring that he is walking on air and drivelling on at a great rate about matters concerning which I don't make the slightest pretence of having any knowledge whatever. I speak with no intention of disparaging such knowledge, if any one has wisdom like that. I trust I may not be brought to trial by Meletus on so grave a count as that. But the truth is, fellow-Athenians, I have nothing to do with physical speculations. I can furnish plenty of witnesses on this point from your own number. I ask those of you who have heard me,—and that is certainly a goodly number,—to speak to your neighbors and tell them whether they have ever heard me saying anything whatsoever about such subjects. . . . There! That answer will show you that the other charges current about me are of the same stripe.

No, there is no truth in any of these charges. And if you have heard any one say that I set myself up as a teacher of men and exact a fee for my services, there's no truth in that either. Not that I don't think it would

be a fine thing to be able to teach men, as Gorgias of
Leontium does, or Prodicus of Ceos, or Hippias of Elis.
Any one of them can go into any city he likes and persuade the young men to forsake the society of their
fellow-citizens, from whom they could choose their
companions at will and without bribes, and to associate
with him and to pay him for the privilege, and be only
too glad to do so. And I've just heard that there is
another wise man, a Parian, who has lately come to
town. The other day I ran across Callias the son of
Hipponicus, a man who has spent more money on the
Sophists than all the rest put together. Knowing he had
two sons I said to him: "Callias, if your sons had been
colts or calves we should have no difficulty in hiring a
trainer who was likely to bring out all the perfections that
belong to their nature: we should get some skilful groom
or farmer. But now, seeing that they are human beings,
whom do you intend to put in charge of their training?
Who is there that has the knowledge of that kind of
excellence, the excellence of the man and of the citizen?
I don't doubt, having sons, you've considered the question. Is there any such person?" "Yes, indeed, there
is," he replied. "Who is he," I said, "and where does
he hail from, and what's his fee?" "His name is
Evenus," he replied, "and he comes from Paros, and he
charges five minæ." And I thought to myself, happy
is Evenus, if he really has this wisdom, and sells it so
cheap. Had I such wisdom I should be fairly puffed
up with pride. But the fact is, fellow-Athenians, I have
it not.

Here perhaps some of you will reply: But, Socrates,
what is this occupation of yours? Whence come these
calumnies? Surely all this rumor and talk would never

have arisen had you not been different from other men. You must have been engaged in some very unusual pursuit. Tell us, then, what it is, that we may not be guilty of judging you off-hand. That, I take it, is a fair challenge; and, if you will give me your attention, I'll try to explain to you what has caused the calumny and given me this reputation. I am afraid some of you will think I am trifling; but, rest assured, I will simply tell you the whole truth. Fellow-Athenians, I have acquired this reputation simply because of a certain kind of wisdom which I do possess. You ask, And what kind of wisdom, pray, is that? I answer, The kind that is, I think, attainable by man. It is just possible I really am wise in that way; whereas the men of whom I was just speaking are wise with what may perhaps be called a superhuman wisdom. I don't know how else to describe it, for I don't pretend to have it myself. No, and whoever says that I do, lies, and is trying to slander me. And I beg of you, fellow-Athenians, that you will not hoot at me even if you think what I am about to say very arrogant; for the words I shall speak are not my own. I shall bring you as their author one who is worthy of your confidence; I shall summon the god of Delphi to testify of my wisdom, whether I have any, and of what sort it is. You remember Chærephon, don't you? He was my comrade from his youth up. And most of you have had him for a comrade; for he went into exile with you, and with you he returned. And of course you remember what sort of a man he was, how impetuously he threw himself into everything he undertook. Well, on one occasion, he went to Delphi and actually had the temerity to put this question to the oracle,—and once more, friends, I beg you not to

cry out against me,—he asked if there was any one wiser
than I. Now the Pythian priestess answered that there
was no man wiser. Chærephon is dead, but his brother
here will bear witness to the truth of what I say.

Now observe why I tell you this. It is because I
mean to show you the origin of the prejudice against
me. When I heard the response of the oracle, I said to
myself: Whatever does the god mean? What is the
explanation of his riddle? For I well know that I am
not a wise man,—not in the least. What then could he
have meant by saying that I am the wisest of men?
He certainly didn't tell a lie: he is a god and couldn't
do that. For a long time I puzzled over his meaning.
Then, after much deliberation, I hit upon this way of
finding it out. I went to one of the citizens who was in
high repute for his wisdom, thinking that there, if anywhere, I could prove the response wrong; and meaning
then to go to the oracle and say: "You said I was the
wisest of men: lo! here is a wiser." Well, I examined
the man,—I needn't mention his name: he was a politician
—and this was my experience with him. As I talked
with him it became apparent that while he passed for a
wise man in the eyes of a great many persons, and most
of all in his own eyes, he was not wise at all. And then
I tried to show him that he was not wise, though he
fancied that he was. The result was, he hated me for it;
and many of those who were standing by hated me too.
And as I walked away I thought to myself, "I am wiser
than that man. Probably neither of us knows anything
very much worth while; but he thinks that he knows,
when in reality he does not; I neither know nor think
that I know. On this small point at any rate I seem to
have the best of him: I do not fancy that I know when

in reality I am in ignorance." And then I went to another man, who was held in still higher repute for his wisdom, and he taught me the same lesson. And there again I made an enemy of him, and of all of his friends.

Well, then, I went to one man after another. I saw that I was making enemies all the while; and I was sorry for that, and feared the result. Still, I couldn't help it; I had to put the command of God above every other consideration. So, in my search for the meaning of the oracle, I must make the rounds, going to all who were reputed to be in any way wise. And I swear to you, fellow-Athenians, by the dog of Egypt I swear,—for I must tell you the truth,—this was the upshot of my divinely appointed quest. The men held in highest esteem for their wisdom proved to be just about the most lacking in it; while others who are looked down upon as people of the common sort were really wiser than they.

Now I must tell you the tale of my wanderings, of the Herculean labors I endured, only to find in the end that the oracle was irrefutable. After I had made trial of the politicians I went to the poets, tragic, dithyrambic, and the rest, thinking that there I should be flagrantly trapped in my ignorance. So I would take up their poems upon which they had apparently bestowed most pains, and would ask them what they meant, hoping that thereby I might learn something from them. Well, my friends, I am almost ashamed to tell you the truth, but I can't help it. The fact is, there is hardly a person present who could not discuss the works of the poets better than the poets themselves. So it didn't take long to discover that the poets, in making their poems, are guided, not by wisdom, but by a sort of divine frenzy like that which possesses the prophets and the soothsayers. They too say many beautiful things without knowing the meaning of what they say. It was clear to me that the poets had come under some such spell. And at the same time I observed that, because of their skill in poetry, they fancied themselves the wisest of men in other matters too, which they didn't know at all. So as I went away I thought to myself that I had the same advantage over them that I had over the politicians.

Last of all I went to the artisans. I was well aware that I knew nothing of any consequence, and I was sure that I should find them possessed of much admirable knowledge. And I was not mistaken about this: they did know things I am ignorant of, and, in so far, were wiser than I. But, fellow-Athenians, I found that even the skilled artisans made the same mistake as the poets. Every man of them, because he was skilled in his particular craft, fancied himself mighty wise in other matters,—and matters of the greatest importance; and this fault of theirs cast their wisdom in the shade. And so I asked myself, on behalf of the oracle, whether I would rather remain as I am, having neither their wisdom nor their ignorance, or have their wisdom together with their ignorance. And the answer I made to myself and to the oracle was: "I am better off as I am."

It is this inquisitorial task, fellow-Athenians, that has made me so many enemies of the most fierce and bitter kind. It is this that has given me the name of "wise man," and that is responsible for all their calumnious charges. For the bystanders always think that I myself possess the wisdom that I show to be lacking in others. But, my friends, I suspect that God alone is truly wise, and, by that oracular response, he meant to say that our human wisdom is of little or no worth.

Apparently he wasn't speaking of me, Socrates. I think he just used my name, and took me for an illustration, as if he would say to mankind: "He is wisest among you who, like Socrates, has found out that in truth his wisdom is worth nothing at all."   And so I still go about, obedient to God's command, probing and testing any one whom I take to be wise, whether he be a citizen or a stranger. And whenever I find that he is not wise, I show him that he is not, and thereby serve Apollo. This occupation has kept me so busy that I have had no time to take any part worth mentioning in public affairs, or even to look after my private interests. I am in deep poverty because of my service to God.

And besides all this (there is another reason for my unpopularity). The young of the richer class, who have a lot of spare time, follow me about of their own accord, and take delight in hearing men cross-examined. And they often imitate me themselves, and try their hand at cross-examining others. And I suspect they find no end of men who think they know a great deal, when in fact they know precious little. The result is, when their sham wisdom has been shown up, they get angry with me rather than with the young men, and vow, "That fellow Socrates is the plague of the town, and he corrupts the youth." And if any one asks them, "How? What does he do? What does he teach?" they do not know and have nothing to say. But, in order not to seem at a loss, they repeat the old stock charges made against all philosophers,—Prying into things up in the clouds or under the earth, not believing in gods, and making the worse appear the better reason. I can readily believe that they would scarcely relish telling the truth, which is that they have been convicted of lay-

ing claim to a wisdom they do not possess. And I don't
doubt they have been filling your ears this many a day
with their bitter accusations; for there are lots of them,
and they are energetic, and keen for notoriety, and they
speak plausibly, and they are all lined up against me.
This is the reason why Meletus and Anytus and Lycon
have attacked me. Meletus is taking up the quarrel
on behalf of the poets, Anytus on behalf of the crafts-
men and politicians, Lycon on behalf of the rhetoricians.
And so, as I remarked at the outset, I should be surprised if I were able in the short time at my disposal to
remove a prejudice that has taken such deep hold upon
you. There, fellow-Athenians! I have given you the
plain, unvarnished truth, and the whole truth. And
yet I am tolerably sure that it is just this my bluntness
of speech that makes me enemies. That indeed is a
proof that I am telling you the truth, and that the
prejudice against me and its causes are as I have said.
And if you will look into this matter, now or at any
future time, you will find that it is so.

Let this suffice for my defence against the charges
brought by my earliest accusers. I will next attempt
to reply to Meletus,—"noble patriot," as he styles himself,—and to my later accusers. Let us assume them to
be a different set of accusers, and let us once more frame
the indictment. It runs something like this: Socrates is
guilty, it says, in that he corrupts the youth, and does
not believe in the gods of his country, but has other and
strange divinities of his own. So runs the charge. Let
us examine it point by point. The first count is, that I
am guilty in that I corrupt the youth. But for my part,
fellow-Athenians, I charge that Meletus is the culprit,
in thus mixing jest with earnest, and lightly bringing

men to trial, and pretending to be very earnest and very solicitous about matters to which he has never given a moment's thought. And I will try to make it as plain to you as it is to me that such is the case.

"Come, Meletus, take the stand and answer my question. Is it not a fact that you have very much at heart the improvement of the youth?"

"It is."

"Well, then, tell the judges who it is that improves them. You must know, for you care so much about it. You have discovered, as you say, that I am their corrupter, and are bringing me to trial on that charge. Come, name the man who is their improver, tell the judges who he is. You see, Meletus, you are silent; you have nothing to say. And yet don't you think that this is disgraceful? Doesn't your silence sufficiently prove the truth of what I was just saying, that you have never given this matter a moment's thought? Speak up, my good sir, who is it that makes the young men better?"

"The laws."

"But, most noble Meletus, that was not what I asked. I want to know who the man is who makes them better, assuming, of course, that he has to begin with a knowledge of the laws."

"The men before you, Socrates,—the judges."

"What do you mean, Meletus? Are they able to instruct the young, and do they improve them?"

"Certainly."

"All of them, or only some of them?"

"All of them."

"By the goddess Hera, this is good news indeed. There is a regular host of improvers of youth. And how about the audience? Do they improve them too?"

"They do."

"And the senators?"

"The senators, too."

"Well, then, take the members of the assembly. Perchance they corrupt them. Or do they, too, without exception, make them better?"

"They, too, make them better."

"Then apparently all the Athenians, excepting only me, make the young men fair and virtuous. I am their sole corrupter. Is that your meaning?"

"Most emphatically it is."

"Truly you have found me in a sorry plight. But tell me, in the case of horses, does it strike you that it is like that,—I mean, that some one man does them harm while all the rest do them good? Is not the truth precisely the contrary,—that one man, or at most a few, namely the skilled horse-trainers, do them good, while the rest, if they have anything to do with them, or try to break them in, do them harm? And isn't it this way, Meletus, not only with horses, but with all other animals too? Of course it is, whether you and Anytus say yes or no. It were indeed a great piece of good fortune for the young men if they had but one corrupter, and if every one else did them good. But the truth is, Meletus, you have clearly proved that you have never given the slightest thought to the young. You make your carelessness quite evident; you show that you have never paid the slightest heed to the matters about which you are prosecuting me.

"Now, once more, Meletus, will you be good enough to answer a question? Is it better to live among bad citizens or among good ones?   Answer, my friend.   That is surely not a hard question.   Do not the bad citizens do their neighbors harm, and the good citizens do them good?"

"Certainly."

"And is there any one who would deliberately prefer to be harmed rather than to be benefited by those with whom he associates?   Answer, my friend, the law requires you to.   Does any one want to be injured?"

"Of course not."

"Well, then, are you bringing me to trial for corrupting the youth and making them worse intentionally, or for doing so unintentionally?"

"For doing so intentionally."

"What, Meletus, are you so much wiser than I,—you so young, and I so old,—that you have made the discovery that evil men always do evil to their neighbors, and good men good, whereas I, forsooth, have fallen to such a depth of ignorance as not to be aware that if I make a rogue of a fellow-citizen he is likely to do me harm?   And so I commit this great wrong intentionally, as you aver?   Meletus, you will never convince me of that, or any one else, I trust.   No, either I do not corrupt the young men at all, or I do so unintentionally; so that in either case your statement is false.   And if I corrupt them unintentionally, then of such unintentional misdeeds the law takes no cognizance.   You ought rather to have taken me aside and taught me and admonished me.   For it is plain that I shall stop sinning unintentionally when I have been taught better.   But you have always avoided me; you didn't want to instruct me. And now you are bringing me into court, where the law brings men for punishment, not for instruction."

Well, fellow-Athenians, you must find it quite evident by this time that, as I was saying, Meletus has never troubled himself a bit about these matters. "However, tell us, Meletus, in what way, according to you, I corrupt the youth. Or is it plain enough from the indictment you have brought, that it is by teaching them not to believe in the gods our country recognizes, but in other and strange divinities? You say, do you not, that this is the teaching by which I corrupt the youth?"

"Precisely; and I say it most emphatically."

"Then, Meletus, in the name of those very gods of whom we are speaking, tell me and my judges here a little more clearly what you mean. I can't quite make out whether you accuse me of teaching them to believe in some gods—in which case I myself believe in gods and am not a downright atheist. I don't offend in that way. My offence is rather that I believe in strange divinities, and not in the gods of my country. Or whether you accuse me of not believing in gods at all, and of making atheists of others too."

"I mean that you are a downright atheist."

"My good fellow, what makes you say that? Do you mean to say that I don't even believe, like other men, that the sun and the moon are gods?"

"Judges, I swear, by heaven I swear, he does not; for he says the sun is a stone and the moon earth."

"My dear Meletus, you must think you are prosecuting Anaxagoras! Have you such a poor opinion of the judges, and do you think them so unlettered as not to know that the works of Anaxagoras of Clazomenæ are chock full of those doctrines? So the young men actually learn those doctrines from me, do they? when for a drachma at most they can often hear them at the theatre,

and laugh Socrates to scorn if he pretends they are his,
—such very odd doctrines, too. No, but honestly, Meletus, do you really think I don't believe in any god at all?"

"I do. I swear by heaven that you do not believe
in any god at all."

"Nobody believes you, Meletus. Indeed, I feel sure
you don't believe yourself." It seems to me, fellow-
Athenians, that my accuser is an insolent and impertinent
young man, and that he has brought this indictment in
a spirit of sheer insolence and youthful audacity. He
is like a man who tries to pose you by putting a paradox.
And he is saying to himself: Will the wise Socrates see
that I am jesting and contradicting myself, or shall I
succeed in befuddling him and the rest of my hearers?
For he plainly contradicts himself in the indictment,
just as if he were to say: Socrates is a wicked man because
he does not believe in gods, but believes in gods.

If you will follow me, friends, you will see how I find
him thus inconsistent. "Answer me, Meletus." And
I hope that you, my judges, will remember the request
I made at the beginning, and quietly suffer me to talk
in my usual way.

"Is there any one in the world, Meletus, who believes
there are things human, while at the same time not
believing there are any humans?" I wish, friends, that
he would answer without these continual interruptions.
" Is there any one who believes that horsemanship exists, but no horses; flute-playing, but no flute-players?
There is no one, my dear man; I'll tell you and the judges
that, if you don't choose to answer. But at least answer
my next question: Is there any one who believes there
are divine agencies, while at the same time not believing
that there are divinities?"

"There is no one."

"I am delighted that the judges have at last managed to pull an answer from you. Well, then, you say that I believe in, and teach others to believe in divine agencies —no matter whether new or old—at all events I believe in divine agencies. I have your own word for that; you swore to it in your indictment. Now, if I believe in divine agencies, surely I must of necessity believe that there are divinities. That follows, doesn't it? Well, it does. I assume from your silence that you admit that. And by 'divinities' we mean, do we not, either gods or sons of gods? Yes or no?"

"Yes, certainly."

"You admit then that I believe in divinities. Now if these divinities are a species of gods, then there is my proof that you are trifling and speaking in riddles, and are saying in one and the same breath that I do not believe in gods and that I do believe in gods, inasmuch as I believe in divinities. If, on the other hand, these divinities are sons of gods, their natural sons, as it were, by nymphs or some other mortal mothers, as rumor makes them,—why, then, let me ask you, is there any one in the world who could suppose that there are sons of gods, and at the same time that there are no gods? That would be just as absurd as to hold that there are mules, and to hold at the same time that there are neither horses nor asses! No, Meletus, you must surely have brought this indictment against me in order to make trial of me,—or else, because you couldn't find any real offence to charge me with. But you will never succeed, by hook or by crook, in persuading any one who has a scrap of intelligence, that one and the same man can believe in supernatural and divine agencies, and yet not believe that there are divinities, gods and heroes."

But really, fellow-Athenians, I don't think I need make a long speech in order to show that I am not guilty of the crime charged by Meletus. I have said enough for that. But it is only too true, as I remarked before, that I have made many and bitter enemies. That is what will convict me, if I am convicted,—not Meletus, nor Anytus, but the prejudice and ill-will of the multitude. These things have convicted many another innocent man, and they will, I dare say, continue to do so: there is no fear that I shall be the last.

Possibly some one will here interpose: Are you not ashamed, Socrates, to have led a life of such a kind that it has brought you into imminent danger of death? To him I should say, and my answer would be just: You are wrong, my friend, if you think a man who is good for anything at all ought, when he acts, to be calculating his chances of life and death, instead of paying heed to this, and this alone: Is he doing right or wrong, are his deeds the deeds of a good man or of a bad? Why, your theory would make worthless men of all the heroes who fell at Troy, and especially of Thetis's son who despised danger when the alternative was disgrace. For when he was bent on slaying Hector his goddess mother spoke to him in words, I believe, something like this: "My son, if you avenge the death of your comrade Patroclus, and slay Hector, you yourself will die. For straightway after Hector's death," said she, "your doom awaits you." He listened to her warning, and, scorning danger and death, but greatly dreading to live a coward's life, with his friend unavenged, he exclaimed: "Let death come, but let me first punish the murderer of my friend, that I may not remain here by the beaked ships the scorn of men, a mere cumberer of the earth." You don't suppose he had any anxiety about danger and death? And, fellow-Athenians, this is just as it should be. In whatever post a man finds himself, whether he has chosen it, thinking it the best, or whether he has been placed there by his superior, there he ought, I am sure, to remain, whatever the risks, taking no thought of death, or of anything else save disgrace.

Fellow-Athenians, when the generals whom you had chosen to place over me assigned me my post at Potidæa, at Amphipolis, and at Delium, I remained where they had put me, facing death like any other man. Strange indeed then would be my conduct if, through fear of death or of anything else, I were now to desert the post where God has placed me, as I am firmly persuaded that he has, commanding me to spend my life in the search after truth and in examining myself and others. Yes, that would indeed be strange. Then surely I might with justice be brought to trial on the charge of not believing in the gods, for I should be disobeying the oracle through fear of death, fancying myself wise when I am not. For to fear death means simply to think you are wise when you are not; for it is equivalent to thinking you know what you do not know. No one knows what death is, whether it be not the greatest blessing that can befall a man. Yet men fear it as if they knew for certain that it is the greatest of evils. And isn't this just ignorance of that disgraceful sort, thinking we know what we do not know? Here too, friends, very likely I differ from most men in this, and if I should venture to say that I am wiser than another in anything it would be in this, that having no clear knowledge of the other world I do not delude myself into thinking that I have. But this I do know, that to do wrong, and to be disloyal to a superior—whether God or man—is base and dishonorable. And I shall always fear and flee from the evils that I know to be evils, rather than from reputed evils which, for all I know, may be blessings.

And so if you should let me go free now, notwithstanding the plea of Anytus that either you ought never to have brought me to trial at all, or, having done so, you cannot possibly do anything but put me to death, because, as he tells you, if I escape now your sons will all forthwith practise what Socrates teaches and be utterly ruined,—if you were to say to me, in view of his argument: "Socrates, this time we shall not listen to Anytus. We shall let you go free, but on this condition, that you give up this quest of yours and philosophize no more. If you are caught at it again you shall die." If, I say, you were to let me off on these terms, I should reply: "Fellow-Athenians, I love you, I am devoted to you; but I shall obey God rather than you. And while breath and strength hold out I shall never cease from pursuing wisdom, or from exhorting any one of you whom I may meet, speaking frankly to him, and saying in my usual fashion: "My friend, as a citizen of Athens, a city greatest and most famous for its wisdom and power, are you not ashamed to be so greedy for wealth and name and fame, so careless and so thoughtless about wisdom and truth and the perfecting of your own soul?" And if he contradicts me, and says that he does care about these things, I shall not take him at his word and straightway let him go, but I shall question him and cross-question him and test him, and if I find that he is not virtuous, but only says that he is, I shall rebuke

him for prizing least what is of most value and prizing
more what is of less worth. This service I shall render
to every one I meet, young or old, citizen or alien, but
especially to you citizens, for you are more nearly akin
to me. Be assured, this is God's command. And I
hold that no greater blessing has ever befallen you in
Athens than this my service to God. For I spend all
my time going about among you, persuading you, old
and young alike, not to be so solicitous about your bodies
or your possessions, but first of all, and most earnestly,
to consider how to make your souls as perfect as possible;
and telling you that wealth does not bring virtue: rather,
virtue brings wealth and every other human good,
private or public. If then by such teaching I corrupt
the youth, these must be pernicious doctrines. But if
any one asserts that I teach anything else than this he
lies. Wherefore, Athenians, either listen to Anytus or
do not, acquit me or not; but rest assured, I shall never
alter my way of life—no, not though many deaths
await me.

Do not interrupt me, fellow-Athenians; stand by me
in the request I made that you should listen patiently
to my words. For I think that it will be to your advantage to hear them. I hesitate to speak, for the fact
is what I am going to say is pretty sure to make you
shouting mad; but you simply mustn't let it do so. If
you put me to death, my character being such as I tell
you it is, you may be very sure that you will do greater
harm to yourselves than to me. Neither Meletus nor
Anytus could possibly do me any real injury; it isn't in
their power to do so; for I take it Providence will never
permit a bad man to harm one better than himself.
Meletus may indeed compass my death, he may have me

banished or deprived of my rights as a citizen. And
very likely he, and other men too, imagine that these
things are very great evils. I do not. Nay, I hold that
it is a much greater evil to do what he is doing now,—
trying to put a man to death unjustly.

So, fellow-Athenians, I am not making the present
defence just to save my own life, as might be supposed.
Not at all. I am doing so to save you from sinning
against God and rejecting his gift to you by condemning
me. For if you kill me you will not easily find another
man who like me will, at God's bidding, literally stick
to the state like a gadfly to a horse,—if you'll pardon a
rather ludicrous comparison. For the state is like a
huge horse of noble breed, but rather sluggish from his
very size, and needing the gadfly to wake him up. And
I think God has given me to the state to play the part
of just such a gadfly, and I keep lighting upon you any
and everywhere, and spend the livelong day waking you
up, and persuading you and rebuking you. My friends,
you will not easily find another man like that, and if
you take my advice you will spare my life. However,
it is quite possible that you are irritated, like drowsy
men when they are awakened, and that you will listen
to Anytus and crush this gadfly, lightly putting me to
death. Then you could sleep on in peace for the rest
of your days,—unless God in his care for you were to
send you another tormentor. That it is God himself
who has given me to the state you can see from this:
no mere human motive would account for my having
neglected all my own affairs, allowing my private interests
to go to ruin during all these years, while at the same
time always looking after your welfare, going to you all,
one by one, like a father or an elder brother, and urging

you to pay heed to virtue. If I had taken a fee for my exhortations and made any money out of them my conduct could be accounted for. But now you yourselves see that my accusers, though they have accused me of everything else with such effrontery, hadn't the face to try to show that I ever either asked or received any fee. I offer you, I fancy, in my actual poverty an incontrovertible witness to the truth of my words.

Well, very likely it has the air of inconsistency to be going about in private offering you my advice and busying myself with your affairs, while not venturing to come forward in public in your assemblies to give the state the benefit of my advice. The reason for this you have heard me give over and again, and in divers places: a certain supernatural and divine sign comes to me,— and it is this that Meletus has caricatured in his indictment. I have had it ever since I was a child. It is a sort of voice that speaks to me, and whenever I hear it it always dissuades me from doing what I was on the point of doing, but never urges me on. This is what forbids my taking part in public life; and it does so wisely, I think. For I am very sure, fellow-Athenians, that had I attempted to take part in public life I should have perished long ago, without doing any good either to you or to myself. And don't be angry with me for telling the truth, but the fact is that there is no man whose life will be safe, here or anywhere else, if he sets himself genuinely in opposition to the multitude, and tries to prevent the many unjust and lawless deeds done in the state. No, he who would really battle for the right must do so in private and not in public life if he means to live even for a short season.

I will give you a striking proof of this, not words but,

what has more weight with you,—deeds. Listen, and I'll tell you some of my experiences, that you may be convinced that I would give way to no man through fear of death, although, for not giving way, I should have to die on the spot. The tale I am going to tell is common enough and may weary you, but it is true. I never held any office in the state, Athenians, except that of senator. And it chanced that my tribe, Antiochus, had the presidency at the time when you proposed to try in a body, and contrary to the law, as you all afterward realized, the ten generals who had not rescued their men after the battle of Arginusæ. On that occasion I was the only one of the presidents who opposed your illegal action and voted against it. In spite of your orators, who were ready to arrest me and lay an information against me, in spite of your shouts and your threats, I deemed it my duty to face every risk, with the law and the right on my side, rather than join you in your iniquitous designs through fear of imprisonment and death.

This happened while the government was still a democracy. And again, when the oligarchy was established, the Thirty summoned me and four others to the council chamber and ordered us to bring Leon the Salaminian from Salamis to be put to death. You know that was a way they had; they gave orders like that to a great many other men too, for they wanted to implicate as many as possible in their guilty deeds. However, there again I showed, not by my professions but by my practice, that, if you'll pardon the slang, I didn't care a fig for death; my great and only care was to do nothing wrong or impious. Strong as was the tyranny of the Thirty, it was not strong enough to frighten me into doing wrong. When we left the council chamber the four others went over to Salamis and brought Leon back, but I went off home. No doubt I should have lost my life for my disobedience had not the government of the Thirty been overthrown soon afterward. You can have plenty of witnesses to the truth of what I say.

Do you imagine for a moment that I should have survived all these years had I taken part in public affairs and, like an honest man, always stood for the right and, as in duty bound, made that my chief concern? Certainly not, fellow-Athenians,—nor I nor any other man. Throughout my whole life, whenever I have had occasion to take part in public affairs, you will find me always the same, and the same in private life too, never swerving from the path of justice through complaisance to any man,—to any of those whom my traducers call my disciples, or to any one else. The fact is, I never was any man's teacher; but if any one, young or old, wants to hear me talking, as I pursue my mission, he is welcome to do so. And I do not talk for a fee and refuse to talk unless paid. I am at the service of rich and poor alike. Any one may question me, or, if he prefers, answer my questions, and may listen to what I say. And whether he turns out to be a good citizen or otherwise, I cannot rightly be held responsible, for I have never taught or promised to teach any one of them anything. And if any one says he has ever learned or heard anything from me in private other than what all the rest of you have heard you may surely put him down for a liar.

But, you will ask, why is it then that people like to spend so much time in my company? You have my answer already, fellow-Athenians. I have told you the whole truth. They like to hear me cross-examining men who think they are wise when they are not. You know, it is rather amusing. This mission, as I say, has been assigned to me by God who has made his will known through oracles, dreams, and in every other way by which the divine providence has ever imposed any duty upon man. This is the truth, Athenians, and may easily be proved. For if I am corrupting some of the young men, and have corrupted others, surely some of them ought to come forward to-day as my accusers and take their revenge, if, now that they are grown up, they have discovered that I ever gave them bad advice in their youth. And if they themselves were unwilling to do so, some of their kinsmen—fathers, brothers, or other relatives—ought now to remember it and take their revenge if I had done their kinsmen any wrong. Certainly I see plenty of them here in court. First there is Crito, a man of my age and of my own deme, and there is his son, Critobulus. Then there is Lysanias of Sphettus, and there is his son, Æschines; and there is Antiphon, too, the father of Epigenes. Then here are others whose brothers have associated with me, Nicostratus, son of Theozotides, and brother of Theodotus—and Theodotus is dead so he at least cannot bind his brother to silence. And here is Paralus, son of Demodocus, who had a brother Theages; and here is Adeimantus, son of Ariston, and there is his brother Plato; and there is Æantodorus with his brother Apollodorus. And I could name many others to you. Surely, during the course of his speech, Meletus ought to have produced one of them as a witness against me. If he forgot it then, let him do so now,— I will make way for him,—and let him tell us if he has any such evidence. But you will find, my friends, that, on the contrary, they are all ready to defend me,—me the corrupter, the man who has worked evil to those of their own household, if we are to take the word of Meletus and Anytus.   To be sure, those who have themselves been corrupted might have their reason for supporting me; but the uncorrupted, their kinsmen who are already advanced in years—what reason have they for defending me, except the true and just one: they know Meletus is a liar and that I am speaking the truth.

Well, gentlemen, this, and possibly more of the same sort, is about all I have to say in my defence.   Perhaps there is some one among you who will be angry when he recalls how he himself, when a defendant in a case of far less importance than this, wept copiously, and begged and implored the judges, bringing his children into court and a great many others, kinsmen and friends, to arouse as much as possible your feelings of compassion; and when he finds that I shall do none of these things, although, in all likelihood, my life is at stake.   And so, as he thinks of this, he may harden his heart against me, and be angry with me for this very reason, and cast his vote in anger.   If there is any one of you in this case —I don't think there should be, but if there is, I think I might very properly say to him: My friend, doubtless I too have a few kinsmen, for, to borrow Homer's words, "I am born not of wood nor of stone, but of woman."   And so I have kinsmen, yes, and sons, fellow-Athenians—three of them.   One is already a youth, the others are mere boys.   Nevertheless, I will not bring one of them here, nor beg you for an acquittal.   And why not?   Not because I am stubborn, nor because I fail in my respect for you, fellow-Athenians.   Whether or not I face death with courage is not the question now.   But I think that for me, at my time of life and with my reputation for wisdom, whether deserved or not, to do any of those things would spell dishonor to me and to you and to the whole state. Whatever the fact, it is the commonly received opinion that Socrates is in some way superior to the general run of mankind. It were surely a disgrace if those of you who are held to excel in wisdom or courage, or in any other virtue, were to act like men whom I've often seen,—men of some reputation too,—who when brought to trial behaved in the strangest manner, as if they were convinced that it was a most terrible thing to die, and as if they expected to live forever provided you did not put them to death. I think such men bring dishonor to our state, so that any stranger would suppose that the Athenians, who excel in virtue, and who are chosen by their fellow-citizens for public offices and other dignities, are no better than women. Fellow-Athenians, it is not right for us who have any reputation at all to behave this way; and if we do, then you ought to put a stop to it. On the other hand you ought to make it plain that you will be much more likely to condemn the man who gets up these piteous farces, thereby making the city ridiculous, than the man who keeps calm.

But, my friends, apart from the question of reputation, I think it is not right to implore a judge for mercy and receive acquittal as a favor. It is one's duty to enlighten and convince him; for he sits as judge to determine what is just and not to curry favor with his verdicts. And he has taken oath to judge according to the laws, and not to favor those whom it may please him to favor. And so it is not right that we should get you in the habit of perjuring yourselves, or that you should acquire that habit, for there would be no piety in that either for you or for me.   Therefore, fellow-citizens, do not require me to do, where you are concerned, what I hold to be neither honorable nor right nor pious, no, not at any time, and least of all when I am being prosecuted by Meletus on the charge of impiety.   For I should clearly be teaching you to believe that there are no gods if I were to persuade you and were to overpower your oaths by my importunings.   In my very defence I should literally be accusing myself of believing that there are no gods.   But that is far from being the case.   Fellow-Athenians, I do believe in the gods, more firmly than any of my accusers, and to you and to God I commend my cause, to be decided in the way that will prove best for you as well as for me.

[Socrates is found guilty by a vote of 281 to 220.   The penalty of death has been proposed by Meletus, and it is now Socrates's privilege to propose a counter penalty.]

Fellow-Athenians, I am not greatly displeased at the verdict you have brought in, and that for many reasons. I was quite prepared for this result.   But I am greatly surprised at the way the votes were divided.   I had no idea the majority against me would be so small; I expected it to be overwhelming.   But now it seems that if only thirty votes had changed sides I should have been acquitted.   Indeed, as it is, I think that I have escaped Meletus.   And not only that; it must be apparent to all that had Anytus and Lycon not come forward to join him in the accusation he would not have obtained the fifth part of your votes, and so would have been fined a thousand drachmas.

So Meletus proposes death as the penalty.   Very good.

And what shall I propose to you, fellow-Athenians, as a counter penalty? Obviously, what I deserve. And what is that? What penalty should I suffer, what fine should I pay because I didn't spend my life in ease; because I cared not for what most men prize—making and hoarding money, military commands, speech-making in the assembly, public offices, and the conspiracies and factions of our state, thinking myself really too conscientious a man to go in for such things and live; because I didn't enter upon a career which would prevent my doing any good to you or to myself, but adopted the course that would enable me, as I have said, to do the greatest possible service to each of you individually, and tried to persuade each of you to take thought for himself and consider how he could make himself as good and as wise as possible before he took thought for his affairs, and in the same way to take thought for the state itself before concerning himself with the state's affairs, and in all cases to follow the same order in his solicitudes? What then do I deserve for such a life? Something good, fellow-Athenians, if I must really fix the penalty according to my deserts, and moreover a good such as would be suitable for me to accept. What then is a fit recompense for a benefactor who is poor and who requires leisure that he may exhort you? Fellow-Athenians, there is none that is more fitting for a man of that sort than that he be maintained in the Prytaneum at the public expense. It is far more suitable to give him such a reward than to give it to one of your number who has been victorious in a horse-race, or in a two- or four-horse chariot-race, at the Olympic games. He gives you the appearance of happiness; I give you the reality. Besides, he is not in want; I am. And so if I must propose the

penalty which I justly deserve I should propose this:
maintenance in the Prytaneum at the public expense.

Well, very likely you will think that I am saying this
from sheer obstinacy, interpreting this pretty much as
you did what I said about wailing and begging for mercy.
But such is not the fact, Athenians. The truth rather
is that I speak as I do because I am convinced that I
never wronged any man intentionally, though I cannot
convince you of that. We have had too short a time to
discuss the matter. If it were the law here, as it is in
other lands, that in a case where the penalty is death
the trial must continue for several days, and not one
only, I might have convinced you. As it is, it is not easy
to do away with formidable calumnies all in a moment.
I am firmly convinced that I never wronged any man,
and I certainly shall not wrong myself. And I shall not
accuse myself of deserving any evil, nor shall I propose
anything of the sort for myself as a penalty. What fear
could drive me to that? Fear lest I suffer the penalty
Meletus proposes, when, as I say, I do not know whether
it be a good or an evil? Would you have me propose
instead things which I know to be evils? What penalty
shall I propose? Imprisonment? And why should I
spend my life in prison, a slave to the Elevens successively
appointed as jailers? Or shall it be a fine, with imprisonment until it is paid? But for me that would be
equivalent to life imprisonment. For I have no money
to pay a fine with. Or shall it be exile? Perhaps you
would agree to that punishment. I must indeed be
madly in love with life if I am so lost to reason as not
to be able to reflect that, if you who are my fellow-citizens
were unable to tolerate my discussions and my arguments,
and have found them so troublesome and so odious that

you are now seeking to be quit of them, strangers will scarcely find it easy to bear with me. Far from it, Athenians, a fine life it would be for an old man like me to leave my native town and pass my days in wandering from city to city, always being driven out. For I am sure that wherever I go the young men will listen to my arguments, just as they do here. And if I drive them away they will persuade their elders to drive me away. If I do not drive them away, their fathers and kinsmen will expel me for their sakes.

But perhaps some one may say: Socrates, when you quit us, won't it be possible for you to refrain from talking and to hold your peace? This is just the point that it is most difficult to make you understand, for if I say that that means to disobey God, and that therefore I cannot hold my peace, you will not believe me, you will say that I am not speaking candidly. If on the other hand I tell you that it is also the very best thing a man can do, to be applying his reason every day to the question of virtue and to the other matters you hear me conversing about, as I examine myself and others; and if I add that the unexamined life is not worthy to be lived by man,—you are still less likely to believe me. I am but telling you the truth, friends, though it is not easy for me to persuade you. For the rest, I have not been accustomed to think myself deserving of any evil. If I had money I should have proposed a fine as large as I could pay. That would not have hurt me any. As it is, I haven't the money for that, unless you are willing to impose a fine within the possibility of my slender means. Very likely I could pay a mina of silver. Well, I propose that.— Fellow-Athenians, Plato here, and Crito, and Critobulus, bid me make it thirty minæ and offer to be my sureties.

So I propose that amount. You will have in them ample security for the money.

[Socrates's half-ironical proposition is not accepted and the penalty of death is imposed. Socrates continues:]

You have not gained much time, fellow-Athenians, and the price you will pay is the evil name which those who wish to abuse our city will give you. They will blame you for having put to death Socrates, a wise man. For those who will want to reproach you will say that I am wise even though I am not. If you had had patience to wait for a little while you would have gained your end in the course of nature. For as you see I am already far advanced in years, and near to death. I say this not to all of you, but only to those who voted for my death. And I have something else to say to them. You may perhaps think, gentlemen, that I have been convicted because I was lacking in the kind of arguments necessary to persuade you,—that is, if I had thought it right to leave nothing unsaid or undone in order to escape punishment. Far from it. I have been convicted because I was lacking, not in argument, but in effrontery and shamelessness, and because I was unwilling to speak to you as you would have liked to have me speak, weeping and lamenting, and doing and saying many other things the like of which you have been wont to hear from other men, but which, as I have said, are unworthy of me. When I was making my defence I thought I ought not to do anything unworthy of a freeman just because I was in danger, and I have no misgivings now over the manner of my defence. No, I would far rather defend myself as I did, and die, than owe my life to a craven defence. For it is wrong for me, and for any one else, either in a lawsuit or in battle, to resort to every possible device in order to escape death. In battle it is often plain that a man may at least save his life by throwing down his arms and imploring quarter of his pursuers. And in other kinds of danger there are plenty of devices whereby a man may save his life, if he has the audacity to say and do any and everything. But, my friends, I suspect the difficulty is, not to escape death, but rather to escape wickedness. For wickedness runs swifter than death, and now I who am old and slow have been caught by the slower runner, while my accusers who are clever and swift have been caught by the faster runner, which is wickedness. And now I depart having been condemned to death by you. They, too, depart condemned by truth to pay the penalty of depravity and unrighteousness. I abide by my punishment; let them abide by theirs. I suppose these things are destined so to be; and I think that it is all for the best.

And now I want to prophesy the future to you who have condemned me. For I am about to die, and that is the time when men are most gifted with prophetic power. I say to you, you who have condemned me to death, that the moment I am gone punishment will overtake you, yes, by heaven, a punishment far more severe than the penalty of death which you have inflicted upon me. You have now done this thing in the belief that you are going to be free from the necessity of giving an account of your lives. I assure you that the result will be quite to the contrary. There will be many more to call you to account, men whom I have thus far been holding in check though you didn't perceive it.

And they are younger, and will be so much the harder upon you, and you will be so much the more angry with them. For you are much mistaken if you think that by putting men to death you can keep people from reproaching you for your evil lives. That way of escape is certainly not possible, nor is it honorable. The way that is at once easiest and most honorable is, not to be silencing the reproaches of others, but to be making yourselves as perfect as you can. With this prophecy, then, I take my leave of you who have condemned me.

But with you who have voted to acquit me I would gladly converse about this thing that has happened, while the officers are busy, and before I go where I must go to die. Pray stay that long with me, my friends, for there is no reason why we should not talk together about our beliefs while we may. I want to explain to you who are my friends the meaning of what has just befallen me. For a very strange thing has happened to me, my judges —for I am surely right in addressing *you* as judges,—my familiar prophetic voice, the divine sign, has up to the present time always been in the habit of opposing me even in most trifling matters, when I was on the point of acting wrongly. But now you yourselves see what has just happened to me, a thing which one might think, which is generally considered, the greatest possible evil. But the divine sign did not oppose me as I was leaving my house this morning, nor as I was mounting the platform here in court, nor did it oppose me once in my speech in what I was about to say. Yet often on other occasions it has stopped me right in the middle of a speech. But now, in this affair, it has not opposed a single word or deed of mine. What do I take to be the meaning of this? I will tell you. This thing that has happened to me must be a blessing, and we who think that death is an evil are surely mistaken in our belief. I have received striking evidence of this, for it is impossible that the divine sign should not have opposed me, unless indeed I am going to fare well.

Again, look at the matter in this light too, and we discover high hopes for believing that death is a blessing. There are just two alternatives with regard to death: either the dead man has lost all power of perception, and wholly ceased to be; or else, as tradition has it, the soul at death changes its habitation, moving from its home here to its home yonder. And if there is no perception at all, and death is like a sound sleep unbroken even by a dream, then it is a wonderful gain. For I think if one were called upon to select the night in which he slept so soundly that he did not even dream, and to compare all the other days and nights of his life with that night, and to declare after careful consideration how many days and nights of his life he had passed better or more agreeable than that night, I think that no one, whether private citizen or even the great king himself, would find them very easy to count in comparison with all the rest. If then that is what death is like I for one say it is a gain, for in that case all eternity is but a single night. If on the other hand death is a journey to another world, and if the traditional belief is true that all the dead are there, what blessing could be greater than this, O my judges? If, on arriving in the under world, one is free from these pretended judges here, and finds the true judges who are said to sit in judgment there, Minos and Rhadamanthus and Æacus and Triptolemus, and all the other demigods who in life were themselves just—

wouldn't that be a journey worth taking! Again, to
associate with Orpheus and Musæus and Hesiod—what
would you not give for that privilege! For my part I am
ready to die over and over again if these beliefs are true;
for I should find wondrous pleasure in the life over there,
meeting with Palamedes and Ajax, the son of Telamon,
or any of the other men of old who met their death
through an unjust judgment. It would be no small
pleasure, I take it, to compare my own experiences with
theirs. And, best of all, I could spend my time examining and questioning the men over there, as I do the
men here on earth, finding out which of them are wise,
and which of them thinks himself wise when he is not.
What would one not give, O my judges, to examine him
who led the great expedition against Troy, or Odysseus
or Sisyphus or countless other men and women who
might be named? What inconceivable happiness to be
with them, to converse with them, and examine them!
One thing at least is certain: they do not put a man to
death over there for asking questions. For the men of
that world, besides being happier than we are in all other
respects, are once and for all immortal, if the tales that
are told are true. You too, my judges, are to face death
full of hope. You ought to meditate on this truth: no
evil can possibly befall a good man, in this life or after
death. His interests are not neglected by the gods.
And it is no mere chance that has brought him to this
pass. No, I see clearly, that it is better for me to die
now and be released from trouble. That is why the
oracle did not once turn me back; that is why I am not
at all angry with these men who have condemned me, or
with my accusers. To be sure it was not with this in
mind that they condemned me, or brought the accusa-

tion against me, but because they thought to do me harm. For that indeed I may fairly blame them.

However, I have this request to make of them. When my sons grow up take your revenge on them, gentlemen; plague them just as I have plagued you, if you find them setting their hearts on riches, or on anything else more than on virtue. If they think they are something when in reality they are nothing, reproach them, as I have reproached you, for not caring for the things they ought to care for and for thinking they are worth something when they are worth nothing at all. If you do this I shall have received justice at your hands, I and my sons, too.

But the time has come for us to depart—I to die, you to live. Which of us is going to the better lot God alone clearly knows.

XI

THE LESSER SOCRATICS

THE CYRENAICS—ARISTIPPUS

The[1] Cyrenaics said that the feelings were the criteria of truth, that they alone could be apprehended and were not misleading. On the other hand the causes of the feelings, one and all, are incomprehensible and the source of false opinion. For whenever we experience a white color or a sweet taste we can speak without fear of being misled or refuted; but what it is that causes the feeling white or sweet, that we cannot tell.

**
* **

It[2] is not the man who abstains who is pleasure's master, but rather the man who enjoys pleasure without being completely carried off his feet. Just as in the case of a ship or a horse one does not show one's mastery by refraining from use, but by knowing how to direct them whithersoever he will. . . .

**
* **

He[3] (Aristippus) was capable of adapting himself to place, time and person, and of playing his part appropriately under whatever circumstances. Hence he found more favor than anybody else with Dionysius, because he could always turn the situation to good account. He derived pleasure from what was present, and did not

[1] Sext. Emp. *Math. Adv.* VII. 191.

[2] Aristippus ap. Stob. *Florileg.* 17, 18.

[3] From Diogenes Laertius, beginning Book II, 66; Hicks's translation, Vol. I, p. 195 ff.

toil to procure the enjoyment of something not present. Hence Diogenes called him the king's poodle. Timon, too, sneered at him for luxury in these words: Such was the delicate nature of Aristippus, who groped after error by touch. . . .

Those then who adhered to the teaching of Aristippus and were known as Cyrenaics held the following opinions. They laid down that there are two states, pleasure and pain, the former a smooth, the latter a rough motion, and that pleasure does not differ from pleasure nor is one pleasure more pleasant than another. The one state is agreeable and the other repellent to all living things. However, the bodily pleasure which is the end is, according to Panætius in his work *On the Sects,* not the settled pleasure following the removal of pains, or the sort of freedom from discomfort which Epicurus accepts and maintains to be the end. They also hold that there is a difference between "end" and "happiness." Our end is particular pleasure, whereas happiness is the sum total of all particular pleasures, in which are included both past and future pleasures.

Particular pleasure is desirable for its own sake, whereas happiness is desirable not for its own sake but for the sake of particular pleasures. That pleasure is the end is proved by the fact that from our youth up we are instinctively attracted to it, and, when we obtain it, seek for nothing more, and shun nothing so much as its opposite, pain. Pleasure is good even if it proceed from the most unseemly conduct, as Hippobotus says in his work *On the Sects.* For even if the action be irregular, still, at any rate, the resultant pleasure is desirable for its own sake and is good. The removal of pain, however, which is put forward in Epicurus, seems to them not to be pleasure at all, any more than the absence of pleasure is pain. For both pleasure and pain they hold to consist in motion, whereas absence of pleasure like absence of pain is not motion, since painlessness is the condition of one who is, as it were, asleep. They assert that some people may fail to choose pleasure because their minds are perverted; not all mental pleasures and pains, however, are derived from bodily counterparts. For instance, we take disinterested delight in the prosperity of our country which is as real as our delight in our own prosperity. Nor again do they admit that pleasure is derived from the memory or expectation of good, which was a doctrine of Epicurus. For they assert that the movement affecting the mind is exhausted in course of time. Again they hold that pleasure is not derived from sight or from hearing alone. At all events, we listen with pleasure to imitation of mourning, while the reality causes pain. They gave the names of absence of pleasure and absence of pain to the intermediate conditions. However, they insist that bodily pleasures are far better than mental pleasures, and bodily pains far worse than mental pains, and that this is the reason why offenders are punished with the former. For they assumed pain to be more repellent, pleasure more congenial. For these reasons they paid more attention to the body than to the mind. Hence, although pleasure is in itself desirable, yet they hold that the things which are productive of certain pleasures are often of a painful nature, the very opposite of pleasure; so that to accumulate the pleasures which are productive of happiness appears to them a most irksome business. . . . And they abandoned the study of nature because of its apparent uncertainty, but fastened on logical inquiries because of their utility. . . . They also held that nothing is just or honorable or base by nature, but only by convention and custom. Nevertheless the good man will be deterred from wrong-doing by the penalties imposed and the prejudices that it would arouse. . . .

THE CYNICS—ANTISTHENES AND DIOGENES

To [4] begin with, he (Antisthenes) became a pupil of Gorgias the rhetorician. . . . Later on, however, he came into touch with Socrates, and derived so much benefit from him that he used to advise his own disciples to become fellow-pupils with him of Socrates. He lived in the Peiræus, and every day would tramp the five miles to Athens in order to hear Socrates. From Socrates he learned his hardihood, emulating his disregard of feeling, and thus he inaugurated the Cynic way of life. He demonstrated that pain is a good thing by instancing the great Heracles and Cyrus, drawing the one example from the Greek world and the other from the barbarians. . . . He used repeatedly to say, "I'd rather be mad than feel pleasure, . . ."

* *

Favorite themes with him were the following: He would prove that virtue can be taught; that nobility belongs to none other than the virtuous. And he held virtue to be sufficient in itself to ensure happiness, since it needed nothing else except the strength of a Socrates.

[4] From Diogenes Laertius, beginning Book VI, 2; Hicks's translation, Vol. II, pp. 3 ff.

And he maintained that virtue is an affair of deeds and
does not need a store of words or learning; that the wise
man is self-sufficing, for all the goods of others are his;
that ill repute is a good thing and much the same as pain;
that the wise man will be guided in his public acts not
by the established laws but by the law of virtue; . . .

Diocles records the following sayings of his: To the
wise man nothing is foreign or impracticable. A good
man deserves to be loved. Men of worth are friends.
Make allies of men who are at once brave and just. Virtue is a weapon that cannot be taken away. It is better
to be with a handful of good men fighting against all
the bad, than with hosts of bad men against a handful
of good men. Pay attention to your enemies, for they
are the first to discover your mistakes. Esteem an honest
man above a kinsman. Virtue is the same for women as
for men. Good actions are fair and evil actions foul.
Count all wickedness foreign and alien.

Wisdom is a most sure stronghold which never crum-
bles away nor is betrayed. Walls of defence must be
constructed in our own impregnable reasonings. . . .

**
* *

They (the Cynics) are content then, . . . to do away
with the subjects of Logic and Physics and to devote
their whole attention to Ethics. . . . They also dispense
with the ordinary subjects of instruction. At least
Antisthenes used to say that those who had attained dis-
cretion had better not study literature, lest they should
be perverted by alien influences. So they get rid of
geometry and music and all such studies. . . . They hold
further that "Life according to Virtue" is the End to be
sought, as Antisthenes says in his *Heracles*: exactly like

the Stoics. For indeed there is a certain close relation-
ship between the two schools. . . . They also hold that
we should live frugally, eating food for nourishment only
and wearing a single garment. Wealth and fame and
high birth they despise. Some at all events are vege-
tarians and drink cold water only and are content with
any kind of shelter or tubs, like Diogenes, who used to
say that it was the privilege of the gods to need nothing
and of god-like men to want but little. . . .

*
* *

He (Diogenes), used to affirm that training was of two
kinds, mental and bodily: . . . and the one half of this
training is incomplete without the other, good health and
strength being just as much included among the essential
things, whether for body or soul. . . . Nothing in life,
however, he maintained, has any chance of succeeding
without strenuous practice; and this is capable of over-
coming anything. Accordingly, instead of useless toils
men should choose such as nature recommends, whereby
they might have lived happily. Yet such is their madness that they choose to be miserable. For even the despising of pleasure is itself most pleasurable, when we are
habituated to it; and just as those accustomed to a life
of pleasure feel disgust when they pass over to the opposite experience, so those whose training has been of the
opposite kind derive more pleasure from despising pleasure than from the pleasures themselves. . . .

XII

PLATO

[427–347 B.C.]

AFTER[1] the philosophers we have described[2] appeared the philosophical system of Plato which agreed with their views in many points, but had its own peculiar tenets which distinguished it from the philosophy of the Italic school. For from his youth up Plato had been familiar with Cratylus and with the opinions of the Heraclitean school—that all things of sense are in perpetual flux and that no real knowledge of them is possible. These views Plato held in later life as well. But while Socrates was occupying himself with ethical investigations, and not at all with nature as a whole, and yet in these investigations was in search of the general law and was the first to direct his attention to the task of definition,—Plato accepted this view too, but drew the conclusion that the definition had for its object something distinct from the objects of sense, for it was impossible that there should be a common definition of any one of the objects of sense, since these are continually changing. And such realities he called ideas; but he held that the objects of sense existed over and above ideas and were all named after them; for the many things that are called by the same name with the ideas exist only through "participation" in them. This ex-

---

[1] Arist. *Met.* I. 6, 987 a 29.   [2] I. e., the Pythagoreans

148

pression "participation" is but a new name for an older view, for the Pythagoreans declared that things that are exist through "imitation" of numbers; Plato, changing the name, says it is through participation. But exactly what is the nature of this participation or of this imitation they have alike failed to explain. Furthermore Plato holds that over and above the objects of sense and the ideas exist the objects with which mathematics deals, occupying an intermediate position, differing from the objects of sense in being eternal and immovable, and differing on the other hand from the ideas in that there are many fac-similes of each, whereas every self-existent idea is one and one only.

From the Phædrus[3]
DIALECTIC VERSUS RHETORIC

Socrates.—But let me ask you, friend: have we not reached the plane-tree to which you were conducting us?

Phædrus.—Yes, this is the tree.

Soc.—By Herè, a fair resting-place, full of summer sounds and scents. Here is this lofty and spreading plane-tree, and the agnus castus high and clustering, in the fullest blossom and the greatest fragrance; and the stream which flows beneath the plane-tree is deliciously cold to the feet. Judging from the ornaments and images, this must be a spot sacred to Achelous and the Nymphs. How delightful is the breeze:—so very sweet; and there is a sound in the air shrill and summer-like which makes answer to the chorus of the cicadæ. But the greatest charm of all is the grass, like a pillow gently sloping to the head. My dear Phædrus, you have been an admirable guide.

[3] From Plato's *Phædrus*, Jowett's translation, beginning p. 230 A.

Phœdr.—What an incomprehensible being you are, Socrates: when you are in the country, as you say, you really are like some stranger who is led about by a guide. Do you ever cross the border? I rather think that you never venture even outside the gates.

Soc.—Very true, my good friend; and I hope that you will excuse me when you hear the reason, which is, that I am a lover of knowledge, and the men who dwell in the city are my teachers, and not the trees or the country. Though I do indeed believe that you have found a spell with which to draw me out of the city into the country, like a hungry cow before whom a bough or bunch of fruit is waved. For only hold up before me in like manner a book, and you may lead me all round Attica, and over the wide world. And now having arrived, I intend to lie down, and do you choose any posture in which you can read best.

[Referring to the love-myth which he had unfolded in the Phædrus Socrates comments as follows:] [4]

The composition was mostly playful. Yet in these chance fancies of the hour were involved two principles of which we should be too glad to have a clearer description if art could give us one.

Phœdr.—What are they?

Soc.—First, the comprehension of scattered particulars in one idea; as in our definition of love, which whether true or false certainly gave clearness and consistency to the discourse, the speaker should define his several notions and so make his meaning clear.

Phœdr.—What is the other principle, Socrates?

[4] From Plato's *Phædrus*, Jowett's translation, beginning p. 265 **D.**

Soc.—The second principle is that of division into species according to the natural formation, where the joint is, not breaking any part as a bad carver might. Just as our two discourses, alike assumed, first of all, a single form of unreason; and then, as the body which from being one becomes double and may be divided into a left side and right side, each having parts right and left of the same name—after this manner the speaker proceeded to divide the parts of the left side and did not desist until he found in them an evil or left-handed love which he justly reviled; and the other discourse leading us to the madness which lay on the right side, found another love, also having the same name, but divine, which the speaker held up before us and applauded and affirmed to be the author of the greatest benefits.

Phœdr.—Most true.

Soc.—I am myself a great lover of these processes of division and generalization; they help me to speak and to think. And if I find any man who is able to see "a One and Many" in nature, him I follow, and "walk in his footsteps as if he were a god." And those who have this art, I have hitherto been in the habit of calling dialecticians; but God knows whether the name is right or not. . . .

***

Oratory [5] is the art of enchanting the soul, and therefore he who would be an orator has to learn the differences of human souls—they are so many and of such a nature, and from them come the differences between man and man. Having proceeded thus far in his analysis, he will next divide speeches into their different classes: "Such and such persons," he will say, "are

[5] From Plato's *Phœdrus*, Jowett's translation, beginning p. 271 D.

affected by this or that kind of speech in this or that way," and he will tell you why.   The pupil must have a good theoretical notion of them first, and then he must have experience of them in actual life, and be able to follow them with all his senses about him, or he will never get beyond the precepts of his masters.   But when he understands what persons are persuaded by what arguments, and sees the person about whom he was speaking in the abstract actually before him, and knows that it is he, and can say to himself, "This is the man or this is the character who ought to have a certain argument applied to him in order to convince him of a certain opinion"; he who knows all this, and knows also when he should speak and when he should refrain, and when he should use pithy sayings, pathetic appeals, sensational effects, and all the other modes of speech which he has learned; when, I say, he knows the times and seasons of all these things, then, and not till then, he is a perfect master of his art; but if he fail in any of these points, whether in speaking or teaching or writing them, and yet declares that he speaks by rules of art, he who says, "I don't believe you," has the better of him.

From the Symposium [6]

ON LOVE

I will rehearse a tale of love which I heard from Diotima of Mantineia, a woman wise in this and in many other kinds of knowledge, who in the days of old, when the Athenians offered sacrifice before the coming of the plague, delayed the disease ten years.   She was my instructress in the art of love, and I shall repeat to you

[6] From Plato's *Symposium*, Jowett's translation, beginning p. 201 D.

what she said to me. . . . "What then is Love?" I asked. "Is he mortal?" "No." "What then?" "As in the former instance, he is neither mortal nor immortal, but in a mean between the two." "What is he, Diotima?" "He is a great spirit (δαίμων), and like all spirits he is intermediate between the divine and the mortal." "And what," I said, "is his power?" "He interprets," she replied, "between gods and men, conveying and taking across to the gods the prayers and sacrifices of men, and to men the commands and replies of the gods; he is the mediator who spans the chasm which divides them, and therefore in him all is bound together, and through him the arts of the prophet and the priest, their sacrifices and mysteries and charms, and all prophecy and incantation, find their way. For God mingles not with man; but through Love all the intercourse and converse of God with man, whether awake or asleep, is carried on. The wisdom which understands this is spiritual; all other wisdom, such as that of arts and handicrafts, is mean and vulgar. Now these spirits or intermediate powers are many and diverse, and one of them is Love. . . .

"You may say generally that all desire of good and happiness is only the great and subtle power of love; but they who are drawn toward him by any other path, whether the path of money-making or gymnastics or philosophy, are not called lovers—the name of the whole is appropriated to those whose affection takes one form only—they alone are said to love, or to be lovers." "I dare say," I replied, "that you are right." "Yes," she added, "and you hear people say that lovers are seeking for their other half; but I say that they are seeking neither for the half of themselves nor for the whole, unless the half or the whole be also a good. And they will cut off their own hands and feet and cast them away, if they are evil; for they love not what is their own, unless perchance there be some one who calls what belongs to him the good, and what belongs to another the evil. For there is nothing which men love but the good. Is there anything?" "Certainly, I should say, that there is nothing." "Then," she said, "the simple truth is, that men love the good." "Yes," I said. "To which must be added that they love the possession of the good?" "Yes, that must be added." "And not only the possession, but the everlasting possession of the good?" "That must be added too." "Then love," she said, "may be described generally as the love of the everlasting possession of the good?" "That is most true."

"Then if this be the nature of love, can you tell me further," she said, "what is the manner of the pursuit? what are they doing who show all this eagerness and heat which is called love? and what is the object which they have in view? Answer me." "Nay, Diotima," I replied, "if I had known, I should not have wondered at your wisdom, neither should I have come to learn from you about this very matter." "Well," she said, "I will teach you: The object which they have in view is birth in beauty whether of body or soul. . . . . .

"These are the lesser mysteries of love, into which even you, Socrates, may enter; to the greater and more hidden ones which are the crown of these, and to which, if you pursue them in a right spirit, they will lead, I know not whether you will be able to attain. But I will do my utmost to inform you, and do you follow if you can. For he who would proceed aright in this matter should begin in youth to visit beautiful forms; and first, if he be guided by his instructor aright, to love one such form only—out of that he should create fair thoughts; and soon he will of himself perceive that the beauty of one form is akin to the beauty of another; and then if beauty of form in general is his pursuit, how foolish would he be not to recognize that the beauty in every form is one and the same! And when he perceives this he will abate his violent love of the one, which he will despise and deem a small thing, and will become a lover of all beautiful forms; in the next stage he will consider that the beauty of the mind is more honorable than the beauty of the outward form. So that if a virtuous soul have but a little comeliness, he will be content to love and tend him, and will search out and bring to the birth thoughts which may improve the young, until he is compelled to contemplate and see the beauty of institutions and laws, and to understand that the beauty of them all is of one family, and that personal beauty is a trifle; and after laws and institutions he will go on to the sciences, that he may see their beauty, being not like a servant in love with the beauty of one youth or man or institution, himself a slave mean and narrow-minded, but drawing toward and contemplating the vast sea of beauty, he will create many fair and noble thoughts and notions in boundless love of wisdom; until on that shore he grows and waxes strong, and at last the vision is revealed to him of a single science, which is the science of beauty everywhere. To this I will proceed; please to give me your very best attention:

"He who has been instructed thus far in the things of love, and who has learned to see the beautiful in due order and succession, when he comes toward the end will suddenly perceive a nature of wondrous beauty (and this, Socrates, is the final cause of all our former toils)— a nature which in the first place is everlasting, not growing and decaying, or waxing and waning; secondly, not fair in one point of view and foul in another, or at one time or in one relation or at one place fair, at another time or in another relation or at another place foul, as if fair to some and foul to others, or in the likeness of a face or hands or any other part of the bodily frame, or in any form of speech or knowledge, or existing in any other being, as for example, in an animal, or in heaven, or in earth, or in any other place; but beauty absolute, separate, simple, and everlasting, which without diminution and without increase, or any change, is imparted to the ever-growing and perishing beauties of all other things.   He who from these ascending under the influence of true love, begins to perceive that beauty, is not far from the end.   And the true order of going, or being led by another, to the things of love, is to begin from the beauties of earth and mount upward for the sake of that other beauty, using these as steps only, and from one going on to two, and from two to all fair forms, and from fair forms to fair practices, and from fair practices to fair notions, until from fair notions he arrives at the notion of absolute beauty, and at last knows what the essence of beauty is.   This, my dear Socrates," said the stranger of Mantineia, "is that life above all others which man should live, in the contemplation of beauty absolute; a beauty which if you once beheld, you would see not to be after the measure of gold, and garments, and fair boys and youths, whose presence now entrances you; and you and many a one would be content to live seeing them only and conversing with them without meat or drink, if that were possible—you only want to look at them and to be with them. But what if man had eyes to see the true beauty—the divine beauty, I mean, pure and clear and unalloyed, not clogged with the pollutions of mortality and all the colors and vanities of human life—thither looking, and holding converse with the true beauty simple and divine? Remember how in that communion only, beholding beauty with the eye of the mind, he will be enabled to bring forth, not images of beauty, but realities (for he has hold not of an image, but of a reality), and bringing forth and nourishing true virtue to become the friend of God and be immortal, if mortal man may. Would that be an ignoble life?"

Such, Phædrus—and I speak not only to you, but to all of you—were the words of Diotima; and I am persuaded of their truth. And being persuaded of them, I try to persuade others, that in the attainment of this end human nature will not easily find a helper better than love. And therefore, also, I say that every man ought to honor him as I myself honor him, and walk in his ways, and exhort others to do the same, and praise the power and spirit of love according to the measure of my ability now and ever.

From the Philebus [1]

PLEASURE AND THE OTHER GOODS

Socrates.—Then, Protarchus, you will proclaim everywhere, by word of mouth to this company, and by messengers bearing the tidings far and wide, that pleasure is not the first of possessions, nor yet the second, but that in measure, and the mean, and the suitable, and the like, the eternal nature has been found.

[1] From the *Philebus,* p. 66 A, Jowett's translation.

Protarchus.—Yes, that seems to be the result of what has been now said.

Soc.—In the second class is contained the symmetrical and beautiful and perfect or sufficient, and all which are of that family.

Pro.—True.

Soc.—And if you reckon in the third class mind and wisdom, you will not be far wrong, if I divine aright.

Pro.—I dare say.

Soc.—And would you not put in the fourth class the goods which we were affirming to appertain specially to the soul—sciences and arts and true opinions as we called them? These come after the third class, and form the fourth, as they are certainly more akin to good than pleasure is.

Pro.—Surely.

Soc.—The fifth class are the pleasures which were defined by us as painless, being the pure pleasures of the soul herself, as we termed them, which accompany, some the sciences, and some the senses.

Pro.—Perhaps.

Soc.—And now, as Orpheus says:

> With the sixth generation cease the glory of my song.

Here, at the sixth award, let us make an end; all that remains is to set the crown on our discourse.

Pro.—True.

Soc.—Then let us sum up and reassert what has been said, thus offering the third libation to the saviour Zeus.

Pro.—How?

Soc.—Philebus affirmed that pleasure was always and absolutely the good.

Pro.—I understand; this third libation, Socrates, of which you spoke, meant a recapitulation.

Soc.—Yes, but listen to the sequel; convinced of what I have just been saying, and feeling indignant at the doctrine, which is maintained, not by Philebus only, but by thousands of others, I affirmed that mind was far better and far more excellent, as an element of human life, than pleasure.

Pro.—True.

Soc.—But, suspecting that there were other things which were also better, I went on to say that if there was anything better than either, then I would claim the second place for mind over pleasure, and pleasure would lose the second place as well as the first.

Pro.—You did.

Soc.—Nothing could be more satisfactorily shown than the unsatisfactory nature of both of them.

Pro.—Very true.

Soc.—The claims both of pleasure and mind to be the absolute good have been entirely disproven in this argument, because they are both wanting in self-sufficiency and also in adequacy and perfection.

Pro.—Most true.

Soc.—But, though they must both resign in favor of another, mind is ten thousand times nearer and more akin to the nature of the conqueror than pleasure.

Pro.—Certainly.

Soc.—And, according to the judgment which has now been given, pleasure will rank fifth.

Pro.—True.

Soc.—But not first; no, not even if all the oxen and horses and animals in the world by their pursuit of enjoyment proclaim her to be so;—although the many trusting in them, as diviners trust in birds, determine that pleasures make up the good of life, and deem the lusts of animals to be better witnesses than the inspirations of divine philosophy.

From the Timæus [8]

THE CREATION OF THE WORLD

Timæus.—All men, Socrates, who have any degree of right feeling, at the beginning of every enterprise, whether small or great, always call upon God. And we, too, who are going to discourse of the nature of the universe, how created or how existing without creation, if we be not altogether out of our wits, must evoke the aid of gods and goddesses and pray that our words may be acceptable to them and consistent with themselves. Let this, then, be our invocation of the gods, to which I add an exhortation of myself to speak in such manner as will be most intelligible to you, and will most accord with my own intent.

First then, in my judgment, we must make a distinction and ask, What is that which always is and has no becoming; and what is that which is always becoming and never is? That which is apprehended by intelligence and reason is always in the same state; but that which is conceived by opinion with the help of sensation and without reason, is always in a process of becoming and perishing and never really is. Now everything that becomes or is created must of necessity be created by some cause, for without a cause nothing can be created. The work of the creator, whenever he looks to the unchangeable and fashions the form and nature of his work after an unchangeable pattern, must necessarily be made

[8] From the *Timæus*, beginning page 27 C, Jowett's translation.

fair and perfect; but when he looks to the created only,
and uses a created pattern, it is not fair or perfect. Was
the heaven then or the world, whether called by this or
by any other more appropriate name—assuming the
name, I am asking a question which has to be asked at
the beginning of an inquiry about anything—was the
world, I say, always in existence and without beginning?
or created, and had it a beginning? Created, I reply,
being visible and tangible and having a body, and
therefore sensible; and all sensible things are apprehended
by opinion and sense and are in a process of creation and
created. Now that which is created must, as we affirm,
of necessity be created by a cause. But the father and
maker of all this universe is past finding out; and even if
we found him, to tell of him to all men would be impossible. And there is still a question to be asked about
him: Which of the patterns had the artificer in view when
he made the world,—the pattern of the unchangeable,
or of that which is created? If the world be indeed fair
and the artificer good, it is manifest that he must have
looked to that which is eternal; but if what cannot be
said without blasphemy is true, then to the created
pattern. Every one will see that he must have looked
to the eternal; for the world is the fairest of creations
and he is the best of causes. And having been created
in this way, the world has been framed in the likeness
of that which is apprehended by reason and mind and is
unchangeable, and must therefore of necessity, if this
is admitted, be a copy of something. Now it is all-
important that the beginning of everything should be
according to nature. And in speaking of the copy and
the original we may assume that words are akin to the
matter which they describe; when they relate to the

lasting and permanent and intelligible, they ought to be lasting and unalterable, and, as far as their nature allows, irrefutable and immovable—nothing less. But when they express only the copy or likeness and not the eternal things themselves, they need only be likely and analogous to the real words. As being is to becoming, so is truth to belief. If then, Socrates, amid the many opinions about the gods and the generation of the universe, we are not able to give notions which are altogether and in every respect exact and consistent with one another, do not be surprised. Enough, if we adduce probabilities as likely as any others; for we must remember that I who am the speaker, and you who are the judges, are only mortal men, and we ought to accept the tale which is probable and inquire no further.

Soc.—Excellent, Timæus; and we will do precisely as you bid us. The prelude is charming, and is already accepted by us—may we beg of you to proceed to the strain?

Tim.—Let me tell you then why the Creator made this world of generation. He was good, and the good can never have any jealousy of anything. And being free from jealousy, he desired that all things should be as like himself as they could be. This is in the truest sense the origin of creation and of the world, as we shall do well in believing on the testimony of wise men: God desired that all things should be good and nothing bad, so far as this was attainable. Wherefore also finding the whole visible sphere not at rest, but moving in an irregular and disorderly fashion, out of disorder he brought order, considering that this was in every way better than the other. Now the deeds of the best could never be or have been other than the fairest; and the Creator, reflecting

on the things which are by nature visible, found that no
unintelligent creature taken as a whole was fairer than
the intelligent taken as a whole; and that intelligence
could not be present in anything which was devoid of
soul. For which reason, when he was framing the
universe, he put intelligence in soul, and soul in body,
that he might be the creator of a work which was by
nature fairest and best. Wherefore, using the language
of probability, we may say that the world became a
living creature truly endowed with soul and intelligence
by the providence of God.

This being supposed, let us proceed to the next stage:
In the likeness of what animal did the Creator make
the world? It would be an unworthy thing to liken it to
any nature which exists as a part only; for nothing can
be beautiful which is like any imperfect thing; but let us
suppose the world to be the very image of that whole
of which all other animals both individually and in their
tribes are portions. For the original of the universe
contains in itself all intelligible beings, just as this world
comprehends us and all other visible creatures. For the
Deity, intending to make this world like the fairest and
most perfect of intelligible beings, framed one visible
animal comprehending within itself all other animals
of a kindred nature. Are we right in saying that there
is one world, or that they are many and infinite? There
must be one only, if the created copy is to accord with
the original. For that which includes all other intelligible creatures cannot have a second or companion;
in that case there would be need of another living being
which would include both, and of which they would be
parts, and the likeness would be more truly said to
resemble not them, but that other which included them.

In order then that the world might be solitary, like the perfect animal, the Creator made not two worlds or an infinite number of them; but there is and ever will be one only-begotten and created heaven.

Such was the whole plan of the eternal God about the god that was to be, to whom for this reason he gave a body, smooth and even, having a surface in every direction equidistant from the centre, a body entire and perfect, and formed out of perfect bodies. And in the centre he put the soul, which he diffused throughout the body, making it also to be the exterior environment of it; and he made the universe a circle moving in a circle, one and solitary, yet by reason of its excellence, able to converse with itself, and needing no other friendship or acquaintance. Having these purposes in view he created the world a blessed god.

Now God did not make the soul after the body, although we are speaking of them in this order; for having brought them together he would never have allowed that the elder should be ruled by the younger; but this is a random manner of speaking which we have, because somehow we ourselves too are very much under the dominion of chance. Whereas he made the soul in origin and excellence prior to and older than the body, to be the ruler and mistress, of whom the body was to be the subject. And he made her out of the following elements and on this wise: Out of the indivisible and unchangeable, and also out of that which is divisible and has to do with material bodies, he compounded a third and intermediate kind of essence, partaking of the nature of the same and of the other, and this compound he placed accordingly in a mean between the indivisible and the divisible and material. He took the three elements of the same, the other and the essence, and mingled them into one form, compressing by force the reluctant and unsociable nature of the other into the same. When he had mingled them with the essence and out of the three made one, he again divided this whole into as many portions as was fitting, each portion being a compound of the same, the other, and the essence.

Now when the Creator had framed the soul according to his will, he formed within her the corporeal universe, and brought the two together, and united them centre to centre. The soul, infused everywhere from the centre to the circumference of heaven, of which also she is the external envelopment, herself turning in herself, began a divine beginning of never-ceasing and rational life enduring throughout all time. The body of heaven is visible, but the soul is invisible, and partakes of reason and harmony, and being made by the best of intellectual and everlasting natures, is the best of things created.

When the Father and Creator saw the creature which he had made moving and living, the created image of the eternal gods, he rejoiced, and in his joy determined to make the copy still more like the original; and as this was eternal, he sought to make the universe eternal, so far as might be. Now the nature of the ideal being was everlasting, but to bestow this attribute in its fulness upon a creature was impossible. Wherefore he resolved to have a moving image of eternity, and when he set in order the heaven, he made this image eternal but moving according to number, while eternity itself rests in unity; and this image we call time. For there were no days and nights and months and years before the heaven was created, but when he constructed the heaven he created them also. They are all parts of time, and the past and future are created species of time, which we unconsciously but wrongly transfer to the eternal essence; for we say that he "was," he "is," he "will be," but the truth is that "is" alone is properly attributed to him, and that "was" and "will be" are only to be spoken of becoming in time, for they are motions, but that which is immovably the same cannot become older or younger by time, nor ever did or has become, or hereafter will be, older or younger, nor is subject at all to any of those states which affect moving and sensible things and of which generation is the cause. These are the forms of time, which imitates eternity and revolves according to a law of number. Moreover, when we say that what has become *is* become and what becomes *is* becoming, and that what will become *is* about to become and that the non-existent *is* non-existent—all these are inaccurate modes of expression. But perhaps this whole subject will be more suitably discussed on some other occasion. . . . .

This new beginning of our discussion of the universe requires a fuller division than the former; for then we made two classes, now a third must be revealed. The two sufficed for the former discussion; one, which we assumed, was a pattern intelligible and always the same; and the second was only the imitation of the pattern, generated and visible. There is also a third kind which we did not distinguish at the time, conceiving that the two would be enough. But now the argument seems to require that we should set forth in words another kind, which is difficult of explanation and dimly seen. What nature are we to attribute to this new kind of being? We reply, that it is the receptacle, and in a manner the nurse, of all generation. . . .

Do all those things which we call self-existent exist? or are only those things which we see, or in some way perceive through the bodily organs, truly existent, and nothing whatever besides them? And is all that which we call an intelligible essence nothing at all, and only a name? Here is a question which we must not leave unexamined or undetermined, nor must we affirm too confidently that there can be no decision; neither must we interpolate in our present long discourse a digression equally long, but if it is possible to set forth a great principle in a few words, that is just what we want.

Thus I state my view: If mind and true opinion are two distinct classes, then I say that there certainly are these self-existent ideas unperceived by sense, and apprehended only by the mind; if, however, as some say, true opinion differs in no respect from mind, then everything that we perceive through the body is to be regarded as most real and certain. But we must affirm them to be distinct, for they have a distinct origin and are of a different nature; the one is implanted in us by instruction, the other by persuasion; the one is always accompanied by true reason, the other is without reason; the one cannot be overcome by persuasion, but the other can; and lastly, every man may be said to share in true opinion, but mind is the attribute of the gods and of very few men. Wherefore also we must acknowledge that there is one kind of being which is always the same, uncreated and indestructible, never receiving anything into itself from without, nor itself going out to any other, but invisible and imperceptible by any sense, and of which the contemplation is granted to intelligence only. And there is another nature of the same name with it,

and like to it, perceived by sense, created, always in
motion, becoming in place and again vanishing out of
place, which is apprehended by opinion and sense.   And
there is a third nature, which is space, and is eternal,
and admits not of destruction and provides a home for all
created things, and is apprehended without the help of
sense, by a kind of spurious reason, and is hardly real;
which we beholding as in a dream, say of all existence
that it must of necessity be in some place and occupy
a space, but that what is neither in heaven nor in earth
has no existence.   Of these and other things of the same
kind, relating to the true and waking reality of nature,
we have only this dream-like sense, and we are unable to
cast off sleep and determine the truth about them.   For
an image, since the reality, after which it is modelled,
does not belong to it, and it exists ever as the fleeting
shadow of some other, must be inferred to be in another
[i. e., in space], grasping existence in some way or other,
or it could not be at all.   But true and exact reason,
vindicating the nature of true being, maintains that
while two things [i. e., the image and space] are different
they cannot exist one of them in the other and so be one
and also two at the same time.

From the Parmenides [9]

PUZZLES PRESENTED BY THE THEORY OF IDEAS

'I understand," said Socrates, "and quite accept
your account.   But tell me, Zeno, do you not further
think that there is an idea of likeness in itself, and another idea of unlikeness, which is the opposite of likeness,
and that in these two you and I, and all other things to
which we apply the term many, participate—things which

[9] From the *Parmenides*, Jowett's translation, beginning p. 128 E.

participate in likeness become in that degree and manner like; and so far as they participate in unlikeness become in that degree unlike, or both like and unlike in the degree in which they participate in both? And may not all things partake of both opposites, and be both like and unlike, by reason of this participation? Where is the wonder? Now if a person could prove the absolute like to become unlike, or the absolute unlike to become like, that, in my opinion, would indeed be a wonder; but there is nothing extraordinary, Zeno, in showing that the things which only partake of likeness and unlikeness experience both. Nor, again, if a person were to show that all is one by partaking of one, and at the same time many by partaking of many, would that be very astonishing? But if he were to show me that the absolute one was many, or the absolute many one, I should be truly amazed. And so of all the rest: I should be surprised to hear that the natures or ideas themselves had these opposite qualities; but not if a person wanted to prove of me that I was many and also one. When he wanted to show that I was many he would say that I have a right and a left side, and a front and a back, and an upper and a lower half, for I cannot deny that I partake of multitude; when, on the other hand, he wants to prove that I am one, he will say, that we who are here assembled are seven, and that I am one, and partake of the one. In both instances he proves his case. So again, if a person shows that such things as wood, stones, and the like, being many are also one, we admit that he shows the co-existence of the one and many, but he does not show that the many are one or the one many; he is uttering not a paradox but a truism. If, however, as I just now suggested, some one were to abstract simple notions of like, unlike, one, many, rest, motion, and similar ideas, and then to show that these admit of admixture and separation in themselves, I should be very much astonished. This part of the argument appears to be treated by you, Zeno, in a very spirited manner; but, as I was saying, I should be far more amazed if any one found in the ideas themselves which are apprehended by reason, the same puzzle and entanglement which you have shown to exist in visible objects."

While Socrates was speaking, Pythodorus thought that Parmenides and Zeno were not altogether pleased at the successive steps of the argument; but still they gave the closest attention, and often looked at one another, and smiled as if in admiration of him. When he had finished, Parmenides expressed their feelings in the following words:

"Socrates," he said, "I admire the bent of your mind toward philosophy; tell me now, was this your own distinction between ideas in themselves and the things which partake of them? and do you think that there is an idea of likeness apart from the likeness which we possess, and of the one and many, and of the other things which Zeno mentioned?"

"I think that there are such ideas," said Socrates.

Parmenides proceeded: "And would you also make absolute ideas of the just and the beautiful and the good, and of all that class?"

"Yes," he said, "I should."

"And would you make an idea of man apart from us and from all other human creatures, or of fire and water?"

"I am often undecided, Parmenides, as to whether I ought to include them or not."

"And would you feel equally undecided, Socrates,

about things of which the mention may provoke a smile?
—I mean such things as hair, mud, dirt, or anything
else which is vile and paltry; would you suppose that
each of these has an idea distinct from the actual objects
with which we come into contact, or not?"

"Certainly not," said Socrates; "visible things like
these are such as they appear to us, and I am afraid that
there would be an absurdity in assuming any idea of
them, although I sometimes get disturbed, and begin to
think that there is nothing without an idea; but then
again, when I have taken up this position, I run away,
because I am afraid that I may fall into a bottomless pit
of nonsense, and perish; and so I return to the ideas of
which I was just now speaking, and occupy myself with
them."

"Yes, Socrates," said Parmenides; "that is because
you are still young; the time will come, if I am not mistaken, when philosophy will have a firmer grasp of you,
and then you will not despise even the meanest things;
at your age, you are too much disposed to regard the
opinions of men. But I should like to know whether
you mean that there are certain ideas of which all other
things partake, and from which they derive their names;
that similars, for example, become similar, because they
partake of similarity; and great things become great,
because they partake of greatness; and that just and
beautiful things become just and beautiful because they
partake of justice and beauty?"

"Yes, certainly," said Socrates, "that is my meaning."

"Then each individual partakes either of the whole of
the idea or else of a part of the idea? Can there be any
other mode of participation?"

"There cannot be," he said.

"Then do you think that the whole idea is one, and yet, being one, is in each one of the many?"

"Why not, Parmenides?" said Socrates.

"Because one and the same thing will exist as a whole at the same time in many separate individuals, and will therefore be in a state of separation from itself."

"Nay, but the idea may be like the day which is one and the same in many places at once, and yet continuous with itself; in this way each idea may be one and the same in all at the same time."

"I like your way, Socrates, of making one in many places at once. You mean to say, that if I were to spread out a sail and cover a number of men, there would be one whole including many—is not that your meaning?"

"I think so."

"And would you say that the whole sail includes each man, or part of it only, and different parts different men?"

"The latter."

"Then, Socrates, the ideas themselves will be divisible, and things which participate in them will have a part of them only and not the whole idea existing in each of them?"

"That seems to follow."

"Then would you like to say, Socrates, that the one idea is really divisible and yet remains one?"

"Certainly not," he said.

"Suppose that you divide absolute greatness, and that of the many great things, each one is great in virtue of a portion of greatness less than absolute greatness—is that conceivable?"

"No."

"Or will each equal thing, if possessing some small portion of equality less than absolute equality, be equal to some other thing by virtue of that portion only?"

"Impossible."

"Or suppose one of us to have a portion of smallness; this is but a part of the small, and therefore the absolutely small is greater; if the absolutely small be greater, that to which the part of the small is added will be smaller and not greater than before."

"How absurd!"

"Then in what way, Socrates, will all things participate in the ideas, if they are unable to participate in them either as parts or wholes?"

"Indeed," he said, "you have asked a question which is not easily answered."

"Well," said Parmenides, "and what do you say of another question?"

"What question?"

"I imagine that the way in which you are led to assume one idea of each kind is as follows: You see a number of great objects, and when you look at them there seems to you to be one and the same idea (or nature) in them all; hence you conceive of greatness as one."

"Very true," said Socrates.

"And if you go on and allow your mind in like manner to embrace in one view the idea of greatness and of great things which are not the idea, and to compare them, will not another greatness arise, which will appear to be the source of all these?"

"It would seem so."

"Then another idea of greatness now comes into view over and above absolute greatness, and the individuals which partake of it; and then another, over and above all these, by virtue of which they will all be great, and so each idea instead of being one will be infinitely multiplied."

"But may not the ideas," asked Socrates, "be thoughts only, and have no proper existence except in our minds, Parmenides? For in that case each idea may still be one, and not experience this infinite multiplication."

"And can there be individual thoughts which are thoughts of nothing?"

"Impossible," he said.

"The thought must be of something?"

"Yes."

"Of something which is or which is not?"

"Of something which is."

"Must it not be of a single something, which the thought recognizes as attaching to all, being a single form or nature?"

"Yes."

"And will not the something which is apprehended as one and the same in all, be an idea?"

"From that, again, there is no escape."

"Then," said Parmenides, "if you say that everything else participates in the ideas, must you not say either that everything is made up of thoughts, and that all things think; or that they are thoughts but have no thought?"

"The latter view, Parmenides, is no more rational than the previous one. In my opinion, the ideas are, as it were, patterns fixed in nature, and other things are like them, and resemblances of them—what is meant by the participation of other things in the ideas, is really assimilation to them."

"But if," said he, "the individual is like the idea, must not the idea also be like the individual, in so far as the individual is a resemblance of the idea? That which is like, cannot be conceived of as other than the like of like."

"Impossible."

"And when two things are alike, must they not partake of the same idea?"

"They must."

"And will not that of which the two partake, and which makes them alike, be the idea itself?"

"Certainly."

"Then the idea cannot be like the individual, or the individual like the idea; for if they are alike, some further idea of likeness will always be coming to light, and if that be like anything else, another; and new ideas will be always arising, if the idea resembles that which partakes of it?"

"Quite true."

"The theory, then, that other things participate in the ideas by resemblance, has to be given up, and some other mode of participation devised?"

"It would seem so."

"Do you see then, Socrates, how great is the difficulty of affirming the ideas to be absolute?"

"Yes, indeed."

"And, further, let me say that as yet you only understand a small part of the difficulty which is involved if you make of each thing a single idea, parting it off from other things."

"What difficulty?" he said.

"There are many, but the greatest of all is this: If an opponent argues that these ideas, being such as we say they ought to be, must remain unknown, no one can prove to him that he is wrong, unless he who denies their existence be a man of great ability and knowledge, and is willing to follow a long and laborious demonstration; he will remain unconvinced, and still insist that they cannot be known."

"What do you mean, Parmenides?" said Socrates.

"In the first place, I think, Socrates, that you, or any one who maintains the existence of absolute essences, will admit that they cannot exist in us."

"No," said Socrates; "for then they would be no longer absolute."

"True," he said; "and therefore when ideas are what they are in relation to one another, their essence is determined by a relation among themselves, and has nothing to do with the resemblances, or whatever they are to be termed, which are in our sphere and from which we receive this or that name when we partake of them. And the things which are within our sphere and have the same names with them, are likewise only relative to one another, and not to the ideas which have the same names with them, but belong to themselves and not to them."

"What do you mean?" said Socrates.

"I may illustrate my meaning in this way," said Parmenides: "A master has a slave; now there is nothing absolute in the relation between them, which is simply a relation of one man to another. But there is also an idea of mastership in the abstract, which is relative to the idea of slavery in the abstract. These natures have nothing to do with us, nor we with them; they are concerned with themselves only, and we with ourselves. Do you see my meaning? "

"Yes," said Socrates, "I quite see your meaning."

"And will not knowledge—I mean absolute knowledge —answer to absolute truth?"

"Certainly."

"And each kind of absolute knowledge will answer to each kind of absolute being?"

"Yes."

"But the knowledge which we have, will answer to the truth which we have; and again, each kind of knowledge which we have, will be a knowledge of each kind of being which we have?"

"Certainly."

"But the ideas themselves, as you admit, we have not, and cannot have?"

"No, we cannot."

"And the absolute natures or kinds are known severally by the absolute idea of knowledge?"

"Yes."

"And we have not got the idea of knowledge?"

"No."

"Then none of the ideas are known to us, because we have no share in absolute knowledge?"

"I suppose not."

"Then the nature of the beautiful in itself, and of the good in itself, and all other ideas which we suppose to exist absolutely, are unknown to us?"

"It would seem so."

"I think that there is a stranger consequence still."

"What is it?"

"Would you, or would you not say, that absolute knowledge, if there is such a thing, must be a far more exact knowledge than our knowledge; and the same of beauty and of the rest?"

"Yes."

"And if there be such a thing as participation in absolute knowledge, no one is more likely than God to have this most exact knowledge?"

"Certainly."

"But then, will God, having absolute knowledge, have a knowledge of human things?"

"Why not?"

"Because, Socrates," said Parmenides, "we have admitted that the ideas are not valid in relation to human things; nor human things in relation to them; the relations of either are limited to their respective spheres."

"Yes, that has been admitted."

"And if God has this perfect authority, and perfect knowledge, His authority cannot rule us, nor His knowledge know us, or any human thing; just as our authority does not extend to the gods, nor our knowledge know anything which is divine, so by parity of reason they, being gods, are not our masters, neither do they know the things of men."

"Yet, surely," said Socrates, "to deprive God of knowledge is monstrous."

"These, Socrates," said Parmenides, "are a few, and only a few of the difficulties in which we are involved if ideas really are and we determine each one of them to be an absolute unity. He who hears what may be said against them will deny the very existence of them—and even if they do exist, he will say that they must of necessity be unknown to man; and he will seem to have reason on his side, and as we were remarking just now, will be very difficult to convince; a man must be gifted with very considerable ability before he can learn that everything has a class and an absolute essence; and still more remarkable will he be who discovers all these things for himself, and having thoroughly investigated them is able to teach them to others."

"I agree with you, Parmenides," said Socrates; "and what you say is very much to my mind."

"And yet, Socrates," said Parmenides, "if a man, fixing his attention on these and the like difficulties, does away with ideas of things and will not admit that every individual thing has its own determinate idea which is always one and the same, he will have nothing on which his mind can rest; and so he will utterly destroy the power of reasoning, as you seem to me to have particularly noted."

"Very true," he said.

"But then, what is to become of philosophy? Whither shall we turn, if the ideas are unknown?"

"I certainly do not see my way at present."

"Yes," said Parmenides; "and I think that this arises, Socrates, out of your attempting to define the beautiful, the just, the good, and the ideas generally, without sufficient previous training."

XIII

PLATO—(*Continued*)

From The Republic

THE NATURE OF VIRTUE

"Tell [1] me, do you think there is such a thing as a horse's function?"

"I do."

"Would you, then, describe the function of a horse, or of anything else whatever, as that work, for the accomplishment of which it is either the sole or the best instrument?"

"I do not understand."

"Look at it this way. Can you see with anything besides eyes?"

"Certainly not."

"Can you hear with anything besides ears?"

"No."

"Then should we not justly say that seeing and hearing are the functions of these organs?"

"Yes, certainly."

"Again, you might cut off a vine shoot with a carving knife, or chisel, or many other tools?"

"Undoubtedly."

"But with no tool, I imagine, so well as with the pruning knife made for the purpose."

[1] Plato's *Republic*, Book I. p. 352 E. The translations from *The Republic* included in this section are all taken from the version of Davies and Vaughan.

"True."

"Then shall we not define pruning to be the function of the pruning knife?"

"By all means."

"Now then, I think, you will better understand what I wished to learn from you just now, when I asked whether the function of a thing is not that work for the accomplishment of which it is either the sole or the best instrument?"

"I do understand, and I believe that this is in every case the function of a thing."

"Very well: do you not also think that everything which has an appointed function has also a proper *virtue*? Let us revert to the same instances; we say that the eyes have a function?"

"They have."

"Then have the eyes a virtue also?"

"They have."

"And the ears: did we assign them a function?"

"Yes."

"Then have they a virtue also?"

"They have."

"And is it the same with all other things?"

"The same."

"Attend then: Do you suppose that the eyes could discharge their own function well if they had not their own proper virtue—that virtue being replaced by a vice?"

"How could they? You mean, probably, if sight is replaced by blindness."

"I mean, whatever their virtue be; for I am not come to that question yet. At present I am asking whether it is through their own peculiar virtue that things perform their proper functions well, and through their own peculiar vice that they perform them ill?"

"You cannot be wrong in that."

"Then if the ears lose their own virtue, will they execute their functions ill?"

"Certainly."

"May we include all other things under the same proposition?"

"I think we may."

"Come, then, consider this point next. Has the soul any function which could not be executed by means of anything else whatsoever? For example, could we in justice assign superintendence and government, deliberation, and the like, to anything but the soul, or should we pronounce them to be peculiar to it?"

"We could ascribe them to nothing else."

"Again, shall we declare life to be a function of the soul?"

"Decidedly."

"Do we not also maintain that the soul has a virtue?"

"We do."

"Then can it ever so happen, Thrasymachus, that the soul will perform its functions well when destitute of its own peculiar virtue, or is that impossible?"

"Impossible."

"Then a bad soul must needs exercise authority and superintendence ill, and a good soul must do all these things well."

THE FOUR CARDINAL VIRTUES

"What [2] at the commencement we laid down as a universal rule of action, when we were founding our

---

[2] Plato's *Republic*, Book IV. 433 A.

state, this, if I mistake not, or some modification of it, is justice. I think we affirmed, if you recollect, and frequently repeated, that every individual ought to have some one occupation in the state, which should be that to which his natural capacity was best adapted."

"We did say so."

"And again, we have often heard people say, that to mind one's own business, and not be meddlesome, is justice; and we have often said the same thing ourselves."

"We have said so."

"Then it would seem, my friend, that to do one's own business, in some shape or other, is justice. Do you know whence I infer this?"

"No; be so good as to tell me."

"I think that the remainder left in the state, after eliminating the qualities which we have considered, I mean temperance, and courage, and wisdom, must be that which made their entrance into it possible, and which preserves them there so long as they exist in it. Now we affirmed that the remaining quality, when three out of the four were found, would be justice. . . ."

"Here then," I proceeded, " after a hard struggle, we have, though with difficulty, reached the land; and we are pretty well satisfied that there are corresponding divisions, equal in number, in a state, and in the soul of every individual."

"True."

"Then does it not necessarily follow that, as and whereby the state was wise, so and thereby the individual is wise?"

"Without doubt it does."

"And that as and whereby the individual is brave, so and thereby is the state brave; and that everything conducing to virtue which is possessed by the one, finds its counterpart in the other?"

"It must be so."

"Then we shall also assert, I imagine, Glaucon, that a man is just, in the same way in which we found the state to be just."

"This too is a necessary corollary."

"But surely we have not allowed ourselves to forget, that what makes the state just, is the fact of each of the three classes therein doing its own work."

"No; I think we have not forgotten this."

"We must bear in mind, then, that each of us also, if his inward faculties do severally their proper work, will, in virtue of that, be a just man, and a doer of his proper work."

"Certainly, it must be borne in mind."

"Is it not then essentially the province of the rational principle to command, inasmuch as it is wise, and has to exercise forethought in behalf of the entire soul, and the province of the spirited principle to be its subject and ally?"

"Yes, certainly."

"And will not the combination of music and gymnastic bring them, as we said, into unison; elevating and foster-ing the one with lofty discourses and scientific teachings, and lowering the tone of the other by soothing address, till its wildness has been tamed by harmony and rhythm?"

"Yes, precisely so."

"And so these two, having been thus trained, and having truly learned their parts and received a real education, will exercise control over the concupiscent principle, which in every man forms the largest portion

of the soul, and is by nature most insatiably covetous.
And they will watch it narrowly, that it may not so
batten upon what are called the pleasures of the body
as to grow large and strong, and forthwith refuse to do
its proper work, and even aspire to absolute dominion
over the classes which it has no right according to its
kind to govern, thus overturning fundamentally the life
of all."

"Certainly they will."

"And would not these two principles be the best
qualified to guard the entire soul and body against
enemies from without; the one taking counsel, and the
other fighting its battles, in obedience to the governing power, to whose designs it gives effect by its
bravery?"

"True."

"In like manner, I think, we call an individual brave,
in virtue of the spirited element of his nature, when this
part of him holds fast, through pain and pleasure, the
instructions of the reason as to what is to be feared, and
what is not."

"Yes, and rightly."

"And we call him wise, in virtue of that small part
which reigns within him, and issues these instructions,
and which also in its turn contains within itself a true
knowledge of what is advantageous for the whole community composed of these three principles, and for each
member of it."

"Exactly so."

"Again, do we not call a man temperate, in virtue of
the friendship and harmony of these same principles,
that is to say, when the two that are governed agree with
that which governs in regarding the rational principle

as the rightful sovereign, and set up no opposition to its
authority?"

"Certainly," he replied; "temperance is nothing else
than this, whether in state or individual."

"Lastly, a man will be just, in the way and by the
means which we have repeatedly described."

THE HIGHER EDUCATION LEADING UP TO THE IDEA OF THE GOOD

"WELL,[3] then, this part of the subject having been
laboriously completed, shall we proceed to discuss the
questions still remaining, in what way, and by the help
of what pursuits and studies, we shall secure the presence
of a body of men capable of preserving the constitution
unimpaired, and what must be the age at which these
studies are severally undertaken?"

"Let us do so, by all means."

"I have gained nothing," I continued, "by my old
scheme of omitting the troublesome questions involved
in the treatment of the women and children, and the
appointment of the magistrates; which I was induced to
leave out from knowing what odium the perfectly correct
method would incur, and how difficult it would be to
carry into effect. Notwithstanding all my precautions,
the moment has now arrived when these points must be
discussed. It is true the question of the women and
children has been already settled, but the inquiry concerning the magistrates must be pursued quite afresh.
In describing them, we said, if you recollect, that, in
order to place their patriotism beyond the reach of suspicion, they must be tested by pleasure and by pain, and
proved never to have deserted their principles in the
midst of toil and danger and every vicissitude of fortune,

'Plato's *Republic*, Book VI. p. 502 D.

on pain of forfeiting their position if their powers of endurance fail; and that whoever comes forth from the trial without a flaw, like gold tried in the fire, must be appointed to office, and receive, during life and after death, privileges and rewards. This was pretty nearly the drift of our language, which, from fear of awakening the question now pending, turned aside and hid its face."

"Your account is quite correct," he said; "I remember perfectly."

"Yes, my friend, I shrank from making assertions which I have since hazarded; but now let me venture upon this declaration, that we must make the most perfect philosophers guardians."

"We hear you," he replied.

"Now consider what a small supply of these men you will, in all probability, find. For the various members of that character, which we described as essential to philosophers, will seldom grow incorporate: in most cases that character grows disjointed."

"What do you mean?"

"You are aware that persons endowed with a quick comprehension, a good memory, sagacity, acuteness, and their attendant qualities, do not readily grow up to be at the same time so noble and lofty-minded, as to consent to live a regular, calm, and steady life: on the contrary, such persons are drifted by their acuteness hither and thither, and all steadiness vanishes from their life."

"True."

"On the other hand, those steady and invariable characters, whose trustiness makes one anxious to employ them, and who in war are slow to take alarm, behave in the same way when pursuing their studies; that is to say, they are torpid and stupid, as if they were benumbed, and are constantly dozing and yawning, whenever they have to toil at anything of the kind."

"That is true."

"But we declare that, unless a person possesses a pretty fair amount of both qualifications, he must be debarred all access to the strictest education, to honor, and to government."

"We are right."

"Then do you not anticipate a scanty supply of such characters?"

"Most assuredly I do."

"Hence we must not be content with testing their behavior in the toils, dangers, and pleasures, which we mentioned before; but we must go on to try them in ways which we then omitted, exercising them in a variety of studies, and observing whether their character will be able to support the highest subjects, or whether it will flinch from the trial, like those who flinch under other circumstances."

"No doubt it is proper to examine them in this way. But pray which do you mean by the highest subjects?"

"I presume you remember, that, after separating the soul into three specific parts, we deduced the several natures of justice, temperance, fortitude, and wisdom?"

"Why, if I did not remember, I should deserve not to hear the rest of the discussion."

"Do you also remember the remark which preceded that deduction?"

"Pray, what was it?"

"We remarked, I believe, that to obtain the best possible view of the question, we should have to take a different and a longer route, which would bring us to a thorough insight into the subject: still that it would be possible to subjoin a demonstration of the question, flowing from our previous conclusions. Thereupon you said that such a demonstration would satisfy you; and then followed those investigations which, to my own mind, were deficient in exactness; but you can tell me whether they contented you."

"Well, to speak for myself, I thought them fair in point of measure; and certainly the rest of the party held the same opinion."

"But, my friend, no measure of such a subject, which falls perceptibly short of the truth, can be said to be quite fair, for nothing imperfect is a measure of anything: though people sometimes fancy that enough has been done, and that there is no call for further investigation."

"Yes," he said, "that is a very common habit, and arises from indolence."

"Yes, but it is a habit remarkably undesirable in the guardian of a state and its laws."

"So I should suppose."

"That being the case, my friend, such a person must go round by that longer route, and must labor as devotedly in his studies as in his bodily exercises. Otherwise, as we were saying just now, he will never reach the goal of that highest science, which is most peculiarly his own."

"What!" he exclaimed, "are not these the highest? Is there still something higher than justice and those other things which we have discussed?"

"Even so," I replied; "and here we must not contemplate a rude outline, as we have been doing: on the contrary, we must be satisfied with nothing short of the

most complete elaboration. For would it not be ridiculous
to exert one's self on other subjects of small value, taking
all imaginable pains to bring them to the most exact
and spotless perfection; and at the same time to ignore
the claim of the highest subjects to a corresponding
exactitude of the highest order?"

"The sentiment is a very just one. But do you suppose that any one would let you go without asking what
that science is which you call the highest, and of what it
treats?"

"Certainly not," I replied; "so put the question yourself. Assuredly you have heard the answer many a
time; but at this moment either you have forgotten it,
or else you intend to find me employment by raising
objections. I incline to the latter opinion; for you have
often been told that the essential Form of the Good (ἡ τοῦ
ἀγαθοῦ ἰδέα) is the highest object of science, and that this
essence, by blending with just things and all other created
objects, renders them useful and advantageous. And at
this moment you can scarcely doubt that I am going to
assert this, and to assert, besides, that we are not sufficiently acquainted with this essence. And if so,—if, I
say, we know everything else perfectly, without knowing
this,—you are aware that it will profit us nothing; just as
it would be equally profitless to possess everything without possessing what is good. Or do you imagine it would
be a gain to possess all possessible things, with the single
exception of things good; or to apprehend every conceivable object, without apprehending what is good,—
in other words, to be destitute of every good and beautiful
conception?"

"Not I, believe me."

"Moreover, you doubtless know besides, that the chief

good is supposed by the multitude to be pleasure,—by the more enlightened, insight?"

"Of course I know that."

"And you are aware, my friend, that the advocates of this latter opinion are unable to explain what they mean by insight, and are compelled at last to explain it as insight into that which is good."

"Yes, they are in a ludicrous difficulty."

"They certainly are: since they reproach us with ignorance of that which is good, and then speak to us the next moment as if we knew what it was. For they tell us that the chief good is insight into good, assuming that we understand their meaning, as soon as they have uttered the term 'good.'"

"It is perfectly true."

"Again: are not those, whose definition identifies pleasure with good, just as much infected with error as the preceding? For they are forced to admit the existence of evil pleasures, are they not?"

"Certainly they are."

"From which it follows, I should suppose, that they must admit the same thing to be both good and evil. Does it not?"

"Certainly it does."

"Then is it not evident that this is a subject often and severely disputed?"

"Doubtless it is."

"Once more: is it not evident, that though many persons would be ready to do and seem to do, or to possess and seem to possess, what seems just and beautiful, without really being so; yet, when you come to things good, no one is content to acquire what only seems such; on the contrary, everybody seeks the reality, and semblances are here, if nowhere else, treated with universal contempt?"

"Yes, that is quite evident."

"This good, then, which every soul pursues, as the end of all its actions, divining its existence, but perplexed and unable to apprehend satisfactorily its nature, or to enjoy that steady confidence in relation to it which it does enjoy in relation to other things, and therefore doomed to forfeit any advantage which it might have derived from those same things;—are we to maintain that, on a subject of such overwhelming importance, the blindness we have described is a desirable feature in the character of those best members of the state in whose hands everything is to be placed?"

"Most certainly not."

"At any rate, if it be not known in what way just things and beautiful things come to be also good, I imagine that such things will not possess a very valuable guardian in the person of him who is ignorant on this point. And I surmise that none will know the just and the beautiful satisfactorily till he knows the good."

"You are right in your surmises."

"Then will not the arrangement of our constitution be perfect, provided it be overlooked by a guardian who is scientifically acquainted with these subjects?"

" Unquestionably it will."

THE IDEA OF THE GOOD AS THE SOURCE OF TRUTH AND OF REALITY

"Pray,[4] Socrates, do *you* assert the chief good to be science or pleasure or something different from either?"

"Ho, ho, my friend! I saw long ago that you would

* Plato's *Republic*, p. 506 B.

certainly not put up with the opinions of other people on these subjects."

"Why, Socrates, it appears to me to be positively wrong in one who has devoted so much time to these questions, to be able to state the opinions of others, without being able to state his own."

"Well," I said, "do you think it right to speak with an air of information on subjects on which one is not well informed?"

"Certainly not with an air of information; but I think it right to be willing to state one's opinion for what it is worth."

"Well, but have you not noticed that opinions divorced from science are all ill-favored? At the best they are blind. Or do you conceive that those who, unaided by the pure reason, entertain a correct opinion, are at all superior to blind men, who manage to keep the straight path?"

"Not at all superior," he replied.

"Then is it your desire to contemplate objects that are ill-favored, blind, and crooked, when it is in your power to learn from other people about bright and beautiful things?"

"I implore you, Socrates," cried Glaucon, "not to hang back, as if you had come to the end. We shall be content even if you only discuss the subject of the chief good in the style in which you discussed justice, temperance, and the rest."

"Yes, my friend, and I likewise should be thoroughly content. But I distrust my own powers, and I feel afraid that my awkward zeal will subject me to ridicule. No, my good sirs: let us put aside, for the present at any rate, all inquiry into the real nature of the chief good. For, methinks, it is beyond the measure of this our enterprise to find the way to what is, after all, only my present opinion on the subject. But I am willing to talk to you about that which appears to be an offshoot of the chief good, and bears the strongest resemblance to it, provided it is also agreeable to you; but if it is not, I will let it alone."

"Nay, tell us about it," he replied. "You shall remain in our debt for an account of the parent."

"I wish that *I* could pay, and you receive, the parent sum, instead of having to content ourselves with the interest springing from it. However, here I present you with the fruit and scion of the essential good. Only take care that I do not involuntarily impose upon you by handing in a forged account of this offspring."

"We will take all the care we can; only proceed."

"I will do so, as soon as we have come to a settlement together, and you have been reminded of certain statements made in a previous part of our conversation, and renewed before now again and again."

"Pray what statements?"

"In the course of the discussion we have distinctly maintained the existence of a multiplicity of things that are beautiful, and good, and so on."

"True, we have."

"And also the existence of an essential beauty, and an essential good, and so on;—reducing all those things which before we regarded as manifold, to a single form and a single entity in each case, and addressing each as an independent being."

"Just so."

"And we assert that the former address themselves to the eye, and not to the pure reason; whereas the forms address themselves to the reason, and not to the eye."

"Certainly."

"Now with what part of ourselves do we see visible objects?"

"With the eyesight."

"In the same way we hear sounds with the hearing, and perceive everything sensible with the other senses, do we not?"

"Certainly."

"Then have you noticed with what transcendent costliness the architect of the senses has wrought out the faculty of seeing and being seen?"

"Not exactly," he replied.

"Well, then, look at it in this light. Is there any other kind of thing which the ear and the voice require to enable the one to hear, and the other to be heard, in the absence of which third thing the one will not hear, and the other will not be heard?"

"No, there is not."

"And I believe that very few, if any, of the other senses require any such third thing. Can you mention one that does?"

"No, I cannot."

"But do you not perceive that, in the case of vision and visible objects, there is a demand for something additional?"

"How so?"

"Why, granting that vision is seated in the eye, and that the owner of it is attempting to use it, and that color is resident in the objects, still, unless there be present a third kind of thing, devoted to this especial purpose, you are aware that the eyesight will see nothing, and the colors will be invisible."

"Pray what is the third thing to which you refer?"

"Of course I refer to what you call light."

"You are right."

"Hence it appears, that of all the pairs aforesaid, the sense of sight, and the faculty of being seen, are coupled by the noblest link, whose nature is anything but insignificant, unless light is an ignoble thing."

"No, indeed; it is very far from being ignoble."

"To whom, then, of the gods in heaven can you refer as the author and dispenser of this blessing? And whose light is it that enables our sight to see so excellently well, and makes visible objects appear?"

"There can be but one opinion on the subject," he replied: "your question evidently alludes to the sun."

"Then the relation subsisting between the eyesight and this deity is of the following nature, is it not?"

"Describe it."

"Neither the sight itself, nor the eye, which is the seat of sight, can be identified with the sun."

"Certainly not."

"And yet, of all the organs of sensation, the eye, methinks, bears the closest resemblance to the sun."

"Yes, quite so."

"Further, is not the faculty which the eye possesses dispensed to it from the sun, and held by it as something adventitious?"

"Certainly it is."

"Then is it not also true, that the sun, though not identical with sight, is nevertheless the cause of sight, and is moreover seen by its aid?"

"Yes, quite true."

"Well then," I continued, "believe that I meant the sun, when I spoke of the offspring of the chief good, begotten by it in a certain resemblance to itself,—that is to

say, bearing the same relation in the visible world to
sight and its objects, which the chief good bears in the
intellectual world to pure reason and its objects."

"How so? Be so good as to explain it to me more at
length."

"Are you aware, that whenever a person makes an
end of looking at objects, upon which the light of day is
shedding color, and looks instead at objects colored by
the light of the moon and stars, his eyes grow dim and
appear almost blind, as if they were not the seat of distinct vision?"

"I am fully aware of it."

"But whenever the same person looks at objects on
which the sun is shining, these very eyes, I believe, see
clearly, and are evidently the seat of distinct vision?"

"Unquestionably it is so."

"Just in the same way understand the condition of the
soul to be as follows: Whenever it has fastened upon an
object, over which truth and real existence are shining,
it seizes that object by an act of reason, and knows it,
and thus proves itself to be possessed of reason: but
whenever it has fixed upon objects that are blent with
darkness,—the world of birth and death,—then it rests in
opinion, and its sight grows dim, as its opinions shift
backward and forward, and it has the appearance of
being destitute of reason."

"True, it has."

"Now, this power, which supplies the objects of real
knowledge with the truth that is in them, and which
renders to him who knows them the faculty of knowing
them, you must consider to be the essential Form of
Good (τὴν τοῦ ἀγαθοῦ ἰδέαν), and you must regard it as
the origin of science, and of truth, so far as the latter

comes within the range of knowledge: and though knowledge and truth are both very beautiful things, you will be right in looking upon good as something distinct from them, and even more beautiful. And just as, in the analogous case, it is right to regard light and vision as resembling the sun, but wrong to identify them with the sun; so, in the case of science and truth, it is right to regard both of them as resembling good, but wrong to identify either of them with good; because, on the contrary, the quality of the good ought to have a still higher value set upon it."

"That implies an inexpressible beauty, if it not only is the source of science and truth, but also surpasses them in beauty; for, I presume, you do not mean by it pleasure."

"Hush!" I exclaimed, "not a word of that. But you had better examine the illustration further, as follows."

"Show me how."

"I think you will admit that the sun ministers to visible objects, not only the faculty of being seen, but also their vitality, growth, and nutriment, though it is not itself equivalent to vitality."

"Of course it is not."

"Then admit that, in like manner, the objects of knowledge not only derive from the good the gift of being known, but are further endowed by it with a real and essential existence; though the good, far from being identical with real existence, actually transcends it in dignity and power."

Hereupon Glaucon exclaimed with a very amusing air, "Good heavens! what a miraculous superiority!"

"Well," I said, "you are the person to blame, because you compel me to state my opinions on the subject."

"Nay, let me entreat you not to stop, till you have at

all events gone over again your similitude of the sun, if you are leaving anything out."

"Well, to say the truth, I am leaving out a great deal."

"Then pray do not omit even a trifle."

"I fancy I shall leave much unsaid; however, if I can help it under the circumstances, I will not intentionally make any omission."

"Pray do not."

REALITY AND APPEARANCE—KNOWLEDGE AND OPINION

"Now [5] understand that, according to us, there are two powers reigning, one over an intellectual, and the other over a visible region and class of objects;—if I were to use the term 'firmament' you might think I was playing on the word. Well, then, are you in possession of these as two kinds,—one visible, the other intellectual?"

"Yes, I am."

"Suppose you take a line divided into two unequal parts,—one to represent the visible class of objects, the other the intellectual,—and divide each part again into two segments on the same scale. Then, if you make the lengths of the segments represent degrees of distinctness or indistinctness, one of the two segments of the part which stands for the visible world will represent all images: meaning, by images, first of all, shadows; and, in the next place, reflections in water, and in close-grained, smooth, bright substances, and everything of the kind, if you understand me."

"Yes, I do understand."

"Let the other segment stand for the real objects corresponding to these images,—namely, the animals about us, and the whole world of nature and of art."

[•] Plato's *Republic*, p. 509 D.

"Very good."

"Would you also consent to say that, with reference to this class, there is, in point of truth and untruthfulness, the same distinction between the copy and the original, that there is between what is matter of opinion and what is matter of knowledge?"

"Certainly I should."

"Then let us proceed to consider how we must divide that part of the whole line which represents the intellectual world."

"How must we do it?"

"Thus: one segment of it will represent what the soul is compelled to investigate by the aid of the segments of the other part, which it employs as images, starting from hypotheses, and travelling not to a first principle, but to a conclusion. The other segment will represent the objects of the soul, as it makes its way from an hypothesis to a first principle which is not hypothetical, unaided by those images which the former division employs, and shaping its journey by the sole help of real essential forms."

"I have not understood your description so well as I could wish."

"Then we will try again. You will understand me more easily when I have made some previous observations. I think you know that the students of subjects like geometry and calculation, assume by way of materials, in each investigation, all odd and even numbers, figures, three kinds of angles, and other similar data. These things they are supposed to know, and having adopted them as hypotheses, they decline to give any account of them, either to themselves or to others, on the assumption that they are self-evident; and, making these their starting point, they proceed to travel through the remainder of the subject, and arrive at last, with perfect unanimity, at that which they have proposed as the object of investigation."

"I am perfectly aware of the fact," he replied.

"Then you also know that they summon to their aid visible forms, and discourse about them, though their thoughts are busy not with these forms, but with their originals, and though they discourse not with a view to the particular square and diameter which they draw, but with a view to the absolute square and the absolute diameter, and so on. For while they employ by way of images those figures and diagrams aforesaid, which again have their shadows and images in water, they are really endeavoring to behold those abstractions which a person can only see with the eye of thought."

"True."

"This, then, was the class of things which I called intellectual; but I said that the soul is constrained to employ hypotheses while engaged in the investigation of them,—not travelling to a first principle (because it is unable to step out of, and mount above, its hypotheses), but using, as images, just the copies that are presented by things below,—which copies, as compared with the originals, are vulgarly esteemed distinct and valued accordingly."

"I understand you to be speaking of the subject-matter of the various branches of geometry and the kindred arts."

"Again, by the second segment of the intellectual world understand me to mean all that the mere reasoning process apprehends by the force of dialectic, when it avails itself of hypotheses not as first principles, but as genuine hypotheses, that is to say, as stepping-stones and impulses, whereby it may force its way up to something that is not hypothetical, and arrive at the first principle of everything, and seize it in its grasp; which done, it turns round, and takes hold of that which takes hold of this first principle, till at last it comes down to a conclusion, calling in the aid of no sensible object whatever, but simply employing abstract, self-subsisting forms, and terminating in the same."

"I do not understand you so well as I could wish, for I believe you to be describing an arduous task; but at any rate I understand that you wish to declare distinctly, that the field of real existence and pure intellect, as contemplated by the science of dialectic, is more certain than the field investigated by what are called the arts, in which hypotheses constitute first principles, which the students are compelled, it is true, to contemplate with the mind and not with the senses; but, at the same time, as they do not come back, in the course of inquiry, to a first principle, but push on from hypothetical premises, you think that they do not exercise pure reason on the questions that engage them, although taken in connection with a first principle these questions come within the domain of the pure reason. And I believe you apply the term understanding, not pure reason, to the mental habit of such people as geometricians,—regarding understanding as something intermediate between opinion and pure reason."

"You have taken in my meaning most satisfactorily; and I beg you will accept these four mental states, as corresponding to the four segments,—namely, pure reason corresponding to the highest, understanding to the second, belief to the third, and conjecture to the last;

and pray arrange them in gradation, and believe them to partake of distinctness in a degree corresponding to the truth of their respective objects."

"I understand you," said he. "I quite agree with you, and will arrange them as you desire."

THE ALLEGORY OF THE DEN—SHADOWS AND REALITIES

"Now [6] then," I proceeded to say, "go on to compare our natural condition, so far as education and ignorance are concerned, to a state of things like the following. Imagine a number of men living in an underground cavernous chamber, with an entrance open to the light, extending along the entire length of the cavern, in which they have been confined, from their childhood, with their legs and necks so shackled that they are obliged to sit still and look straight forward, because their chains render it impossible for them to turn their heads round; and imagine a bright fire burning some way off, above and behind them, and an elevated roadway passing between the fire and the prisoners, with a low wall built along it, like the screens which conjurers put up in front of their audience, and above which they exhibit their wonders."

"I have it," he replied.

"Also figure to yourself a number of persons walking behind this wall, and carrying with them statues of men, and images of other animals, wrought in wood and stone and all kinds of materials, together with various other articles, which overtop the wall; and, as you might expect, let some of the passers-by be talking, and others silent."

"You are describing a strange scene, and strange prisoners."

[6] Plato's *Republic*, Book VII. p. 514 D.

"They resemble us," I replied. "For let me ask you, in the first place, whether persons so confined could have seen anything of themselves or of each other, beyond the shadows thrown by the fire upon the part of the cavern facing them?"

"Certainly not, if you suppose them to have been compelled all their lifetime to keep their heads unmoved."

"And is not their knowledge of the things carried past them equally limited?"

"Unquestionably it is."

"And if they were able to converse with one another, do you not think that they would be in the habit of giving names to the objects which they saw before them?"

"Doubtless they would."

"Again: if their prison-house returned an echo from the part facing them, whenever one of the passers-by opened his lips, to what, let me ask you, could they refer the voice, if not to the shadow which was passing?"

"Unquestionably they would refer it to that."

"Then surely such persons would hold the shadows of those manufactured articles to be the only realities."

"Without doubt they would."

"Now consider what would happen if the course of nature brought them a release from their fetters, and a remedy for their foolishness, in the following manner: Let us suppose that one of them has been released, and compelled suddenly to stand up, and turn his neck round and walk with open eyes toward the light; and let us suppose that he goes through all these actions with pain, and that the dazzling splendor renders him incapable of discerning those objects of which he used formerly to see the shadows. What answer should you expect him to make, if some one were to tell him that in those days he was watching foolish phantoms, but that now he is somewhat nearer to reality, and is turned toward things more real, and sees more correctly; above all, if he were to point out to him the several objects that are passing by, and question him, and compel him to answer what they are? Should you not expect him to be puzzled, and to regard his old visions as truer than the objects now forced upon his notice?"

"Yes, much truer."

"And if he were further compelled to gaze at the light itself, would not his eyes, think you, be distressed, and would he not shrink and turn away to the things which he could see distinctly, and consider them to be really clearer than the things pointed out to him?"

"Just so."

"And if some one were to drag him violently up the rough and steep ascent from the cavern, and refuse to let him go till he had drawn him out into the light of the sun, would he not, think you, be vexed and indignant at such treatment, and on reaching the light, would he not find his eyes so dazzled by the glare as to be incapable of making out so much as one of the objects that are now called true?"

"Yes, he would find it so at first."

"Hence, I suppose, habit will be necessary to enable him to perceive objects in that upper world. At first he will be most successful in distinguishing shadows; then he will discern the reflections of men and other things in water, and afterward the realities; and after this he will raise his eyes to encounter the light of the moon and stars, finding it less difficult to study the heavenly bodies and the heaven itself by night, than the sun and the sun's light by day."

"Doubtless."

"Last of all, I imagine, he will be able to observe and contemplate the nature of the sun, not as it *appears* in water or on alien ground, but as it *is* in itself in its own territory."

"Of course."

"His next step will be to draw the conclusion, that the sun is the author of the seasons and the years, and the guardian of all things in the visible world, and in a manner the cause of all those things which he and his companions used to see."

"Obviously, this will be his next step."

"What then? When he recalls to mind his first habitation, and the wisdom of the place, and his old fellow-prisoners, do you not think he will congratulate himself on the change, and pity them?"

"Assuredly he will."

"And if it was their practice in those days to receive honor and commendations one from another, and to give prizes to him who had the keenest eye for a passing object, and who remembered best all that used to precede and follow and accompany it, and from these data divined most ably what was going to come next, do you fancy that he will covet these prizes, and envy those who receive honor and exercise authority among them? Do you not rather imagine that he will feel what Homer describes, and wish extremely

> ' To drudge on the lands of a master,
>   Under a portionless wight,'

and be ready to go through anything, rather than entertain those opinions, and live in that fashion?"

"For my own part," he replied, "I am quite of that

opinion. I believe he would consent to go through anything rather than live in that way."

"And now consider what would happen if such a man were to descend again and seat himself on his old seat? Coming so suddenly out of the sun, would he not find his eyes blinded with the gloom of the place?"

"Certainly, he would."

"And if he were forced to deliver his opinion again, touching the shadows aforesaid, and to enter the lists against those who had always been prisoners, while his sight continued dim, and his eyes unsteady,—and if this process of initiation lasted a considerable time, would he not be made a laughing-stock, and would it not be said of him, that he had gone up only to come back again with his eyesight destroyed, and that it was not worth while even to attempt the ascent? And if any one endeavored to set them free and carry them to the light, would they not go so far as to put him to death, if they could only manage to get him into their power?"

"Yes, that they would."

"Now this imaginary case, my dear Glaucon, you must apply in all its parts to our former statements, by comparing the region which the eye reveals to the prison-house, and the light of the fire therein to the power of the sun: and if, by the upward ascent and the contemplation of the upper world, you understand the mounting of the soul into the intellectual region, you will hit the tendency of my own surmises, since you desire to be told what they are; though, indeed, God only knows whether they are correct. But, be that as it may, the view which I take of the subject is to the following effect: In the world of knowledge, the essential Form of Good (ἡ τοῦ ἀγαθοῦ ἰδέα) is the limit of our inquiries, and can barely be

perceived; but, when perceived, we cannot help conclud-
ing that it is in every case the source of all that is bright
and beautiful,—in the visible world giving birth to light
and its master, and in the intellectual world dispensing,
immediately and with full authority, truth and reason;
and that, whosoever would act wisely, either in private or
in public, must set this Form of Good before his eyes."

"To the best of my power," said he, "I quite agree with
you."

"That being the case," I continued, "pray agree with
me on another point, and do not be surprised that those
who have climbed so high are unwilling to take a part in
the affairs of men, because their souls are ever loath to
desert that upper region. For how could it be otherwise, if the preceding simile is indeed a correct representation of their case?"

"True, it could scarcely be otherwise."

"Well: do you think it a marvellous thing, that a
person who has just quitted the contemplation of divine
objects for the study of human infirmities should betray
awkwardness, and appear very ridiculous, when with his
sight still dazed, and before he has become sufficiently
habituated to the darkness that reigns around, he finds
himself compelled to contend in courts of law, or elsewhere, about the shadows of justice, or images which
throw the shadows, and to enter the lists in questions
involving the arbitrary suppositions entertained by
those who have never yet had a glimpse of the essential
features of justice?"

"No, it is anything but marvellous."

"Right: for a sensible man will recollect that the eyes
may be confused in two distinct ways and from two
distinct causes—that is to say, by sudden transitions

either from light to darkness, or from darkness to light. And, believing the same idea to be applicable to the soul, whenever such a person sees a case in which the mind is perplexed and unable to distinguish objects, he will not laugh irrationally, but he will examine whether it has just quitted a brighter life, and has been blinded by the novelty of darkness, or whether it has come from the depths of ignorance into a more brilliant life, and has been dazzled by the unusual splendor; and not till then will he congratulate the one upon its life and condition, and compassionate the other; and if he chooses to laugh at it, such laughter will be less ridiculous than that which is raised at the expense of the soul that has descended from the light of a higher region."

"You speak with great judgment."

"Hence, if this be true, we cannot avoid adopting the belief, that the real nature of education is at variance with the account given of it by certain of its professors, who pretend, I believe, to infuse into the mind a knowledge of which it was destitute, just as sight might be instilled nto blinded eyes."

"True; such are their pretensions."

"Whereas, our present argument shows us that there is a faculty residing in the soul of each person, and an instrument enabling each of us to learn; and that, just as we might suppose it to be impossible to turn the eye round from darkness to light without turning the whole body, so must this faculty, or this instrument, be wheeled round, in company with the entire soul, from the perishing world, until it be enabled to endure the contemplation of the real world and the brightest part thereof, which, according to us, is the Form of Good. Am I not right?"

"You are."

"Hence," I continued, "this very process of revolution must give rise to an art, teaching in what way the change will most easily and most effectually be brought about. Its object will not be to generate in the person the power of seeing. On the contrary, it assumes that he possesses it, though he is turned in a wrong direction, and does not look toward the right quarter; and its aim is to remedy this defect."

"So it would appear."

"Hence, while, on the one hand, the other so-called virtues of the soul seem to resemble those of the body, inasmuch as they really do not preëxist in the soul, but are formed in it in the course of time by habit and exercise; the virtue of wisdom, on the other hand, does most certainly appertain, as it would appear, to a more divine substance, which never loses its energy, but by change of position becomes useful and serviceable, or else remains useless and injurious. For you must, ere this, have noticed how keen-sighted are the puny souls of those who have the reputation of being clever but vicious, and how sharply they see through the things to which they are directed, thus proving that their powers of vision are by no means feeble, though they have been compelled to become the servants of wickedness, so that the more sharply they see, the more numerous are the evils which they work."

"Yes, indeed, it is the case."

"But," I proceeded, " if from earliest childhood these characters had been shorn and stripped of those leaden, earth-born weights, which grow and cling to the pleasures of eating and gluttonous enjoyments of a similar nature, and keep the eye of the soul turned upon the things below; if, I repeat, they had been released from these snares, and turned round to look at objects that are true, then these very same souls of these very same men would have had as keen an eye for such pursuits as they actually have for those in which they are now engaged."

"Yes, probably it would be so."

"Once more: is it not also probable, or rather is it not a necessary corollary to our previous remarks, that neither those who are uneducated and ignorant of truth, nor those who are suffered to linger over their education all their life, can ever be competent overseers of a state,— the former, because they have no single mark in life, which they are to constitute the end and aim of all their conduct both in private and in public; the latter, because they will not act without compulsion, fancying that, while yet alive, they have been translated to the islands of the blest."

"That is true."

"It is, therefore, our task," I continued, "to constrain the noblest characters in our colony to arrive at that science which we formerly pronounced the highest, and to set eyes upon the good, and to mount that ascent we spoke of; and, when they have mounted and looked long enough, we must take care to refuse them that liberty which is at present permitted them."

"Pray what is that?"

"The liberty of staying where they are, and refusing to descend again to those prisoners, or partake of their toils and honors, be they mean or be they exalted."

"Then are we to do them a wrong, and make them live a life that is worse than the one within their reach?"

"You have again forgotten, my friend, that the law does not ask itself how some one class in a state is to live extraordinarily well.   On the contrary, it tries to bring about this result in the entire state; for which purpose it links the citizens together by persuasion and by constraint, makes them share with one another the benefit which each individual can contribute to the common weal, and does actually create men of this exalted character in the state, not with the intention of letting them go each on his own way, but with the intention of turning them to account in its plans for the consolidation of the state."

"True," he replied; "I had forgotten."

"Therefore reflect, Glaucon, that far from wronging the future philosophers of our state, we shall only be treating them with strict justice, if we put them under the additional obligation of watching over their fellow-citizens, and taking care of them. . . . And in this way you and we shall find that the life of the state is a substance, and not a phantom like the life of our present states, which are mostly composed of men who fight among themselves for shadows, and are at feud for the administration of affairs, which they regard as a great boon.   Whereas I conceive the truth stands thus: That city in which the destined rulers are least eager to rule, will inevitably be governed in the best and least factious manner, and a contrary result will ensue if the rulers are of a contrary disposition. . . . But if beggars, and persons who hunger after private advantages, take the reins of the state, with the idea that they are privileged to snatch advantage from their power, all goes wrong.   For the post of magistrate is thus made an object of strife; and civil and intestine conflicts of this nature ruin not only the contending parties, but also the rest of the state."

DIALECTIC THE COPING-STONE OF THE SCIENCES

[The allegory of the den suggests the question: How is the soul drawn upward from the shifting shadows of sense to the eternal world of reality?) Plato, through Socrates, points out that the contradictions and confusions of our sense-impressions stimulate reflection. The application of number, fixing, as it were, the "one in many," begins to bring order out of chaos. The development of the sciences,—arithmetic, geometry, astronomy,—further tends to draw the soul upward to the intelligible world, and this process is finally completed by dialectic, the nature and function of dialectic being thus described:]

"Whenever [7] a person strives, by the help of dialectic, to start in pursuit of every reality by a simple process of reason, independent of all sensuous information,—never flinching, until by an act of the pure intelligence he has grasped the real nature of good,—he arrives at the very end of the intellectual world, just as the last-mentioned person arrived at the end of the visible world."

"Unquestionably."

"And this course you name dialectic, do you not?"

"Certainly I do."

"On the other hand, the release of the prisoners from their chains, and their transition from the shadows of the images to the images themselves and to the light, and their ascent from the cavern into the sunshine;—and, when there, the fact of their being able to look, not at the animals and vegetables and the sun's light, but still only at their reflections in water, which are indeed divine and shadows of things real, instead of being shadows of images thrown by a light which may itself be called an

[7] Plato's *Republic*, p. 532 A.

image, when compared with the sun;—these points, I say, find their counterpart in all this pursuit of the above-mentioned arts, which possesses this power of elevating the noblest part of the soul, and advancing it toward the contemplation of that which is most excellent in the things that really exist, just as in the other case the clearest organ of the body was furthered to the contemplation of that which is brightest in the corporeal and visible region. . . . And may I not also affirm, that the faculty of dialectic can alone reveal the truth to one who is master of the sciences which we have just enumerated; and that in no other way is such knowledge possible?"

"Yes, on that point also you are warranted in speaking positively."

"At any rate," I continued, "no one will contradict us when we assert that there is no other method which attempts systematically to form a conception of the real nature of each individual thing. On the contrary, all the arts, with a few exceptions, are wholly addressed to the opinions and wants of men, or else concern themselves about the production and composition of bodies, or the treatment of things which grow and are compounded. And as for these few exceptions, such as geometry and its accompanying sciences, which, according to us, in some small degree apprehend what is real,— we find that, though they may dream about real existence, they cannot behold it in a waking state, so long as they use hypotheses which they leave unexamined, and of which they can give no account. For when a person assumes a first principle which he does not know, on which unknown first principle depends the web of intermediate propositions, and the final conclusion,—by what possibility can such mere admissions ever constitute science?"

"It is indeed impossible."

"Hence the dialectic method, and that alone, adopts the following course. It carries back its hypotheses to the very first principle of all, in order to establish them firmly; and finding the eye of the soul absolutely buried in a swamp of barbarous ignorance, it gently draws and raises it upward, employing as handmaids in this work of revolution the arts which we have discussed. These we have often called sciences, because it is customary to do so, but they require another name, betokening greater clearness than opinion, but less distinctness than science. On some former occasion we fixed upon the term understanding to express this mental process. But it appears to me to be no part of our business to dispute about a name, when we have proposed to ourselves the consideration of such important subjects."

"You are quite right," said he: "we only want a name which when applied to a mental state shall indicate clearly what phenomena it describes."

"Indeed, I am content," I proceeded, "to call as before the first division science, the second understanding, the third belief, and the fourth conjecture,—the two latter jointly constituting opinion, and the two former intelligence. Opinion deals with the changing, intelligence with the real; and as the real is to the changing, so is intelligence to opinion; and as intelligence is to opinion, so is science to belief, and understanding to conjecture. . . .

"Do you also give the title of Dialectician to the person who takes thoughtful account of the essence of each thing? And will you admit that, so far as a person has

no such account to give to himself and to others, so far
he fails to exercise pure reason upon the subject?"

"Yes, I cannot doubt it," he replied.

"Then shall you not also hold the same language concerning the good?   Unless a person can strictly define
by a process of thought the essential Form of the Good,
abstracted from everything else; and unless he can fight
his way as it were through all objections, studying to
disprove them not by the rules of opinion, but by those
of real existence; and unless in all these conflicts he
travels to his conclusion without making one false step
in his train of thought,—unless he does all this, shall you
not assert that he knows neither the essence of good, nor
any other good thing; and that any phantom of it, which
he may chance to apprehend, is the fruit of opinion and
not of science; and that he dreams and sleeps away his
present life, and never wakes on this side of that future
world, in which he is doomed to sleep forever? . . .
Then does it not seem to you that dialectic lies, like
a coping-stone, upon the top of the sciences, and that it
would be wrong to place any other science above it,
because the series is now complete?"

XIV

ARISTOTLE

[384–322 B.C.]

ORIGIN AND NATURE OF PHILOSOPHY

IT [1] was owing to wonder that men began to philosophize in earlier times just as it is to-day, wondering at first about the problems that lie close at hand, and then little by little advancing to the greater perplexities, such as the phenomena of the moon and sun and stars, and the creation of the universe. But one who is perplexed and filled with wonder feels himself to be in ignorance, and so the lover of the myth is in a way the lover of wisdom, for the myth too is made of marvels. And so if men philosophized in order to escape ignorance it is evident that they pursued wisdom just for the sake of knowing, not for the sake of any advantage it might bring. This is shown too by the course of events. For it was only after practically all things that are necessary for the comfort and convenience of life had been provided that this kind of knowledge began to be sought. Clearly then we pursue this knowledge for the sake of no extraneous use to which it may be put, but, just as we call a man free who serves his own and not another's will, so also this science is the only one of all the sciences that is liberal, for it is the only one that exists for its own sake. . . . More necessary, indeed, every other science may be than this, more excellent there is none.

[1] Arist. *Met.* I. 2, 982 b 12.

But [2] somehow the possession of this knowledge inevitably brings us to a position precisely the opposite of that in which we were at the beginning of our investigations. For, as I have said, we all begin by wondering that things are as they are, just as marionettes, or again such things as the turnings of the sun or the incommensurability of the diameter are wonderful to those who do not yet understand the cause; for every one is filled with astonishment on first hearing that there is anything which cannot be measured if the unit of measurement be made small enough. And yet in the end our position is reversed, and "after-thinking is best," as the proverb has it; and so it is in the cases before us when once we reach knowledge. For nothing would so astonish the geometrician as to discover that the diagonal was commensurate with the side.

***

Science [3] arises whenever from a number of notions derived from experience a universal conception is formed comprising all similar cases. To have the conception that when Kallias was sick of such and such a disease such and such a remedy did him good, and the same of Socrates and of many others taken one by one, is the part of experience; but to know that it did good to all such persons comprised in one and the same class, afflicted with the same disease, such as inflammation, or biliousness, or burning fever, is the part of science. In actually achieving results experience is apparently not inferior to science. On the contrary we often find men of experience more successful in reaching their aim than men who have the theory without the experience.

[2] Arist. *Met.* I. 2, 983 a 11.
[3] Ib. I. 1, 981 a 5.

The reason for this is that experience is knowledge of individual cases, whereas science is knowledge of universal principles, and every action and every creative process has to do with individual cases. For example, the physician does not heal mankind, except incidentally, but rather Kallias or Socrates or some other similar individual who happens, to be sure, also to belong to the *genus homo*. If, then, one possesses the theory without the experience, and has a knowledge of the general principles, but does not know how to apply them in the individual case before him, he will very often make a mistake as to the cure required; for it is always the individual case that is to be cured.

Nevertheless we think that knowledge and understanding are properties of science rather than of experience, and we hold men of science to be wiser than men of experience on the ground that in every case wisdom is to be ascribed to one in proportion to the extent of his knowledge. And the reason why we do this is because the former know the reason why, the latter do not; men of experience know the fact, men of science know the wherefore of the fact. . . .

In general the mark of knowledge is ability to impart what one knows to others; and this is why we hold science to be a higher form of knowledge than experience, men of science being able, men of experience being unable to impart their knowledge to others.

Furthermore, we do not attribute wisdom to any of the senses although they are, it is true, the chief means of knowing individual cases. But they do not tell us the wherefore of any fact, as for example, why fire is hot, but simply that it is hot. Consequently it was natural that the first man who discovered any science whatso-

ever that went beyond the knowledge of the senses
which is common to all, was the wonder and admiration of his fellow-men, not only because there was something useful in his discoveries, but because they held
him to be a wise man and superior to his fellows. And
as more and more of the sciences are discovered, some
having to do with the necessities, others with the com-
forts of life, we always hold men who discovered the
latter to be wiser than those who discovered the former,
just because in their case knowledge has nothing to do
with utility. Whence it came about that when all the
different sciences of these two sorts had been discovered
the sciences were discovered which have nothing to do
either with the pleasures or the necessities of life, and
first of all in those places where men had leisure. This
is why the mathematical sciences were developed first
of all in the neighborhood of Egypt, for there the priestly
class was left with plenty of leisure. . . . All men understand as the object of what is called wisdom knowledge of ultimate causes and first principles, so that,
as we said before, the man of experience is superior
in point of wisdom to the man who merely trusts his
senses, whatever the sense may be, and the man of science
is superior to the man of experience, the architect to the
manual laborer, theory to practice. It is evident from
all this that wisdom is the knowledge of causes and first
principles of some kind or other.

ARISTOTLE'S CRITICISM OF THE THEORY OF IDEAS

With [4] regard to the philosophers who introduced ideas
as causes we have in the first place this objection to
offer, that in seeking to find an explanation of the things

----

[4] Arist. *Met.* I. 9, 990 a 34.

that exist they have introduced other realities equal in number; just as if one should try to count a number of objects, and should suppose that he could not do so if the number were small, but that he would have no difficulty if he made the number larger. For the ideas are practically equal in number to,—at any rate they are not less than, the things for the explanation of which they had recourse to the world of ideas. For every individual object has its synonymous reality, and over and above actual existences there are ideas of all other things wherever there is a "one in many," both in the changeable things of this world and in the eternal.

The second objection we have to offer is that of all the proofs which we bring forward for the existence of ideas there is no real evidence; for in the case of some of our arguments the conclusion does not necessarily follow, and in the case of others, ideas are also proved to exist for things for which we do not assume the existence of any ideas. For example, from the proofs which are taken from the existence of the various sciences there will be ideas of all things whatever which can serve as the objects of knowledge; according to the argument which proceeds from the "one in many," ideas will be proved to exist also in the case of negations; on the ground of our thinking what has already perished there will be ideas of things that have perished, for there still remains a certain representation of them.

But the most serious objection of all is this: what in the world do the ideas contribute to the things of sense, either to those that are imperishable or to those that arise and perish? For they are not the cause of any motion or change in them. On the contrary they help us not a whit toward the knowledge of things other than themselves (for they are not the substances of those things, else they would be present in them); nor do they explain their existence, not being present in the things that participate in them. . . .

But again things other than the ideas do not arise from them, at least in any of the usual meanings of that expression. To call the ideas 'patterns,' and to say that other things 'participate' in them, is to use words void of meaning, or to talk in poetical metaphor. For what is it that does the work with its eyes fixed upon the ideas as patterns? It is in truth quite possible that something should come into being like something else without being expressly patterned after it. For instance, whether or not Socrates actually existed a man might arise like Socrates; and it is plain this is equally possible had the existing Socrates been imperishable.

And there must be several patterns of the same thing, consequently several ideas. For example, in the case of man there will be a pattern "animal" and "biped" as well as the pattern "man as such."

Furthermore the ideas must be patterns not only of the things of sense, but also of the ideas themselves,—class, for example, as a class of ideas. And so the same thing will be at once pattern and image. Again it would seem to be impossible that the substance should exist apart from that of which it is the substance. How then if the ideas are the substances of things can they exist apart from them?

In the *Phœdo* Plato speaks as if the ideas were the causes alike of existence and of coming into being. And yet even if we grant the existence of ideas, still the things that participate in them do not come into being unless there is some cause productive of movement. Besides.

many other things come into being, such as a house or a ring, for which we do not assume the existence of ideas. This being the case it is clearly possible that other things also should be or come into being through causes like those operative in the cases just mentioned.

ARISTOTLE'S OWN VIEW REGARDING THE UNIVERSAL

That [5] it is impossible to acquire knowledge through demonstration if we have no knowledge of primary principles immediately known we have shown above. One might, however, raise the question with regard to the knowledge of these immediate principles . . . whether the habits of mind that give this knowledge, not being innate are developed in us, or whether they are innate but have escaped our notice. On the one hand it is absurd to say that we already have them, for then we should be saying that we have, all unknown to us, a knowledge more accurate than demonstration. If on the other hand we suppose that we have to begin with no such immediate principles, how should we ever know or learn them unless some knowledge had preceded? That would be impossible as we said above in treating of demonstration. The obvious inference is that it is impossible that we should already have this knowledge, and equally impossible that it should be developed in us if we are entirely ignorant and have no habits of mind [fitting us to detect them]. We must then have some such faculty, but not of such a kind as to be superior in point of accuracy to the principles themselves. And this faculty seems to be shared by all animals, for they all have an innate critical faculty called sense-perception.

[5] Arist. *An. Post.* II. 19, 99 b 20.

Without [6] the universal it is impossible to have knowledge; but separating [the universal from the individual] was the cause of all the difficulties that attended the theory of ideas.

***

It [7] is not necessary that, if there is to be demonstrative truth, the ideas must exist, or some unity over and above the many individual things; but it is necessary that there should be some unity that may be truly predicated of the many things. Otherwise there will be no universal, and without the universal there would be no middle term, and hence no demonstration.

***

Unless [8] there were something over and above the individual things there would be no object of reason, but all things would be merely objects of sense, and consequently there would be no knowledge of anything, unless indeed one affirm that sense-perception is knowledge.

***

It [9] is evident then that no universals exist over and above the individual objects and separate from them. And those who assume the reality of ideas are right in giving them such independent and separate existence in so far as they are substances; they are wrong, however, in calling the unity which is predicated of many individual things [such a substantial] idea. The cause of their confusion is the fact that they are unable to tell us what such imperishable substances are which exist over and above the individual objects of sense. And so they make them in form the same as the perishable

---

[6] Arist. *Met*. XII. 9, 1086 b 8.
[7] Arist. *An. Post*. I. 11, 77 a 5.
[8] Arist. *Met*. II. 4, 999 b 1.
[9] Arist. *Met*. VI. 16, 1040 b 27.   Cf. *Psych*. III. 18, 432 a 4.

objects of sense (for these we know), and speak of man as such (αὐτοάνθρωπος), horse as such, adding to the objects of sense the expression "as such."

₊

It [10] is apparently impossible that any of the so-called universals should exist as substance.

₊

Of [11] sensuous substances taken individually there is neither definition nor proof possible, because they possess matter, and the nature of matter is such that it is possible for it to be, and, also, not to be.

₊

Substance [12] is the indwelling form or idea, and the concrete substance consists of ideas in conjunction with matter. For example, take the idea "hollowness": this and the nose together give the snub nose or snub-nosedness.

₊

Substance [13] signifies alike substratum (ὑποκείμενον), and the essential notion (τὸ τί ἦν εἶναι), and that which consists of both, and, also, the universal.

THE FOUR CAUSES

One [14] meaning of the word cause is the matter from which anything comes into being. For example, bronze is the material cause of the statue. . . . A second meaning is, form and pattern. This is the same as the essential notion (ὁ λόγος τοῦ τί ἦν εἶναι). . . . In the third place cause means the principle which produces change, or puts a stop to it. For example, one who gives advice

[10] Arist. *Met.* VI. 13, 1038 b 9.
[11] Ib. 15, 1039 b 29.
[12] Ib. 11, 1037 a 29.
[13] Ib. 13, 1038 b 2.
[14] Ib. IV. 2, 1013 a 24.

is cause in this sense, or the father is cause of the child;
. . . Finally, cause is used as meaning end or purpose,
i. e., as that for the sake of which anything is done.
For example, health is the final cause of taking a walk.

***

Since [15] we find that there are several kinds of causes
of natural processes . . . we must determine in regard
to them which is naturally primary, and which secondary.
The primary cause appears to be what we describe as
that for the sake of which [a thing is done], for this gives
the reason (λόγος), and the reason is the first principle
alike in the case of the things that are manufactured
and in the case of the things that arise in the course of
nature. For when by means of discursive reasoning or
sense-perception a physician has determined for himself
the nature of health, or the builder the nature of a house,
they give the reasons and the causes of what they do in
each individual case, and tell why it must be done thus
and so. ***

First [16] and foremost, matter when strictly defined
means the substratum which is the subject of generation
and destruction. ***

I [17] mean by matter what is not yet actually (ἐνεργείᾳ)
an individual object, but is such potentially (δυνάμει).

***

I [18] mean by matter as such neither a definite something nor a quantity nor anything else that can be
described by the categories which define being.

[15] Arist. *De Part. An.* I. 6, 39 b 11.
[16] Ib. *De Gen. et Cor.* I. 4, 320 a 2.
[17] Ib. *Met.* VII. 1, 1042 a 27.
[18] Ib. VI. 3, 1029 a 20.

Matter [19] is the contingent cause of that which occurs incidentally and over and above what regularly takes place.

ARISTOTLE'S CONCEPTION OF GOD

NECESSITY OF ASSUMING A FIRST CAUSE OR A PRIME MOVER

Since,[20] as we have seen, substances are of three kinds, two belonging to the physical world, the third being immovable, we have now to speak of the last, and to show that of necessity there exists some eternal immovable substance.

Of things that exist substances are the first, and if they are all perishable then everything is perishable. But it is impossible that there should be either beginning or end of motion: it is forevermore. And the same is true of time, for it is impossible that there should be either a "before" or an "after" if there is no time. Motion is then unceasing, just as time is, for time is either identical with motion or else it is a certain property of motion. And there is no unceasing motion save motion in space, and of this only circular motion is unceasing. If, however, there were something merely possessing the power to create and to impart motion, but not actually operative, still there is no motion. For it is conceivable that that which possesses potentiality should not be actually operative. Nor are we any better off if we assume eternal substances, like the "ideas" which some have assumed, unless they contain some principle that is capable of bringing about change. And even this would not be sufficient, nor would some other substance over and above the ideas accomplish the purpose; for unless this principle be actually operative there will be no motion. Moreover,

[19] Arist. *Met.* V. 2, 1027 a 14.
[20] Ib. XI. Ch. 6.

even if it be actually operative, but if at the same time its substance be but potentiality, it will not suffice; for still there will be no eternal motion, for it is conceivable that what potentially is should not come into being. It is necessary therefore that there should be a principle of such a nature that its very substance is its being actually operative. Further, substances of this sort must be immaterial; for they must be eternal, if anything at all is eternal. They must therefore be pure actuality.

But here arises a difficulty: It is commonly supposed that everything actual is also potential while not everything potential is actual, from which it would follow that what potentially is is prior to what actually is. But if this were so not a single thing would truly exist; for it is possible that a thing should have the capacity to exist and at the same time not yet truly exist. To be sure, if we accept the view of the theologians that all things sprang from Night, or that of the physical philosophers that all things were originally mixed together, we have to face the same impossibility. For how will the motion get started if there is to be no cause that is actually realized? Matter will not put itself in motion. It is, say, the builder's art that does this.—So, too, menses and earth must be set in motion by semen and seeds.—This is the reason some philosophers, like Leucippus and Plato, assume an eternal actuality; for they say that motion is eternal. But they do not tell us why; nor do they tell us what the motion is, nor how it takes place in each case, nor what causes it. The truth is, nothing is set in motion by chance; there must have been always some underlying cause, just as is the case now; a thing is moved this way by its nature, that way by force—whether of the mind or of something else.

Furthermore, of what sort is the primal motion? It makes a vast deal of difference how we answer this question. But Plato himself is not entitled to say that the principle of movement is what he sometimes assumes it to be, the self-mover; for he says that the soul comes later and is coeval with the heavens.

To suppose that what is potential is prior to what is actual is partly right and partly wrong. How this is so we have explained above. That actuality is prior to potentiality is the view of Anaxagoras, for "mind" is actual, and of Empedocles, too, with his doctrine of Love and Hate, and of all those who, with Leucippus, affirm that motion is eternal. If it is true that actuality is prior to potentiality it follows that we must not suppose that Chaos and Night existed for an indefinite time, but rather that the same things that exist now existed always, moving like a circle returning upon itself, or in some other way. Now if the same world exists always in the circular process there must be something that always abides and that is actually operative in one and the same way. But the process of coming into being and passing away is possible only on the assumption that there is something else that exists always and exerts its activity now in this way and now in that; and so it must exert its activity in one way with reference to itself, in another way with reference to something other than itself. It must therefore exert its activity either with reference to the primal heavens [the heaven of the fixed stars] or with reference to another and a different principle. Now it must of necessity be with reference to the primal heavens, for that in turn is cause both of its own movement and of the movement of the lower heavens [i. e., the planetary

region, the sun, etc.]. And so it is better to say the
heaven of the fixed stars, for it is the cause of the eternally uniform motion while the lower heaven is the cause
of the diversity of motion. Evidently both are causes
of the eternally diverse motion. And in this way too
the different kinds of motion are related to each other.
What need therefore to seek for other principles?

DIVINE REASON AS THE PRIME MOVER

Since [21] the case stands thus—and if it did not stand
thus all things would have to spring from Night, or
from Chaos, or from the non-existent—our difficulties
would appear to be solved. There exists something always moving with ceaseless motion, and its motion is
cyclical. This is shown too not merely by our argument
but also by the actual fact. Consequently the primal
heavens are everlasting. There is therefore also something which imparts motion to them. And since that
which both imparts motion and has motion imparted
to it is in the mean position there exists something
which imparts motion without itself having motion imparted to it—something which is eternal, which is an
individual substance and wholly actual. And this is the
way it imparts motion. It is like the object of desire,
or the object of thought, for these impart motion without
being themselves moved. Fundamentally the object of
desire and the object of thought are the same. The object of desire is that which appears beautiful; the object
of the will is primarily that which *is* beautiful. It is not
the striving that makes a thing seem good; rather we
strive after a thing because it seems good. It is the
thought that comes first. And the mind moves under

[21] Arist. *Met.* XI. Ch. 7.

the instigation of the object of thought. But only the positive series is in itself the thought series, and in this series substance stands first, and substance that is pure and simple and fully actual is first of all. (We must not confound the simple with the one. The "one" signifies measure, but "simple" signifies that the thing itself has a certain quality.) But surely the beautiful and that which is desirable on its own account belong in the same positive series, and here the best, or its likeness, stands first. And that the final cause belongs to the immovable order the method of division makes plain; for purpose is always a purpose which some subject *has*, and of these the one—the purpose itself—is immovable, while the other—the purpose in its relation to a subject—is not. And [this immovable final cause] draws its object unto itself as the beloved the lover; and that which is thus set in motion imparts motion to all other things.

Now if anything is subject to motion it is possible for it to be different from what it is. Consequently if the primal actuality is the motion of the heavens, in so far as it is in motion it is possible for it to be different from what it is—different in position if not in substance. Since, however, there is something that imparts motion, being itself not subject to motion but existing in pure actuality, it is impossible that *it* should be in any respect different from what it is. The first of all changes is motion in space, and, in fact, circular motion. And the prime mover imparts this motion, and is therefore necessarily existent, and in so far as necessarily existent, nobly existent, and thus the first principle of all. (Necessity is a term used in several senses: (1) necessity by force, as contrary to natural impulse; (2) the necessity of that without which the good is not; and (3) the necessity of that which cannot be otherwise, but which absolutely is.) Upon such a principle then heaven and nature depend.

God's life is like that of which we catch a transient glimpse when our life is at its best. Thus indeed his life always is (a thing which is impossible for us), for his very self-activity is bliss. And that is why we find greatest pleasure in being awake, in feeling and in thinking, and in the hopes and memories that come through these activities. But thinking, pure thinking, has for its object that which is in itself the best, and such thinking when most perfect has for its object the supreme good. The intellect thinks itself in grasping the intelligible, for it *becomes* intelligible in laying hold upon and thinking its object. Therefore, the intellect and the intelligible are the same thing; for to be able to receive the intelligible and the real is what we mean by intellect, and the intellect actually lives in doing this. And it is this actual life of the intellect, rather than the intelligible as object, that seems to be the divine element in the intellect, and pure speculative vision is what is best and most enjoyable. If then God is always as well off as we are now and then, how wonderful it is! And if he is always better off, it is still more wonderful. But such is the fact. And life belongs to him; for the activity of the mind is life, and he is that activity. Pure self-activity of reason is God's most blessed and everlasting life. We say that God is living, eternal, perfect; and continuous and everlasting life is God's, for God is eternal life.

And they are wrong who, like Pythagoras and Speusippus, hold that the most beautiful and the best are not found in the first cause, arguing from the fact that while the first cause produces plants and animals, still it is from these that the perfect plant or animal springs. For the seed comes from a complete plant previously existing; the seed is not first, but the complete plant. Just as we should say that man is prior to the germ— not the man who springs from it, but he from whom it comes.

That there is then a substance which is eternal and immovable and separable from the objects of sense is evident from what has been said. And it has also been shown that this substance cannot have extension but is without parts and indivisible. For it imparts motion through endless time, and nothing limited has unlimited potentiality. Now since every magnitude is either limited or unlimited, for the reason given God cannot have limited magnitude; nor yet can he have unlimited magnitude because, in a word, there is no such magnitude.

And further that God is free from passion and from qualitative change has also been shown, for all other changes are subsequent to motion in space. Why these things are so is now clear.

DIVINE REASON AND ITS OBJECT

With [22] regard to the divine reason certain problems arise. For while it passes for the divinest of manifestations still what its nature must be in order that it should be such is a question hard to answer. For if it thinks of nothing wherein would lie its majesty? It were just like a man asleep. On the other hand if it thinks of something and that something, being different from itself, controls its thinking, it cannot be the noblest substance—

[22] Arist. *Met.* XI. Ch. 9

for in that case that which is its substance is not thinking but potentiality. And it is through actual thinking that it gets its noble character.

Further, whether its substance be reason or thinking, what does it think about? Clearly, either itself or something else; and if something else, either always the same thing, or now one thing and now another. Does it forsooth make no difference whether it thinks about what is excellent or whether it simply thinks at random? Are there not some things about which it is absurd that it should think? It is evident therefore that it thinks about what is most divine and most noble, and that it changes not, for it could change only for the worse, and any motion would be already such a change.

Now in the first place if the divine reason is not actual but only potential thinking, it is conceivable that it should find its everlastingness but toil and weariness. And in the second place it is evident that then something else would be nobler than reason, namely, the object of reason. For thinking, and the activity of thinking, would belong also to that which thinks the most ignoble thoughts. And consequently, if this is to be avoided— and there are some things which it is better not to see than to see—then thinking as such would not be the best thing.

The divine reason then, if it is the supremely excellent thing, has itself for its object, and its thinking is a thinking of thinking. But science, perception, opinion, discursive reasoning, seem always to have something other than themselves for their object and only incidentally to be their own object.

Again, if there is a difference between thinking and

being thought, by which of the two does reason get its nobility? For [in the case supposed] thinking and being thought are in essence not the same. However, in some cases knowledge is its own object. In the case of the creative sciences it is the immaterial substance and the essential notion that is the object of knowledge; in the case of the speculative sciences it is reason itself and thinking. Since, then, the mind is not one thing and the object of the mind another, in cases where matter is not involved, the two must be identical, and thinking is one with its object.

Still a puzzle remains if the object of thought is composite, for then there might be change from part to part within the whole. But the fact is everything immaterial is indivisible. And just as the human mind, which has for its object composite things, is related to its object in favored moments—for it does not then grasp the good in this or that part of its object, but rather the best in the whole of it, the object in this case being something different from itself—just so the divine thinking is itself related to itself through all eternity.

XV

ARISTOTLE ON PSYCHOLOGY

WE[1] will now . . . . attempt to determine what soul is, and what is the most comprehensive definition that can be given of it.

Real substance is the name which we assign one class of existing things; and this real substance may be viewed from several aspects, either, *first*, as matter, meaning by matter that which in itself is not any individual thing; or, *secondly*, as form and specific characteristic in virtue of which an object comes to be described as such and such an individual; or, *thirdly*, as the result produced by a combination of this matter and this form.   Further, while matter is merely potential existence, the form is perfect realization (a conception which may be taken in two forms, either as resembling knowledge possessed or as corresponding to observation in active exercise).

These real substances again are thought to correspond for the most part with bodies, and more particularly with natural bodies, because these latter are the source from which other bodies are formed.   Now among such natural bodies, some have, others do not have life, meaning here by life the process of nutrition, increase, and decay from an internal principle.   Thus every natural

---

[1] Arist. *De An.* II. 1, 412 a 4. The passages from Aristotle's *Psychology* which follow are all taken from Wallace's translation

body possessed of life would be a real substance, and a substance which we may describe as composite.

Since then the body, as possessed of life, is of this compound character, the body itself would not constitute the soul: for body is not [like life and soul] something attributed to a subject; it rather acts as the underlying subject and the material basis. Thus then the soul must necessarily be a real substance, as the form which de-. termines a natural body possessed potentially of life. The reality, however, of an object is contained in its perfect realization. Soul therefore will be a perfect realization of a body such as has been described. Perfect realization, however, is a word used in two senses: it may be understood either as an implicit state corresponding to knowledge as possessed, or as an explicitly exercised process corresponding to active observation. Here, in reference to soul, it must evidently be understood in the former of these two senses: for the soul is present with us as much while we are asleep as while we are awake; and while waking resembles active observation, sleep resembles the implicit though not exercised possession of knowledge. Now in reference to the same subject, it is the implicit knowledge of scientific principles which stands prior. Soul therefore is the earlier or implicit perfect realization of a natural body possessed potentially of life.

Such potential life belongs to everything which is possessed of organs. Organs, however, we must remember, is a name that applies also to the parts of plants, except that they are altogether uncompounded. Thus the leaf is the protection of the pericarp and the pericarp of the fruit; while the roots are analogous to the mouth in animals, both being used to absorb nourishment. Thus

then, if we be required to frame some one common definition, which will apply to every form of soul, it would be
that soul is the earlier perfect realization of a natural
organic body.

The definition we have just given should make it
evident that we must no more ask whether the soul and
the body are one, than ask whether the wax and the
figure impressed upon it are one, or generally inquire
whether the material and that of which it is the material
are one; for though unity and being are used in a variety
of senses, their most distinctive sense is that of perfect
realization.

A general account has thus been given of the nature
of the soul: it is, we have seen, a real substance which
expresses an idea. Such a substance is the manifestation of the inner meaning of such and such a body. Suppose, for example, that an instrument such as an axe
were a natural body; then its axehood or its being an axe
would constitute its essential nature or reality, and thus,
so to speak, its soul; because were this axehood taken
away from it, it would be no longer an axe, except in so
far as it might still be called by this same name. The
object in question, however, is as matter of fact only an
axe; soul being not the idea and the manifestation of the
meaning of a body of this kind, but of a natural body
possessing within itself a cause of movement and of rest.

The theory just stated should be viewed also in
reference to the separate bodily parts. If, for example,
the eye were possessed of life, vision would be its soul:
because vision is the reality which expresses the idea of
the eye. The eye itself, on the other hand, is merely
the material substratum for vision: and when this power
of vision fails, it no longer remains an eye, except in so

far as it is still called by the same name, just in the same
way as an eye carved in stone or delineated in painting
is also so described. Now what holds good of the part
must be applied to the living body taken as a whole:
for perception as a whole stands to the whole sensitive
body, as such, in the same ratio as the particular exercise
of sense stands to a single organ of sense.

The part of our definition which speaks of something
as "potentially possessed of life" must be taken to mean
not that which has thrown off its soul, but rather that
which has it: the seed and the fruit is such and such a
body potentially. In the same way then as cutting is
the full realization of an axe, or actual seeing the realization of the eye, so also waking may be said to be the full
realization of the body; but it is in the sense in which
vision is not only the exercise but also the implicit
capacity of the eye that soul is the true realization of
the body. The body on the other hand is merely the
material to which soul gives reality; and just as the eye
is both the pupil and its vision, so also the living animal
is at once the soul and body in connection.

It is not then difficult to see that soul or certain parts
of it (if it naturally admit of partition) cannot be
separated from the body: for in some cases the soul is
the realization of the parts of body themselves. It is,
however, perfectly conceivable that there may be some
parts of it which are separable, and this because they are
not the expression or realization of any particular body.
And indeed it is further matter of doubt whether soul
as the perfect realization of the body may not stand to
it in the same separable relation as a sailor to his boat.

This much may suffice as a description and sketch of
the nature of the soul.

THE ANIMATE AND THE INANIMATE

It [2] may serve as a fresh beginning for our inquiry to say that the animate is distinguished from the inanimate or soulless by the fact of life. There are a number of ways in which a thing is said to live; yet should it possess only one of them—as, for example, reason, sense-perception, local movement and rest, and further movement in respect of nutrition as well as of decay and growth— we say it lives. Hence it is that all plants are thought to live; because they manifestly contain within themselves such a power and principle as enables them to acquire growth and undergo decay in opposite directions; for they do not while growing upwards not grow downwards, but they grow in both directions and on all sides, and they continue to live so long as they can assimilate nourishment. Now this faculty of nutrition may be separated from the other functions; but in the case of mortal creatures the other faculties cannot exist apart from this, as indeed is evident from plants which possess no other psychic power except this faculty of growth.

It is then through this principle of nutrition that life is an attribute of all living things. At the same time the animal strictly so called only begins when we reach sensation; for even those objects which do not move themselves nor change their position but possess sensation are said to be animals and not merely to be living. Among the senses themselves, it is touch which is the fundamental attribute of all animal forms. And just as the nutritive function may exist apart from touch and every form of sense, so also may touch exist without any of the other senses. Thus while nutritive is the name given

[2] Arist. *De An.* II. 2, 413 a 20.

to that part of the soul in which plants share as well as animals, all animals are found to possess the sense of touch.

* * *

[Life,[3] then, and sensation are what mark the animate.] But there are two ways in which we may speak of that by which we live and have sensation, just as also that by which we know may be employed to denote either knowledge or the mind, by both of which we are in the habit of speaking of people as knowing. So also that by which we are in health denotes on the one hand the health itself, on the other hand some portion of the body, or it may be the whole of it. Now of these two uses, knowledge and health are what we may term the determining form and notion and so to speak the realization of the recipient faculty, in the one case of knowledge, in the other of health—for the passive material which is subject to modification is what is taken to be the home of the manifestation of the active forces. Soul then is the original and fundamental ground of all our life, of our sensation and of our reasoning. It follows therefore that the soul must be regarded as a sort of form and idea, rather than as matter and as underlying subject. For the term real substance is, as we have before remarked, employed in three senses: it may denote either the specific form, or the material substratum, or thirdly the combination of the two: and of these different aspects of reality the matter or substratum is but the potential ground, whereas the form is the perfect realization. Since then it is the product of the two that is animate, it cannot be that the body is the full realization or expression of the soul; rather on the contrary it is the soul which is the full realization of some body.

Arist. *De An.* II. 2, 414 a.

NOURISHMENT THE FUNDAMENTAL FUNCTION; TOUCH THE FUNDAMENTAL SENSE

Of [4] the powers of soul which have been mentioned, some organisms, as has been said, possess all, others again a few, while a third class possesses one only.   The powers in question are those of nutrition, of sensation, of desire, of local movement, and of reasoning.   Plants possess the function of nutrition only: other creatures have this and also the faculty of sensation; and if this latter, then they must also have the faculty of desire: for desire includes appetite and passion and wish. Animals, however, without exception possess one at least among the senses—viz., touch: and wherever a faculty of sense is present it is accompanied by a feeling of pleasure and pain, and an object which is pleasant or painful.   But where these are present, there appetite is also: for appetite is the desire of what is pleasant.

Besides, all animals have a sense for nourishment— viz., touch—for it is by means of things dry and moist, hot and cold, that all animals are fed: and touch is the sense which directly perceives these.

THE HIGHER FACULTIES PRESUPPOSE THE LOWER

So [5] likewise animals possessed of the faculties of sense sometimes have, sometimes do not have, the faculty of local movement; while finally the smallest class possess also reflection and understanding.   And all mortals that possess the faculty of reasoning possess also all the other powers, whereas those that possess each of those others do not in every case possess reflection; some in fact do not even possess imagination while others live by the

---

[4] Arist. *De An.* II. 3, 414 a.
[5] Ib. II. 3, 415 a.

aid of this alone. As regards the speculative reason a different account must be given. Meanwhile it is clear that the special definition of each of these powers separately is at the same time the most appropriate account of the soul.

The [6] general character of sense in all its forms is to be found in seeing that sense-perception is that which is receptive of the forms of things sensible without their matter, just in the same way as wax receives the impress of the seal without the iron or the gold of which it is composed, and takes the figure of the gold or bronze, but at the same time not as bronze or gold.

Similarly, sense receives the impress of each object that possesses color, or flavor, or sound, not, however, in so far as each of them is such and such a definite individual, but rather so far as it is of such and such a general character, and relatively to its notion. An organ of sense-perception then is reached so soon as any part displays this power of apprehending the general character of objects. And thus the organ and the faculty of sense are essentially and fundamentally the same, although they manifest themselves in different ways; otherwise, in fact, the faculty perceiving would be as it were a sort of magnitude: whereas neither the essential character of perception nor the faculty of sense can be described as a magnitude—rather it is a power to read the essential notion of the object.

These considerations show why sentient impressions in excess destroy the organ of sense. The reason is that if the movement of the organ of sense be too strong, the

[6] Arist. *De An.* II. 12, 424 a.

relation, which, as we have seen, sense involves, is broken much in the same manner as harmony and tone become discordant when the strings are violently struck. The same fact explains also why plants possess no sense-perception although they have a psychic element and are impressed in some degree by things tangible, becoming, as they do, both hot and cold. The reason is that they do not possess that faculty (which sense implies) of acting as a mean between extremes, and have no funda-mental capacity for receiving the form only of the things of sense: but that, on the contrary, at the same time as they receive the form of anything, they receive the matter likewise.

COGNITION

We [7] must next discuss the cognitive and thinking part of soul, whether it be separated from our other mental faculties or whether it is not separated physically, but be so only by thought and abstraction, and inquire what is the specific character of thought, and how it is that at some stage or another thought begins to operate.

Thinking, we may assume, is like perception, and, if so, consists in being affected by the object of thought or in something else of this nature. Like sense then, thought or reason must be not entirely passive, but receptive of the form—that is, it must be potentially like this form, but not actually identical with it: it will stand, in fact, toward its objects in the same relation as that in which the faculty of sense stands toward the objects of perception. Reason therefore, since it thinks everything, must be free from all admixture, in order that, to use the phrase of Anaxagoras, it may rule the

[7] Arist. *De An.* III. 4, 429 a 10.

world—that is, acquire knowledge: for the adjacent light of any foreign body obstructs it and eclipses it. Its very nature, then, is nothing but just this comprehensive potentiality: and the reason—that is, that function through which the soul is ratiocinative and frames notions—is therefore, previously to the exercise of thought, actually identical with nothing which exists.

This consideration shows how improbable it is that reason should be incorporated with the bodily organism: for if so, it would be of some definite character, either hot or cold, or it would have some organ for its operation, just as is the case with sense. But, as matter of fact, reason has nothing of this character. There is truth, too, in the view of those who say the soul is the source of general ideas: only it is soul not as a whole, but in its faculty of reason: and the forms or ideas in question exist within the mind, not as endowments which we already possess, but only as capacities to be developed.

The difference, however, between the impassivity of the faculty of reason and of the faculty of sense is clear from a consideration of the organs and the processes of sense-perception. Sense, for example, is unable to acquire perception from an object which is in too great excess—cannot, to take an instance, perceive sound from extremely loud noises, nor see nor smell anything from too violent colors and odors. Reason, on the contrary, when it applies itself to something extremely intellectual, does not lessen but rather increases its power of thinking inferior objects, the explanation being that the faculty of sense is not independent of the body, whereas reason is separated from it. And since reason becomes each of its objects in the sense in which he who is in actual possession of knowledge is described as knowing—this resulting when he can apply his knowledge by himself—the reason as a developed capacity is similar to what it was previously as a mere unformed faculty, though not the same as what it was before it learned or discovered: and it may in this final stage be said to think itself.

CREATIVE REASON

The [8] same differences, however, as are found in nature as a whole must be characteristic also of the soul. Now in nature there is on the one hand that which acts as material substratum to each class of objects, this being that which is potentially all of them; on the other hand, there is the element which is causal and creative in virtue of its producing all things, and which stands toward the other in the same relation as that in which art stands toward the materials on which it operates. Thus reason is, on the one hand, of such a character as to *become* all things, on the other hand of such a nature as to *create* all things, acting then much in the same way as some positive quality, such as for instance light: for light also in a way creates actual out of potential color.

This phase of reason is separate from and uncompounded with material conditions, and, being in its essential character fully and actually realized, it is not subject to impressions from without: for the creative is in every case more honorable than the passive, just as the originating principle is superior to the matter which it forms. And thus, though knowledge as an actually realized condition is identical with its object, this knowledge as a potential capacity is in time prior in the individual, though in universal existence it is not even in time thus prior to actual thought. Further,

[8] Arist. *De An.* III. 5, 430 a 10.

this creative reason does not at one time think, at another time not think [it thinks eternally]; and when separated from the body it remains nothing but what it essentially is; and thus it is alone immortal and eternal. Of this unceasing work of thought, however, we retain no memory, because this reason is unaffected by its objects; whereas the receptive passive intellect (which is affected) is perishable, and can really think nothing without the support of the creative intellect.

REASON AND JUDGMENT

With [9] regard then to the exercise of reason, the thinking of isolated single terms falls within a sphere in which there is no falsity: when, on the other hand, we find both falsity and truth, there we reach a certain combination of ideas as constituting one conception; much in the same way as Empedocles said: "Thereupon many there were whose heads grew up neckless entirely," but were afterward brought together by friendship. In a corresponding fashion is it that those notions which are originally separate are afterwards connected, as is, for instance, the case with the two notions incommensurate and diagonal. Should the notions in question be, however, related to the past or to the future, thought then adds on the idea of time to that of mere connection. Falsehood, in fact, always involves combination and connection: even in asserting the white to be not white we bring not-white into a combination. It should be added, at the same time, that all this process might be described, not as combination, but rather as disjunction or division. Anyhow it follows that truth or falsehood is not limited to saying that "Cleon is white," but in-

[9] Arist. De An. III. 6, 430 a 26.

cludes the judgment that he was or will be: and the process of thus reducing our ideas into the unity of a single judgment is in each case the work of reason.

REASON AND ITS OBJECTS

We [10] will now sum up the conclusions we have made about the soul. The soul, we have seen, is in a way all existing things. For the objects of existence are either objects of sense or objects of thought; and while science is in a way identical with the objects of thought, sense again is one with the objects of sense. How this comes about is a point we must investigate.

Scientific thought and sense-perception thus spread themselves over objects, potential sense and science relating to things potential, actual to things actual. Now the sensitive and the scientific faculty in the soul are potentially these objects—that is to say, the objects of scientific thought on the one hand, the objects of sense on the other. It must be then either the things themselves or their forms with which they are identical. The things themselves, however, they are not: it is not the stone, but simply the form of the stone, that is in the soul. The soul, therefore, is like the hand: for just as the hand is the instrument through which we grasp other instruments, so also reason is the form through which we apprehend other forms, while sense-perception is the form of the objects of sense.

[The forms of reason are not, however, something different from the things of sense.] As there is, according to the common opinion, no object outside the magnitudes of sense, it follows that the ideas of reason are contained in the forms of sense, both the so-called

[10] Arist. *De An.* III. 8, 431 b 20.

abstract conceptions and the various qualities and attributes that determine sensible phenomena. And further, without the aid of sense-perception we never come to learn or understand anything; and whenever we consider something in the mind, we must at the same time contemplate some picture of the imagination: for the pictures of the imagination correspond to the impressions of the senses, except that the former are without material embodiment.

At the same time imagination is something different from affirmation and negation, for it is only by a combination of ideas that we attain to truth and falsehood. But, it may be asked, in what respect will our primary ideas differ from mere images of sense? And to this, perhaps, we may reply that they are, as little as other ideas which we frame, mere images of sense, although never framed without the help of such representative images.

THE SPRINGS OF ACTION

There [11] are, however, at least two faculties which are manifestly motive—viz., desire or reason, if we regard imagination as a form of reason. Frequently, in fact, it is the pictures of imagination as against knowledge that people follow, and among animals other than man it is not thought nor ratiocination, but simply this power of representing images of sense, which guides them. Both then reason and desire are fitted to produce and lead to local movement. The reason which is here intended is that which calculates for some purpose—that is, it is the practical reason, distinguished from the speculative by its end. As for desire, *it* is always directed to some object: in fact, it is the object at which desire

[11] Arist. *De An.* III. 10, 433 a 11.

aims that forms the starting-point of the practical reason, although it is some particular detail which forms the beginning of the action.

It is then on good grounds that people have viewed as springs of action these two faculties of desire and practical intellect; for the faculty of desire has itself a motive force, and the intellect excites to action just in so far as the object of desire supplies it with a starting-point; just as, similarly, imagination when it moves to action does not do so independently of desire.

The spring of action thus resolves itself into one single thing, viz., the object of desire. For if there were two faculties acting as springs to action—reason on the one hand, desire on the other—they would have to move in virtue of some common character they shared. Now reason, it is found, does not act as a spring of action independently of desire: for settled wish is a form of desire, and when a man is led to act according to his reasonable conviction he is moved also in a manner corresponding to his wish. Desire, however, excites to action contrarily to reason, appetite, which so acts, being one of the forms of desire. And thus, then, it would seem, reason is always true and right, whereas desire and imagination may be both right and not right.

It is then always the object of desire that moves to action; and this is either the good or the apparent good—not good, however, as a whole, but simply that form of it which relates to action—that is, which is contingent and admits of being other than it is.

XVI

ARISTOTLE ON ETHICS

THE SUMMUM BONUM

EVERY [1] art and every kind of inquiry, and likewise every act and purpose, seems to aim at some good; and so it has been well said that the good is that at which everything aims. . . .

If then in what we do there be some end which we wish for on its own account, choosing all the others as means to this, but not every end without exception as a means to something else (for so we should go on *ad infinitum*, and desire would be left void and objectless), this evidently will be the good or the best of all things.

And surely from a practical point of view it much concerns us to know this good; for then, like archers shooting at a definite mark, we shall be more likely to attain what we want. . . .

We see that there are many ends. But some of these are chosen only as means, as wealth, flutes, and the whole class of instruments. And so it is plain that not all ends are final.

But the best of all things must, we conceive, be something final.

If then there be only one final end, this will be what we are seeking—or if there be more than one, then the most final of them.

[1] Arist. *Ethics*, I. 1, 1. The passages in this section are taken from Peters's translation of Aristotle's *Nichomachean Ethics*.

Now that which is pursued as an end in itself is more final than that which is pursued as means to something else, and that which is never chosen as means than that which is chosen both as an end in itself and as means, and that is strictly final which is always chosen as an end in itself and never as means.

Happiness seems more than anything else to answer to this description: for we always choose it for itself, and never for the sake of something else; while honor and pleasure and reason, and all virtue or excellence, we choose partly indeed for themselves (for, apart from any result, we should choose each of them), but partly also for the sake of happiness, supposing that they will help to make us happy. But no one chooses happiness for the sake of these things, or as a means to anything else at all.

We seem to be led to the same conclusion when we start from the notion of self-sufficiency.

The final good is thought to be self-sufficing (or all-sufficing). In applying this term we do not regard a man as an individual leading a solitary life, but we also take account of parents, children, wife, and, in short, friends and fellow-citizens generally, since man is naturally a social being. Some limit must indeed be set to this; for if you go on to parents and descendants and friends of friends, you will never come to a stop. But this we will consider further on: for the present we will take self-sufficing to mean what by itself makes life desirable and in want of nothing. And happiness is believed to answer to this description.

And further, happiness is believed to be the most desirable thing in the world, and that not merely as one among other good things: if it were merely one among other good things [so that other things could be added to it], it is plain that the addition of the least of other goods must make it more desirable: for the addition becomes a surplus of good, and of two goods the greater is always more desirable.

Thus it seems that happiness is something final and self-sufficing, and is the end of all that man does.

But perhaps the reader thinks that though no one will dispute the statement that happiness is the best thing in the world, yet a still more precise definition of it is needed.

TO FIND IT WE ASK, WHAT IS MAN'S FUNCTION?

This will best be gained, I think, by asking, What is the function of man? For as the goodness and the excellence of a piper or a sculptor, or the practiser of any art, and generally of those who have any function or business to do, lies in that function, so man's good would seem to lie in his function, if he has one.

But can we suppose that, while a carpenter, or a cobbler has a function and a business of his own, man has no business and no function assigned him by nature? Nay, surely as his several members, eye and hand and foot, plainly have each its own function, so we must suppose that man also has some function over and above all these.

What then is it?

Life evidently he has in common even with the plants, but we want that which is peculiar to him. We must exclude, therefore, the life of mere nutrition and growth.

Next to this comes the life of sense; but this too he plainly shares with horses and cattle and all kinds of animals.

There remains then the life whereby he acts—the life of his rational nature, with its two sides or divisions, one rational as obeying reason, the other rational as having and exercising reason.

But as this expression is ambiguous, we must be understood to mean thereby the life that consists in the exercise of the faculties; for this seems to be more properly entitled to the name.

The function of man, then, is exercise of his vital faculties [or soul] on one side in obedience to reason, and on the other side with reason.

But what is called the function of a man of any profession and the function of a man who is good in that profession are generically the same, e. g., of a harper and of a good harper; and this holds in all cases without exception, only that in the case of the latter his superior excellence at his work is added; for we say a harper's function is to harp, and a good harper's to harp well.

Man's function then being, as we say, a kind of life— that is to say, exercise of his faculties and action of various kinds with reason—the good man's function is to do this well and beautifully [or nobly].

But the function of anything is done well when it is done in accordance with the proper excellence of that thing.

Putting all this together, then, we find that the good of man is exercise of his faculties in accordance with excellence or virtue, or, if there be more than one, in accordance with the best and most complete virtue.

But there must also be a full term of years for this exercise; for one swallow or one fine day does not make a spring, nor does one day or any small space of time make a blessed or happy man. . . .

But I think we may say that it makes no small difference whether the good be conceived as the mere possession of something, or as its use—as a mere habit or trained faculty, or as the exercise of that faculty. For the habit or faculty may be present, and yet issue in no good result, as when a man is asleep, or in any other way hindered from his function; but with its exercise this is not possible, for it must show itself in acts and in good acts. And as at the Olympic games it is not the fairest and strongest who receive the crown, but those who contend (for among these are the victors), so in life, too, the winners are those who not only have all the excellences, but manifest these in deed.

And, further, the life of these men is in itself pleasant. For pleasure is an affection of the soul, and each man takes pleasure in that which he is said to love—he who loves horses in horses, he who loves sight-seeing in sight-seeing, and in the same way he who loves justice in acts of justice, and generally the lover of excellence or virtue in virtuous acts or the manifestation of excellence.

And while with most men there is a perpetual conflict between the several things in which they find pleasure, since these are not naturally pleasant, those who love what is noble take pleasure in that which is naturally pleasant. For the manifestations of excellence are naturally pleasant, so that they are both pleasant to them and pleasant in themselves.

Their life, then, does not need pleasure to be added to it as an appendage, but contains pleasure in itself.

Indeed, in addition to what we have said, a man is not good at all unless he takes pleasure in noble deeds.

No one would call a man just who did not take pleasure in doing justice, nor generous who took no pleasure in acts of generosity, and so on.

If this be so, the manifestations of excellence will be pleasant in themselves. But they are also both good and noble, and that in the highest degree—at least, if the good man's judgment about them is right, for this is his judgment.

Happiness, then, is at once the best and noblest and pleasantest thing in the world, and these are not separated, as the Delian inscription would have them to be:

> What is most just is noblest, health is best,
> Pleasantest is to get your heart's desire.

For all these characteristics are united in the best exercises of our faculties; and these, or some one of them that is better than all the others, we identify with happiness.

But nevertheless happiness plainly requires external goods, too, as we said; for it is impossible, or at least not easy, to act nobly without some furniture of fortune. There are many things that can only be done through instruments, so to speak, such as friends and wealth and political influence: and there are some things whose absence takes the bloom off our happiness, as good birth, the blessing of children, personal beauty; for a man is not very likely to be happy if he is very ugly in person, or of low birth, or alone in the world, or childless, and perhaps still less if he has worthless children or friends, or has lost good ones that he had.

As we said, then, happiness seems to stand in need of this kind of prosperity.

HOW VIRTUE IS ACQUIRED

Excellence,[2] then, being of these two kinds, intellectual and moral, intellectual owes its birth and growth mainly to instruction, and so requires time and experience, while moral excellence is the result of habit or custom (ἔθος), and has accordingly in our language received a name formed by a slight change from ἔθος.

From this it is plain that none of the moral excellences or virtues is implanted in us by nature; for that which is by nature cannot be altered by training. For instance, a stone naturally tends to fall downward, and you could not train it to rise upward, though you tried to do so by throwing it up ten thousand times, nor could you train fire to move downward, nor accustom anything which naturally behaves in one way to behave in any other way.

The virtues, then, come neither by nature nor against nature, but nature gives the capacity for acquiring them, and this is developed by training. . . .

But the virtues we acquire by doing the acts, as is the case with the arts too. We learn an art by doing that which we wish to do when we have learned it; we become builders by building, and harpers by harping. And so by doing just acts we become just, and by doing acts of temperance and courage we become temperate and courageous. . . .

But habits or types of character are not only produced and preserved and destroyed by the same occasions and the same means, but they will also manifest themselves in the same circumstances. This is the case with palpable things like strength. Strength is produced by taking plenty of nourishment and doing plenty of hard work, and the strong man, in turn, has the greatest

[2] Arist. *Ethics*, II. 1, 1

capacity for these. And the case is the same with the virtues: by abstaining from pleasure we become temperate, and when we have become temperate we are best able to abstain. And so with courage: by habituating ourselves to despise danger, and to face it, we become courageous; and when we have become courageous, we are best able to face danger.

The pleasure or pain that accompanies the acts must be taken as a test of the formed habit or character.

He who abstains from the pleasures of the body and rejoices in the abstinence is temperate, while he who is vexed at having to abstain is profligate; and again, he who faces danger with pleasure, or, at any rate, without pain, is courageous, but he to whom this is painful is a coward.

For moral virtue or excellence is closely concerned with pleasure and pain. It is pleasure that moves us to do what is base, and pain that moves us to refrain from what is noble. And therefore, as Plato says, man needs to be so trained from his youth up as to find pleasure and pain in the right objects. This is what sound education means. . . .

Virtue, then, is a habit or trained faculty of choice, the characteristic of which lies in observing the mean relatively to the persons concerned, and which is guided by reason, i. e., by the judgment of the prudent man.

And it is a moderation, firstly, inasmuch as it comes in the middle or mean between two vices, one on the side of excess, the other on the side of defect; and, secondly, inasmuch as, while these vices fall short of or exceed the due measure in feeling and in action, it finds and chooses the mean, middling, or moderate amount.

Regarded in its essence, therefore, or according to the

definition of its nature, virtue is a moderation or middle state, but viewed in its relation to what is best and right it is the extreme of perfection.

VIRTUE AND VICE ALIKE VOLUNTARY

We [3] have seen that, while we wish for the end, we deliberate upon and choose the means thereto.

Actions that are concerned with means, then, will be guided by choice, and so will be voluntary.

But the acts in which the virtues are manifested are concerned with means.

Therefore, virtue depends upon ourselves; and vice likewise. For where it lies with us to do, it lies with us not to do. Where we can say no, we can say yes. If then the doing a deed, which is noble, lies with us, the not doing it, which is disgraceful, lies with us; and if the not doing, which is noble, lies with us, the doing, which is disgraceful, also lies with us. But if the doing and likewise the not doing of noble or base deeds lies with us, and if this is, as we found, identical with being good or bad, then it follows that it lies with us to be worthy or worthless men.

And so the saying,

None would be wicked, none would not be blessed,

seems partly false and partly true; no one indeed is blessed against his will; but vice is voluntary.

If we deny this, we must dispute the statements made just now, and must contend that man is not the originator and the parent of his actions, as of his children.

But if those statements commend themselves to us, and if we are unable to trace our acts to any other

[3] Arist. *Ethics*, III. 5, 1.

sources than those that depend upon ourselves, then that whose source is within us must itself depend upon us and be voluntary.

This seems to be attested, moreover, by each one of us in private life, and also by the legislators; for they correct and punish those that do evil (except when it is done under compulsion, or through ignorance for which the agent is not responsible), and honor those that do noble deeds, evidently intending to encourage the one sort and discourage the other. But no one encourages us to do that which does not depend on ourselves, and which is not voluntary; it would be useless to be persuaded not to feel heat or pain or hunger and so on, as we should feel them all the same. . . .

[To the objection that a man's character is responsible for his misdeeds] we reply that men are themselves responsible for acquiring such a character by a dissolute life, and for being unjust or profligate in consequence of repeated acts of wrong, or of spending their time in drinking and so on. For it is repeated acts of a particular kind that give a man a particular character.

This is shown by the way in which men train themselves for any kind of contest or performance: they practise continually.

Not to know, then, that repeated acts of this or that kind produce a corresponding character or habit, shows an utter want of sense.

Moreover, it is absurd to say that he who acts unjustly does not wish to be unjust, or that he who behaves profligately does not wish to be profligate.

If then a man knowingly does acts which must make him unjust, he will be voluntarily unjust; but it does not follow that, if he wishes it, he can cease to be unjust and be just, any more than he who is sick can, if he wishes it, be whole. And it may be that he is voluntarily sick, through living incontinently and disobeying the doctor. At one time, then, he had the option not to be sick, but he no longer has it now that he has thrown away his health. When you have discharged a stone it is no longer in your power to call it back; but nevertheless the throwing and casting away of that stone rest with you; for the beginning of its flight depended upon you.

Just so the unjust or the profligate man at the beginning was free not to acquire this character, and therefore he is voluntarily unjust and profligate; but now that he has acquired it, he is no longer free to put it off.

But it is not only our mental or moral vices that are voluntary; bodily vices also are sometimes voluntary, and then are censured. We do not censure natural ugliness, but we do censure that which is due to negligence and want of exercise. And so with weakness and infirmity; we should never reproach a man who was born blind, or had lost his sight in an illness or by a blow— we should rather pity him; but we should all censure a man who had blinded himself by excessive drinking or any other kind of profligacy.

We see, then, that of the vices of the body it is those that depend on ourselves that are censured, while those that do not depend on ourselves are not censured. And if this be so, then in other fields also those vices that are blamed must depend upon ourselves.

ON FRIENDSHIP

It [4] is said that those who are blessed and self-sufficient have no need of friends; for they are already supplied

ᵃ Arist. *Ethics*, IX. 9, 1.

with good things: as self-sufficient, then they need nothing more, while a friend is an *alter ego* who procures
for you what you cannot procure yourself; whence the
saying—

"When the gods favor you, what need of friends?"

But it seems strange, while endowing the happy man
with all good things, to deny him friends, which are
thought to be the greatest of all external goods. . . .
Again, it is surely absurd to make the happy man a
solitary being: for no one would choose to have all conceivable good things on condition of being alone; for
man is a social being, and by nature adapted to share
his life with others. The happy man, then, must have
this good, since he has whatever is naturally good for
man. But it is obvious that it is better to live with
friends and good people, than with strangers and casual
persons. The happy man, then, must have friends.

What, then, do those who maintain the former opinion
mean? and in what sense are they right? Is it that the
generality of men think that friends means useful people?
Friends in this sense certainly the happy or blessed man
will not need, as he already has whatever is good. And,
again, he will have no need, or but little need, of the
friendship that is based on pleasure; for his life is pleasant
and does not require adventitious pleasure. Because he
does not need these kinds of friends then, people come to
think he does not need friends at all.

But I think we may say that this opinion is not true.
For we said at the outset that happiness is a certain
exercise of our faculties; but the exercise of our faculties
plainly comes to be in time, and is not like a piece of
property acquired once for all. But if happiness con-

sists in living and exercising our faculties; and if the exercise of the good man's faculties is good and pleasant in itself, as we said at the outset; and if the sense that a thing belongs to us is one of the sources of pleasure, but it is easier to contemplate others than ourselves, and others' acts than our own—then the acts of the good men who are his friends are pleasant to the good man; for both the natural sources of pleasure are united in them. The happy or blessed man, then, will need such friends, since he desires to contemplate acts that are good and belong to him, and such are the acts of a good man who is his friend.

Again, it is thought that the happy man's life must be pleasant. Now, if he is solitary, life is hard for him; for it is very difficult to be continuously active by one's self, but not so difficult along with others, and in relation to others. With friends, then, the exercise of his faculties will be more continuous, being pleasant in itself. And this is what ought to be the case with the blessed man; for the good man, as such, delights in acts of virtue and is vexed by acts of vice, just as a musician is pleased by good music and pained by bad. . . . But the good man stands in the same relation to his friend as to himself, for his friend is another self: just as his own existence, then, is desirable to each, so, or nearly so, is his friend's existence desirable.

But existence, we found, is desirable because of the feeling that one's self is good, such a feeling being pleasant in itself.

The good man, then, should be conscious of the existence of his friend also, and this consciousness will be given by living with him and by rational converse with him (for this would seem to be the proper meaning of

living together, when applied to man, and not merely
feeding in the same place, which it means when applied
to beasts).

Putting all this together, then, if his own existence is
desirable in itself to the good man, being naturally good
and pleasant, and if his friend's existence is also desirable
to him in nearly the same way, it follows that a friend is
a desirable thing for him.   But that which is desirable
for him he ought to have, or in that respect he will be
incomplete.   Our conclusion, therefore, is that he who
is to be happy must have good friends.

HIGHEST HAPPINESS FOUND IN THE VISION OF TRUTH

But [5] if happiness be the exercise of virtue, it is reasonable to suppose that it will be the exercise of the highest
virtue; and that will be the virtue or excellence of the
best part of us.

Now, that part or faculty—call it reason or what you
will—which seems naturally to rule and take the lead,
and to apprehend things noble and divine—whether it
be itself divine, or only the divinest part of us—is the
faculty the exercise of which, in its proper excellence,
will be perfect happiness.

That this consists in speculation or contemplation
we have already said.

This conclusion would seem to agree both with what
we have said above, and with known truths.

This exercise of faculty must be the highest possible;
for the reason is the highest of our faculties, and of all
knowable things those that reason deals with are the
highest.

Again, it is the most continuous; for speculation can be

[5] Arist. *Ethics*, X. 7, 1.

carried on more continuously than any kind of action whatsoever.

We think, too, that pleasure ought to be one of the ingredients of happiness; but of all virtuous exercises it is allowed that pleasantest is the exercise of wisdom. At least philosophy is thought to have pleasures that are admirable in purity and steadfastness; and it is reasonable to suppose that the time passes more pleasantly with those who possess, than with those who are seeking knowledge.

Again, what is called self-sufficiency will be most of all found in the speculative life. The necessaries of life, indeed, are needed by the wise man as well as by the just man and the rest; but, when these have been provided in due quantity, the just man further needs persons towards whom, and along with whom, he may act justly; and so does the temperate and the courageous man and the rest; while the wise man is able to speculate even by himself, and the wiser he is the more is he able to do this. He could speculate better, we may confess, if he had others to help him, but nevertheless he is more self-sufficient than anybody else.

Again, it would seem that this life alone is desired solely for its own sake; for it yields no result beyond the contemplation itself, while from all actions we get something more or less besides the action itself.

Again, happiness is thought to imply leisure; for we toil in order that we may have leisure, as we make war in order that we may enjoy peace. . . .

This, then, will be the complete happiness of man, i. e., when a complete term of days is added; for nothing incomplete can be admitted into our idea of happiness.

But a life which realized this idea would be something

more than human; for it would not be the expression of man's nature, but of some divine element in that nature —the exercise of which is as far superior to the exercise of the other kind of virtue [i. e., practical or moral virtue], as this divine element is superior to our compound human nature.

If then reason be divine as compared with man, the life which consists in the exercise of reason will also be divine in comparison with human life. Nevertheless, instead of listening to those who advise us as men and mortals not to lift our thoughts above what is human and mortal, we ought rather, as far as possible, to put off our mortality and make every effort to live in the exercise of the highest of our faculties; for though it be but a small part of us, yet in power and value it far surpasses all the rest.

And indeed this part would even seem to constitute our true self, since it is the sovereign and the better part. It would be strange, then, if a man were to prefer the life of something else to the life of his true self.

HOW THE END IS TO BE REALIZED

Now [6] that we have treated (sufficiently, though summarily) of these matters, and of the virtues, and also of friendship and pleasure, are we to suppose that we have attained the end we proposed? Nay, surely the saying holds good, that in practical matters the end is not a mere speculative knowledge of what is to be done, but rather the doing of it. It is not enough to know about virtue, then, but we must endeavor to possess it and to use it, or to take any other steps that may make us good.

Now, if theories alone were sufficient to make people

[6] Arist. *Ethics*, X. 9, 1.

good, they would deservedly receive many and great rewards, to use the words of Theognis; but, in fact, it seems that though they are potent to guide and to stimulate liberal-minded young men, and though a generous disposition, with a sincere love of what is noble, may by them be opened to the influence of virtue, yet they are powerless to turn the mass of men to goodness. For the generality of men are naturally apt to be swayed by fear rather than by reverence, and to refrain from evil rather because of the punishment that it brings than because of its own foulness. For under the guidance of their passions they pursue the pleasures that suit their nature and the means by which those pleasures may be obtained, and avoid the opposite pains, while of that which is noble and truly pleasant they have not even a conception, as they have never tasted it.

What theories or arguments, then, can bring such men as these to order? Surely it is impossible, or at least very difficult, to remove by any argument what has long been ingrained in the character. For my part, I think we must be well content if we can get some modicum of virtue when all the circumstances are present that seem to make men good.

Now, what makes men good is held by some to be nature, by others habit [or training], by others instruction.

As for the goodness that comes by nature, it is plain that it is not within our control, but is bestowed by some divine agency on certain people who truly deserve to be called fortunate.

As for theory or instruction, I fear that it cannot avail in all cases, but that the hearer's soul must be prepared by training it to feel delight and aversion on the right occasions, just as the soil must be prepared if the seed is to thrive. For if he lives under the sway of his passions, he will not listen to the arguments by which you would dissuade him, nor even understand them. And when he is in this state, how can you change his mind by argument? To put it roundly, passion seems to yield to force only, and not to reason. The character, then, must be already formed, so as to be in some way akin to virtue, loving what is noble and hating what is base.

But to get right guidance from youth up in the road of virtue is hard, unless we are brought up under suitable laws; for to live temperately and regularly is not pleasant to the generality of men, especially to the young. Our nurture, then, should be prescribed by law, and our whole way of life; for it will cease to be painful as we get accustomed to it. And I venture to think that it is not enough to get proper nurture and training when we are young, but that as we ought to carry on the same way of life after we are grown up, and to confirm these habits, we need the intervention of the law in these matters also, and indeed, to put it roundly, in our whole life. For the generality of men are more readily swayed by compulsion than by reason, and by fear of punishment than by desire for what is noble. . . .

Now, the paternal rule has not the requisite force or power of compulsion, nor has the rule of any individual, unless he be a king or something like one; but the law has a compulsory power, and at the same time is a rational ordinance proceeding from a kind of prudence or reason. And whereas we take offence at individuals who oppose our inclinations, even though their opposition is right, we do not feel aggrieved when the law bids us do what is right.

XVII

THE STOICS †

THE [1] Stoics said that wisdom was a knowledge of things human and divine, and that philosophy was the practice of an art contrived to bring that knowledge about. The one art suitable to this purpose, and the highest of all, they said was virtue, but added that there were three generic virtues, the physical, the ethical, and the logical. And for this reason there are also three parts of philosophy, namely, physics, ethics, and logic. Whenever we investigate the cosmos, and the things that it contains, it is physics; when we are busily concerned about human life, it is ethics; when about reason, it is logic, or as it is also called, dialectic.

***

The [2] Stoics said that some of the objects of sense and some of the objects of reason were true. The objects of sense, however, were not true straight off, but only in so far as they carried one back to their attendant objects of reason. True is that which belongs to and corresponds with something or other, false that which does not.

[1] Aetius. *Plac.* I. (D. Dox. 273).
[2] Sext. Emp. *Adv. Math.* VIII. 10.

† Zeno of Citium, the founder of the Stoic school, flourished about 300 B.C. Upon his death in 264 (?) he was succeeded by Cleanthes, who died about 220. Chrysippus was born in 280 and died in 207.

Philosophy,[3] they say, is like an animal, Logic corresponding to the bones and sinews, Ethics to the fleshy parts, Physics to the soul. Another simile they use is that of an egg: the shell is Logic, next comes the white, Ethics, and the yolk in the centre is Physics. Or, again, they liken Philosophy to a fertile field: Logic being the encircling fence, Ethics the crop, Physics the soil or the trees. Or, again, to a city strongly walled and governed by reason.

No single part, some Stoics declare, is independent of any other part, but all blend together. Nor was it usual to teach them separately. Others, however, start their course with Logic, go on to Physics, and finish with Ethics; . . .

Some divide the logical part of the system into the two sciences of rhetoric and dialectic; while some would add that which deals with definitions and another part concerning canons or criteria: some, however, dispense with the part about definitions.

Now the part which deals with canons or criteria they admit as a means for the discovery of truth, since in the course of it they explain the different kinds of perceptions that we have. And similarly the part about definitions is accepted as a means of recognizing truth, inasmuch as things are apprehended by means of general notions. . . .

Demonstration is an argument inferring by means of what is better apprehended something less clearly apprehended.

A presentation (or mental impression) is an imprint on the soul: the name having been appropriately borrowed from the imprint made by the seal upon the wax. There are two species of presentation, the one apprehending a real object, the other not. The former, which they take

[3] From Diogenes Laertius, Book VII, 40; Hicks's translation, Vol. II, pp. 151 ff.

to be the test of reality, is defined as that which proceeds from a real object, agrees with that object itself, and has been imprinted seal-fashion and stamped upon the mind: the latter, or non-apprehending, that which does not proceed from any real object, or, if it does, fails to agree with the reality itself, not being clear or distinct. . . .

"The Stoics agree to put in the forefront the doctrine of presentation and sensation, inasmuch as the standard by which the truth of things is tested is generically a presentation, and again the theory of assent and that of apprehension and thought, which precedes all the rest, cannot be stated apart from presentation. For presentation comes first; then thought, which is capable of expressing itself, puts into the form of a proposition that which the subject receives from a presentation."

There is a difference between the process and the outcome of presentation. The latter is a semblance in the mind such as may occur in sleep, while the former is the act of imprinting something on the soul, that is a process of change, as is set forth by Chrysippus in the second book of his treatise *Of the Soul* (*De anima*). For, says he, we must not take "impression" in the literal sense of the stamp of a seal, because it is impossible to suppose that a number of such impressions should be in one and the same spot at one and the same time. The presentation meant is that which comes from a real object, agrees with that object, and has been stamped, and imprinted, and pressed seal-fashion on the soul, as would not be the case if it came from an unreal object.

According to them some presentations are data of sense and others are not: the former are the impressions conveyed through one or more sense-organs; while the latter, which are not data of sense, are those received through the mind itself, as is the case with incorporeal things and all the other presentations which are received by reason. Of sensuous impressions some are from **real** objects and are accompanied by yielding and assent **on** our part. But there are also presentations that are appearances and no more, purporting, as it were, to come from real objects. . . .

The standard of truth they declare to be the apprehending presentation, *i.e.*, that which comes from a real object—according to Chrysippus in the twelfth book of his *Physics* and to Antipater and Apollodorus. Boëthus, on the other hand, admits a plurality of standards, namely intelligence, sense-perception, appetency, and knowledge; while Chrysippus in the first book of his *Exposition of Doctrine* contradicts himself and declares that sensation and preconception are the only standards, preconception being a general notion which comes by the gift of nature (an innate conception of universals or general concepts). Again, certain others of the older Stoics make Right Reason the standard; . . .

ETHICS—FOLLOWING NATURE

An [4] animal's first impulse, say the Stoics, is to self-preservation, because nature from the outset endears it to itself, as Chrysippus affirms in the first book of his work *On Ends:* his words are, "The dearest thing to every animal is its own constitution and its consciousness thereof"; for it was not likely that nature should estrange the living thing from itself or that she should leave the creature she has made without either estrangement from or affection for its own constitution. We are forced then to conclude that nature in constituting the animal made it near and dear to itself; for so it comes to repel all that is injurious and give free access to all that is serviceable or akin to it.

[4]Op. cit., pp. 193 ff.

As for the assertion made by some people that pleasure is the object to which the first impulse of animals is directed, it is shown by the Stoics to be false. For pleasure, if it is really felt, they declare to be a by-product, which never comes until nature by itself has sought and found the means suitable to the animal's existence or constitution; it is an aftermath comparable to the condition of animals thriving and plants in full bloom. And nature, they say, made no difference originally between plants and animals, for she regulates the life of plants too, in their case without impulse and sensation, just as also certain processes go on of a vegetative kind in us. But when in the case of animals impulse has been superadded, whereby they are enabled to go in quest of their proper aliment, for them, say the Stoics, nature's rule is to follow the direction of impulse. But when reason by way of a more perfect leadership has been bestowed on the beings we call rational, for them life according to reason rightly becomes the natural life. For reason supervenes to shape impulse scientifically.

This is why Zeno was the first (in his treatise *On the Nature of Man*) to designate as the end "life in agreement with nature" (or living agreeably to nature), which is the same as a virtuous life, virtue being the goal towards which nature guides us. So too Cleanthes in his treatise *On Pleasure*, as also Posidonius, and Hecato in his work *On Ends*. Again, living virtuously is equivalent to living in accordance with experience of the actual course of nature, as Chrysippus says in the first book of his *De finibus;* for our individual natures are parts of the nature of the whole universe. And this is why the end may be defined as life in accordance with nature, or, in other words, in accordance with our own human nature as well as that of the universe, a life in which we refrain from every action forbidden by the law common to all things, that is to say, the right reason which pervades all things, and is identical with this Zeus, lord and ruler of all that is. And this very thing constitutes the virtue of the happy man and the smooth current of life, when all actions promote the harmony of the spirit dwelling in the individual man with the will of him who orders the universe. Diogenes then expressly declares the end to be to act with good reason in the selection of what is natural. Archedemus says the end is to live in the performance of all befitting actions.

By the nature with which our life ought to be in accord, Chrysippus understands both universal nature and more particularly the nature of man, whereas Cleanthes takes the nature of the universe alone as that which should be followed, without adding the nature of the individual.

And virtue, he holds, is a harmonious disposition, choiceworthy for its own sake and not from hope or fear or any external motive. Moreover, it is in virtue that happiness consists; for virtue is the state of mind which tends to make the whole of life harmonious. When a rational being is perverted, this is due to the deceptiveness of external pursuits or sometimes to the influence of associates. For the starting-points of nature are never perverse. . . .

It [5] is one of their tenets that sins are all equal: so Chrysippus in the fourth book of his *Ethical Questions*, as well as Persæus and Zeno. For if one truth is not more true than another, neither is one falsehood more false than another, and in the same way one deceit is not more so than another, nor sin than sin. For he who is a hundred furlongs from Canopus and he who is only one furlong away are equally not in Canopus, and so

---

[5] Op. cit., p. 225.

too he who commits the greater sin and he who commits the less are equally not in the path of right conduct. . . .

Now [6] they say that the wise man is passionless, because he is not prone to fall into such infirmity. But they add that in another sense the term apathy is applied to the bad man, when, that is, it means that he is callous and relentless. Further, the wise man is said to be free from vanity; for he is indifferent to good or evil report. However, he is not alone in this, there being another who is also free from vanity, he who is ranged among the rash, and that is the bad man. Again, they tell us that all good men are austere or harsh, because they neither have dealings with pleasure themselves nor tolerate those who have. The term harsh is applied, however, to others as well, and in much the same sense as a wine is said to be harsh when it is employed medicinally and not for drinking at all.

Again, the good are genuinely in earnest and vigilant for their own improvement, using a manner of life which banishes evil out of sight and makes what good there is in things appear. At the same time they are free from pretence; for they have stripped off all pretence or "make-up" whether in voice or in look. Free too are they from all business cares, declining to do anything which conflicts with duty. They will take wine, but not get drunk. Nay more, they will not be liable to madness either; not but what there will at times occur to the good man strange impressions due to melancholy or delirium, ideas not determined by the principle of what is choiceworthy but contrary to nature. Nor indeed will the wise man ever feel grief; seeing that grief is irrational contraction of the soul, as Apollodorus says in his *Ethics*. . . .

[6] Op. cit., pp. 221 ff.

They hold [7] that the virtues involve one another, and that the possessor of one is the possessor of all, inasmuch as they have common principles, . . .

It is a tenet of theirs that between virtue and vice there is nothing intermediate, whereas according to the Peripatetics there is, namely, the state of moral improvement. For, say the Stoics, just as a stick must be either straight or crooked, so a man must be either just or unjust. Nor again are there degrees of justice and injustice; and the same rule applies to the other virtues. Further, while Chrysippus holds that virtue can be lost, Cleanthes maintains that it cannot. According to the former it may be lost in consequence of drunkenness or melancholy; the latter takes it to be inalienable owing to the certainty of our mental apprehension. And virtue in itself they hold to be worthy of choice for its own sake. At all events we are ashamed of bad conduct as if we knew that nothing is really good but the morally beautiful. Moreover, they hold that it is in itself sufficient to ensure well-being. . . .

Again, they say that justice, as well as law and right reason, exists by nature and not by convention: so Chrysippus in his work *On the Morally Beautiful*. Neither do they think that the divergence of opinion between philosophers is any reason for abandoning the study of philosophy, since at that rate we should have to give up life altogether. . . .

Furthermore, the term Duty [8] is applied to that for

[7] Op. cit., pp. 229 ff.

[8] Op. cit., p. 213. "Duty," as Mr. Hicks explains in a note to this passage, is a very inadequate rendering of καθῆκον, which is here made to apply to the proper behavior of plants and animals no less than to that of human beings. But the term is "as near an approach, perhaps, to the idea of duty as can be expected in any ancient system of Ethics, which regards human conduct not as obedience to law, but as determination and pursuit of good."

which, when done, a reasonable defence can be adduced, *e.g.*, harmony in the tenor of life's process, which indeed pervades the growth of plants and animals. For even in plants and animals, they hold, you may discern fitness of behavior.

Zeno was the first to use this term καθῆκον of conduct. Etymologically it is derived from κατά τινας ἥκειν, *i.e.*, reaching as far as, being up to, or incumbent on so and so. And it is an action in itself adapted to nature's arrangements. For of the acts done at the prompting of impulse some, they observe, are fit and meet, others the reverse, while there is a third class which is neither the one nor the other. . . .

THE HYMN OF CLEANTHES

Most [9] glorious of immortals, O thou of many names, all-powerful ever, hail! On thee it is fit all men should call. For we come forth from thee, and have received the gift of imitative speech alone of all that live and move on earth. So will I make my song of thee and chant thy power forever. Thee all this ordered universe, circling around the earth, follows as thou dost guide and evermore is ruled by thee. For such an engine hast thou in thine unswerving hands—the two-edged, blazing, everliving bolt—that at its blow all nature trembles. Herewith thou guidest universal Reason—the moving principle of all the world, joined with the great and lesser lights—which, being born so great, is highest lord of all. Nothing occurs on earth apart from thee, O Lord, nor at the airy sacred pole nor on the sea, save what the wicked work through lack of wisdom. But thou canst

[9] I am indebted to Prof. G. H. Palmer for this translation of the Hymn of Cleanthes.

make the crooked straight, bring order from disorder, and what is worthless is in thy sight worthy. For thou hast so conjoined to one all good and ill that out of all goes forth a single everlasting Reason. This all the wicked seek to shun, unhappy men, who, ever longing to obtain a good, see not nor hear God's universal law; which, wisely heeded, would assure them noble life. They haste away, however, heedless of good, one here, one there; some showing unholy zeal in strife for honor, some turning recklessly toward gain, others to looseness and the body's pleasures. But thou, O Zeus, giver of all, thou of the cloud, guide of the thunder, deliver men from baleful ignorance! Scatter it, father, from our souls, grant us to win that wisdom on which thou thyself relying suitably guidest all; that thus being honored, we may return to thee our honor, singing thy works unceasingly; because there is no higher office for a man— nor for a god—than ever rightly singing of universal law.

PLUTARCH'S REFUTATION OF THE STOIC THEODICY†

In [1] the third book of his Treatise on The Gods Chrysippus writes as follows: "Just as states which have a surplus population send great numbers out to colonies, and stir up wars against their neighbors, so God provides occasions for our destruction." And he cites Euripides and other writers who maintained that the Trojan War

---

[1] Plutarch, *De Stoicorum Repugnantiis*, §§ 32–37.

† For the suggestion to include these interesting and illuminating passages from Plutarch I am indebted to Dr. B. A. G. Fuller, and the translation of them which is here given is his.

was brought about by the gods because of the super-
abundancy of men.

Now leave aside all the other absurdities—for it is
not our business here to inquire whether the Stoics
have spoken the truth, but only whether they have
contradicted themselves—and consider this one point.
They are always giving fine and humane names to God,
yet they attribute to him savage and barbarous deeds,
yea, deeds worthy of the Galatæ. For the enormous
destruction and wholesale slaughter of men such as was
entailed by the Trojan War, or again by the Persian and
the Peloponnesian Campaigns, bears no resemblance to
colonization, unless the gods were intending to found
some underground cities in Hades. Chrysippus rather
makes God like one Deiotarus, chief of the Galatæ. He
had many children born to him, but wished to leave his
power and all his property to one alone. So he killed all
the rest off, just as one might cut back and prune the
new shoots of a vine, in order that some one which was
left might grow strong and big. A vine-dresser, it goes
without saying, does this, while the twigs are still small
and insignificant. And we are merciful to the dog and
destroy the surplus puppies just after they are born
and before their eyes are yet open. But Zeus not only
allows men to grow up; he even begets them himself and
brings them up to manhood, and then, forsooth, carefully
contrives occasions for their death and destruction and
brutally sends them out of the world. I think he had
better not have provided the causes and sources of our
birth.

This, however, is of minor importance compared to
what follows. No war arises among men without viciousness behind it. Love of luxury stirs up the one, avarice

another, ambition a third, lust for power a fourth.
Now if it be God who brings wars to pass, he is also the
cause of our vices, provoking and perverting mankind
as he does.   Nevertheless Chrysippus says in his Treatise
on Law Procedure, and again in the second book of his
Treatise on The Gods, that "it is not reasonable that the
deity should be the cause of base deeds.   For just as a
law cannot be the cause of its contravention, so neither
can the gods be the cause of impiety.   It is then
reasonable that they should not be the causes of anything
base."

But, I say, can anything be more base than that men
should destroy one another?   And for this destruction
Chrysippus says that God is responsible.   I will swear
to it, however, that some one will say that he also praises
the saying of Euripides:

> If gods do aught that's base, they are not gods,

and

> Thou say'st an easy thing—to blame the gods,

as if we were now doing anything but showing up his
contradictory sayings and ideas.

This very saying, however, which now meets with
approval, "Thou say'st an easy thing—to blame the
gods"—can be urged against Chrysippus not once, or
twice, or thrice, but innumerable times.   For in the
first book in the Treatise on Nature, in likening the cause
of motion to a mixture of things whirling and churning
in all directions, he speaks thus, "Since the world-
economy proceeds in this fashion, it is due to it that we
are as we are at every moment, whether contrary to our
proper nature we suffer disease or disability, or be
grammarians or musicians."   And again a little later he

says, "By this reasoning the same holds true of our virtues
and vices, and in general of our skill in the arts or lack
of it, as I have said." And a line or two later, without
any ambiguity he remarks, "No single or slightest thing
can happen except in accordance with the common
nature and its reason." That the common nature and
the common reason of this nature are fate, and providence,
and Zeus, is something of which not even the dwellers
in the antipodes are unaware, for this truth is noised
about by the Stoics everywhere, and Chrysippus remarks
"that Homer rightly said, 'The will of Zeus is done,'
referring to that fate and that nature of the universe
according to which all things are governed."

How now, I ask, can God be the author of nothing base,
and yet at the same time not the slightest thing happen
otherwise than according to the common nature and its
reason? For since evils belong in the sum of events they
are, I presume, to be ascribed to God. Even Epicurus
turns and twists and thinks up subtleties to free and
release the will from the eternal motion of the world-
mechanism, in order that vice may not be left blameless.
Chrysippus, however, concedes to vice complete license,
as something which is not only necessary and destined,
but also in accordance with the divine reason, and
produced agreeably to that nature which is supremely
good. Look, for instance, at this statement of his:
"The common nature is spread throughout all things,
and hence everything whatsoever which happens in the
universe and every part thereof happens in accordance
with it and its reason, and follows therefrom without any
hindrance. For there is nothing outside the universe to
oppose its workings, nor can any one of its parts be
moved or conditioned otherwise than agreeably to the

common nature." What, now, are the conditions and motions of its parts? Evidently the conditions are vices and diseases, avarice, luxury, ambition, fear, injustice; and the motions are adultery, theft, treachery, murder, and parricide. None of these, then, great or small, is thought by Chrysippus to exist contrary to the reason, the law, the justice, the providence of Zeus, nor do lawless acts exist contrary to law, nor injustice to justice, nor evil-doing to providence.

Chrysippus says, however, "that God punishes vice, and does much in the way of punishing wicked men." Likewise in the second book of the Treatise on The Gods he says that "misfortunes happen sometimes to good men, not for punishment as with the wicked, but in accordance with some other line of administration, as in the case of cities." Again, his words run as follows: "In the first place evils are to be understood in pretty much the aforesaid way, and secondly as apportioned according to the reason of Zeus, either for punishment, or agreeably to some other scheme of administration to the advantage of the whole." It is, however, a horrible thing that vice should be both produced and punished agreeably to the reason of Zeus. And Chrysippus pushes the contradiction still further when he writes in the second book of the Treatise on Nature, that "Vice has a peculiar and reasonable fitness viewed in relation to terrible calamities. It is produced in a way agreeably to the universal reason, and its production is not without benefit to the universe. For without it, there would be no good." And this is the man who reproves those who argue with equal force to the opposite conclusion; this man who, wishing in every case to get off some odd and subtle remark about the universe, maintains that cut-pursing and flattery and foolishness are not without their uses, that the good for nothing are good for something, and the noxious and the miserable are not unbeneficial. Again what kind of a being is Zeus—I mean, of course, Chrysippus's Zeus—to punish what is neither responsible for itself nor uselessly produced? For according to Chrysippus's way of arguing, it is not vice that is to be blamed, but Zeus, either because he made vice to no use, or because, having made it to some use, he punishes it.

Once more, in the first book of the Treatise on Justice, Chrysippus says that the gods resist some unjust deeds, yet that "it is neither possible nor expedient to remove vice from the universe." If, however, it be inexpedient to do away with lawlessness, injustice, and foolishness, it is impossible for him to pursue his present argument. For he himself in doing all he can by philosophizing to do away with vice—which it is not expedient to do away with—is doing something repugnant both to reason and to God. Yet when he says as well that the gods resist some unrighteous deeds, he gives the impression that these sins are impious.

In another place where he writes many times that nothing is blameworthy or contemptible in the universe, since everything takes place agreeably to the supremely good nature, there are yet passages where some neglect in small and mean matters is allowed not to be reprehensible. Thus in the third book of the Treatise on Substance, in reminding us that noble and good men are the victims of such neglect, he asks "whether some things may not be neglected, just as in great houses some grains of corn and wheat fall unnoticed, though the household as a whole is well managed? Or is this neglect due to the presence in such cases of evil spirits, in whom a reprehensible carelessness is naturally inherent?" And he adds that there is a large admixture of necessity in things. Now I pass over the recklessness of likening to the unnoticed fall of grains of wheat such misfortunes of good and noble men as the condemnation of Socrates, and the burning alive of Pythagoras by the Cylonians, and the torture and death of Zeno at the hands of the tyrant Demylus, and of Antiphon by Dionysius. But is it not to blame God, to say that evil spirits were providentially appointed to such offices? For God in that case would be like a king who handed over his provinces to evil and stupid satraps and generals, and then overlooked their neglect and ill-treatment of his best subjects. Finally, if there be a large admixture of necessity in things, God is not all powerful and all things are not administered according to his word.

* * *

But [2] what fault can any one find with what I have said if he keeps in mind the passage in the second book of the Treatise on Nature in which Chrysippus shows that evil is produced to some benefit to the universe? It is worth while to take this doctrine and compare it with those sayings of his in which you will find he accuses Xenocrates and Speusippus of not regarding health as indifferent, and wealth as useless, and in the same place defines vice, and discourses about it. "Vice," he says, "is distinguished from other calamities. For it happens agreeably to the rational constitution of nature, and, so to speak, does not happen without some benefit to the universe. For did it not exist there would be no good."

There is then nothing good among the gods when there is nothing evil. When Zeus shall have consumed

[2] *De Communibus Notitiis*, §§ 13–16.

the whole of matter within himself, and shall have become one, having cast out all differences and distinctions, then there will be no good, since there is no evil. Still, one might object, a chorus can sing in harmony, though no one in it sing out of tune; and a body can be healthy even though no part of it be diseased.

However, Chrysippus maintains that virtue cannot exist without vice, and that just as the venom of the serpent or the bile of the hyena is necessary to the efficacy of some medicines, so a suitable admixture of the wickedness of Meletus is necessary to the righteousness of Socrates, or of the vulgarity of Cleon to the nobility of Pericles. How, too, could Zeus create Hercules and Lycurgus, unless he also created Sardanapalus and Phalaris for us? Chrysippus might as reasonably add, also, that tuberculosis promotes human health, and gout swiftness of foot; also that Achilles could not have had a fine head of hair unless Thersites had been bald. For what is the difference between such nonsense and drivel, and saying that wantonness conduces to continence, or unrighteousness to righteousness? And how are we to pray the gods that

Lies and oily words and wily ways

may be ever evil in their sight, if virtue also vanishes and is destroyed when they are done away with?

Would you really like to know, however, the most charming bit of his smoothness and persuasion? "Just as comedians," he says, "put in ridiculous lines which are poor stuff in themselves but lend a certain charm to the whole piece, so what you censure as evil, taken by itself, is not without its use in relation to other things." Now, in the first place, that vice has been produced by

divine providence, as a poor line is intentionally written by the playwright, is the most absurd of opinions.
Supposing it were so, how should the gods be any more
the givers of good than of evil?   How could vice be
inimical to the gods, and hateful in their sight?   What
could we reply to such blasphemy as

> When God will injure mortals he creates the reason why

and

> Which of the gods put strife between the chiefs,
> That they should thus contend? *

In the second place the poor line adorns the comedy
and contributes to its purpose of arousing laughter and
pleasing the audience.   But surely father Zeus, the most
high, the all-just, the all-good creator, as Pindar calls
him, did not make this world as a big and varied and
clever play, but as a commonwealth of gods and men
wherein they might live together as comrades amid
righteousness and virtue in concord and blessedness.
And to this most beautiful and holy end, I say, what
need was there of robbers and murderers, parricides and
tyrants?   For in the eyes of God vice is not a charming
and clever by-play, nor is unrighteousness inflicted for
the sake of coarse joking and laughter and jest, upon
human life—a life such that it will not permit one even
to dream of the Stoics' renowned "harmony."

Again the poor line is but a trivial part of the play
and in all respects occupies but a small place in the
comedy.   There are not many such lines, and they do
not destroy or spoil the charm of such passages as seem
well-written.   But all things are full of vice, and our
whole life from the cradle to the grave is shameful and
disgraceful and troublous, and as there is no part of it

* Bryant's rendering.

pure and blameless, as they themselves say, is the basest
and saddest of all plays.

So it is that I would gladly learn from Chrysippus of
what use vice is in the universe. It is of no use to
heavenly and divine things, he says. For it would be
absurd if for the lack among men of vice and avarice
and lying, and for the want of our ravaging one another's
lands and slandering and murdering one another, the
sun could not accomplish his appointed course, nor the
world enjoy its seasons and its cycles, nor the earth keep
its central position in the universe and provide the
sources of the winds and rains. It is left then for vice to
benefit us and our affairs; and this perhaps is what these
Stoics mean. But are we healthier for being vicious,
or better off as regards the necessities of life? Does
vice benefit our beauty or our strength? They deny it.
Yet where is virtue to be found on earth? "It is," they
say, "a name, an appearance in the night to benighted"
sophists. Vice, however, is exposed to every waking
eye, and plain as day to all men. If, however, we cannot
have a share in anything good for anything, and least
of all in virtue, for heaven's sake what is the good of
being born? And is it not a terrible thing that though
what is of use to the farmer or the pilot or the driver
leads and contributes to its proper end, yet that which is
created by God for virtue destroys and corrupts virtue?

***

Moreover,[3] the Stoic sage doesn't and never will exist
anywhere in this world. But there are innumerable men
as wretched as they can be living in this state and
principality of Zeus with its perfect government. What
now is more contrary to common sense than that, with

De Communibus Notitiis, § 33, 4–34.

Zeus directing all things for the best, we should be doing all things for the worst? It is a blasphemous thing to say, but if Zeus does not care to be considered as savior and merciful and a guardian against evils, but as rather the opposite of all these noble names, certainly nothing could be added to the evils that now exist either in number or magnitude. For, as the Stoics maintain, all men live in the depths of folly and wickedness, and there can be no addition to their viciousness nor increase to their misery.

This, however, is not the worst of the case. We read that rather where they find fault with Menander for saying in one of his acted plays,

> No greater source of evils among men is there than too
> great good . . .

This they say is contrary to common-sense. Yet they make God who is good the origin of evil. "Matter," they say, "cannot produce evil of itself, since it is without quality and gets all the different properties which it is capable of receiving from that which moves and gives it form." The indwelling reason, however, moves and gives it form, and it cannot move or give form to itself. Hence necessarily evil, if it have no cause, comes from not-being, but if it comes through the moving principle, gets its existence from God. For if the Stoics think that Zeus is not the master of his own members, and does not employ each agreeably to his reason, they go contrary to common-sense, and they are inventing an animal whose many members do not obey its will, but employ their several activities and ways of action, without any stimulus from the whole organism and without deriving their power of movement from it. What animal, however, is so badly put together that against its will its feet advance, its tongue makes noises, its horns butt, or its teeth bite? God must do most of these things, though, if, contrary to his will, the wicked men who are parts of him lie and misbehave and thieve, and kill one another. And if, as Chrysippus says, "Not the smallest part exists otherwise than as Zeus wills," and every living thing naturally behaves and moves as Zeus guides and directs and behaves and disposes, then

> More ruinous than the last, this speech.

For it is ten thousand times more decent that the members of Zeus, deranged by his weakness and impotence, should do many absurd things contrary to his nature and will, than that there should be no wantonness and no wickedness of which he was not the cause. Yet for all that "the world is a city, the stars its citizens," and, if you like, its tribesmen and rulers—the sun for instance a counsellor, and the evening star the president of a prytany or a magistrate. If this be the case I do not think that they who deny the doctrines we have been discussing, show themselves to be any more absurd than those who maintain and advocate them.

XVIII

EPICURUS

[341–270 B.C.]

THEORY OF KNOWLEDGE

"In [1] the first place, Herodotus, you must understand what it is that words denote, in order that by reference to this we may be in a position to test opinions, inquiries, or problems, so that our proofs may not run on untested *ad infinitum*, nor the terms we use be empty of meaning. For the primary signification of every term employed must be clearly seen, and ought to need no proving; this being necessary, if we are to have something to which the point at issue or the problem or the opinion before us can be referred.

"Next, we must by all means stick to our sensations, that is, simply to the present impressions whether of the mind or of any criterion whatever, and similarly to our actual feelings, in order that we may have the means of determining that which needs confirmation and that which is obscure.

"When this is clearly understood, it is time to consider generally things which are obscure. . . .

"Besides this,[2] remember that the production of the images is as quick as thought. For particles are continually streaming off from the surface of bodies, though

---

[1] From Diogenes Laertius, Book X, 37; Hicks's translation, Vol. II, beginning on p. 567. This and the following section are taken from Epicurus's letter to Herodotus.

[2] Op. cit., p. 577.

no diminution of the bodies is observed, because other particles take their place. And those given off for a long time retain the position and arrangement which their atoms had when they formed part of the solid bodies, although occasionally they are thrown into confusion. Sometimes such films are formed very rapidly in the air, because they need not have any solid content; and there are other modes in which they may be formed. For there is nothing in all this which is contradicted by sensation, if we in some sort look at the clear evidence of sense, to which we should also refer the continuity of particles in the objects external to ourselves.

"We must also consider that it is by the entrance of something coming from external objects that we see their shapes and think of them. For external things would not stamp on us their own nature of colour and form through the medium of the air which is between them and us, or by means of rays of light or currents of any sort going from us to them, so well as by the entrance into our eyes or minds, to whichever their size is suitable, of certain films coming from the things themselves, these films or outlines being of the same colour and shape as the external things themselves. They move with rapid motion; and this again explains why they present the appearance of the single continuous object, and retain the mutual interconnexion which they had in the object, when they impinge upon the sense, such impact being due to the oscillation of the atoms in the interior of the solid object from which they come. And whatever presentation we derive by direct contact, whether it be with the mind or with the sense-organs, be it shape that is presented or other properties, this shape as presented is the shape of the solid thing, and it is due either to a close coherence of the image as a whole or to a mere remnant of its parts. Falsehood and error always depend upon the intrusion of opinion [when a fact awaits] confirmation or the absence of contradiction, which fact is afterwards frequently not confirmed [or even contradicted] . . . (*following a certain movement in ourselves connected with, but distinct from, the mental picture presented—which is the cause of error*).

"For the presentations which, *e.g.*, are received in a picture or arise in dreams, or from any other form of apprehension by the mind or by the other criteria of truth, would never have resembled what we call the real and true things, had it not been for certain actual things of the kind with which we come in contact. Error would not have occurred, if we had not experienced some other movement in ourselves, conjoined with, but distinct from, the perception of what is presented. And from this movement, if it be not confirmed or be contradicted, falsehood results; while, if it be confirmed or not contradicted, truth results.

"And to this view we must closely adhere, if we are not to repudiate the criteria founded on the clear evidence of sense, nor again to throw all these things into confusion by maintaining falsehood as if it were truth. . . .

PHYSICAL SPECULATIONS

". . . To [3] begin with, nothing comes into being out of what is non-existent. For in that case anything would have arisen out of anything, standing as it would in no need of its proper germs. And if that which disappears had been destroyed and become non-existent, every-

[3] Op. cit., pp. 569 ff.

thing would have perished, that into which the things were dissolved being non-existent. Moreover, the sum total of things was always such as it is now, and such it will ever remain. For there is nothing into which it can change. For outside the sum of things there is nothing which could enter into it and bring about the change.

"Further, . . . the whole of being consists of bodies and space. For the existence of bodies is everywhere attested by sense itself, and it is upon sensation that reason must rely when it attempts to infer the unknown from the known. And if there were no space (which we call also void and place and intangible nature), bodies would have nothing in which to be and through which to move, as they are plainly seen to move. Beyond bodies and space there is nothing which by mental apprehension or on its analogy we can conceive to exist. . . .

"Again, the sum of things is infinite. For what is finite has an extremity, and the extremity of anything is discerned only by comparison with something else. [Now the sum of things is not discerned by comparison with anything else:] hence, since it has no extremity, it has no limit; and, since it has no limit, it must be unlimited or infinite. . . .

"Furthermore, the atoms, which have no void in them —out of which composite bodies arise and into which they are dissolved—vary indefinitely in their shapes; for so many varieties of things as we see could never have arisen out of a recurrence of a definite number of the same shapes. The like atoms of each shape are absolutely infinite; but the variety of shapes, though indefinitely large, is not absolutely infinite. . . .

"The atoms are in continual motion through all eternity. . . . Some of them rebound to a considerable distance from each other, while others merely oscillate in one place when they chance to have got entangled or to be enclosed by a mass of other atoms shaped for entangling.

"This is because each atom is separated from the rest by void, which is incapable of offering any resistance to the rebound; while it is the solidity of the atom which makes it rebound after a collision, however short the distance to which it rebounds, when it finds itself imprisoned in a mass of entangling atoms. Of all this there is no beginning, since both atoms and void exist from everlasting. . . .

"Moreover,[4] we must hold that the atoms in fact possess none of the qualities belonging to things which come under our observation, except shape, weight, and size, and the properties necessarily conjoined with shape. For every quality changes, but the atoms do not change, since, when the composite bodies are dissolved, there must needs be a permanent something, solid and indissoluble, left behind, which makes change possible: not changes into or from the non-existent, but often through differences of arrangement, and sometimes through additions and subtractions of the atoms. Hence these somethings capable of being diversely arranged must be indestructible, exempt from change, but possessed each of its own distinctive mass and configuration. This must remain. . . .

"When [5] they are travelling through the void and meet with no resistance, the atoms must move with equal speed. Neither will heavy atoms travel more quickly

[4] Op. cit., p. 583.   [5] Op. cit., pp. 591 ff.

than small and light ones, so long as nothing meets them,
nor will small atoms travel more quickly than large ones,
provided they always find a passage suitable to their
size, and provided also that they meet with no obstruction. Nor will their upward or their lateral motion,
which is due to collisions, nor again their downward motion, due to weight, affect their velocity. As long as
either motion obtains, it must continue, quick as the
speed of thought, provided there is no obstruction,
whether due to external collision or to the atoms' own
weight counteracting the force of the blow. . . .

"Next, keeping in view our perceptions and feelings
(for so shall we have the surest grounds for belief), we
must recognize generally that the soul is a corporeal
thing, composed of fine particles, dispersed all over the
frame, most nearly resembling wind with an admixture
of heat, in some respects like wind, in others like heat.
But, again, there is the third part which exceeds the other
two in the fineness of its particles and thereby keeps in
closer touch with the rest of the frame. And this is
shown by the mental faculties and feelings, by the ease
with which the mind moves, and by thoughts, and by
all those things the loss of which causes death. Further,
we must keep in mind that soul has the greatest share in
causing sensation. Still, it would not have had sensation, had it not been somehow confined within the rest
of the frame. But the rest of the frame, though it provides this indispensable condition for the soul, itself also
has a share, derived from the soul, of the said quality;
and yet does not possess all the qualities of soul. Hence
on the departure of soul it loses sentience. . . . But the
rest of the frame, whether the whole of it survives or

only a part, no longer has sensation, when once those atoms have departed, which, however few in number, are required to constitute the nature of soul. Moreover, when the whole frame is broken up, the soul is scattered and has no longer the same powers as before, nor the same motions; hence it does not possess sentience either. . . .

THE PRACTICAL PHILOSOPHY OF EPICURUS

"Let [6] no one be slow to seek wisdom when he is young nor weary in the search thereof when he is grown old. For no age is too early or too late for the health of the soul. And to say that the season for studying philosophy has not yet come, or that it is past and gone, is like saying that the season for happiness is not yet or that it is now no more. Therefore, both old and young ought to seek wisdom, the former in order that, as age comes over him, he may be young in good things because of the grace of what has been, and the latter in order that, while he is young, he may at the same time be old, because he has no fear of the things which are to come. So we must exercise ourselves in the things which bring happiness, since, if that be present, we have everything, and, if that be absent, all our actions are directed toward attaining it.

"Those things which without ceasing I have declared unto thee, those do, and exercise thyself therein, holding them to be the elements of right life. First believe that God is a living being immortal and blessed, according to the notion of a god indicated by the common sense of mankind; and so believing, thou shalt not affirm of him

[6] From Diogenes Laertius, Book X, 122; Hicks's translation, Vol. II, pp. 649 ff. This passage is from Epicurus's letter to Menœceus.

aught that is foreign to his immortality or that agrees not with blessedness, but shalt believe about him whatever may uphold both his blessedness and his immortality. For verily there are gods, and the knowledge of them is manifest; but they are not such as the multitude believe, seeing that men do not steadfastly maintain the notions they form respecting them. Not the man who denies the gods worshipped by the multitude, but he who affirms of the gods what the multitude believes about them is truly impious. For the utterances of the multitude about the gods are not true preconceptions but false assumptions; hence it is that the greatest evils happen to the wicked and the greatest blessings happen to the good from the hand of the gods, seeing that they are always favourable to their own good qualities and take pleasure in men like unto themselves, but reject as alien whatever is not of their kind.

"Accustom thyself to believe that death is nothing to us, for good and evil imply sentience, and death is the privation of all sentience; therefore a right understanding that death is nothing to us makes the mortality of life enjoyable, not by adding to life an illimitable time, but by taking away the yearning after immortality. For life has no terrors for him who has thoroughly apprehended that there are no terrors for him in ceasing to live. Foolish, therefore, is the man who says that he fears death, not because it will pain when it comes, but because it pains in the prospect. Whatsoever causes no annoyance when it is present, causes only a groundless pain in the expectation. Death, therefore, the most awful of evils, is nothing to us, seeing that, when we are, death is not come, and, when death is come, we are not.

It is nothing, then, either to the living or to the dead, for with the living it is not and the dead exist no longer. But in the world, at one time men shun death as the greatest of all evils, and at another time choose it as a respite from the evils in life. The wise man does not deprecate life nor does he fear the cessation of life. The thought of life is no offence to him, nor is the cessation of life regarded as an evil. And even as men choose of food not merely and simply the larger portion, but the more pleasant, so the wise seek to enjoy the time which is most pleasant and not merely that which is longest. And he who admonishes the young to live well and the old to make a good end speaks foolishly, not merely because of the desirableness of life, but because the same exercise at once teaches to live well and to die well. Much worse is he who says that it were good not to be born, but when once one is born to pass with all speed through the gates of Hades. For if he truly believes this, why does he not depart from life? It were easy for him to do so, if once he were firmly convinced. If he speaks only in mockery, his words are foolishness, for those who hear believe him not.

"We must remember that the future is neither wholly ours nor wholly not ours, so that neither must we count upon it as quite certain to come nor despair of it as quite certain not to come.

"We must also reflect that of desires some are natural, others are groundless; and that of the natural some are necessary as well as natural, and some natural only. And of the necessary desires some are necessary if we are to be happy, some if the body is to be rid of uneasiness, some if we are even to live. He who has a clear and

certain understanding of these things will direct every
preference and aversion toward securing health of body
and tranquillity of mind, seeing that this is the sum and
end of a blessed life. For the end of all our actions is
to be free from pain and fear, and, when once we have
attained all this, the tempest of the soul is laid; seeing
that the living creature has no need to go in search of
something that is lacking, nor to look for anything else
by which the good of the soul and of the body will be
fulfilled. When we are pained because of the absence
of pleasure, then, and then only, do we feel the need of
pleasure. Wherefore we call pleasure the alpha and
omega of a blessed life. Pleasure is our first and kindred
good. It is the starting-point of every choice and of
every aversion, and to it we come back, inasmuch as we
make feeling the rule by which to judge of every good
thing. And since pleasure is our first and native good,
for that reason we do not choose every pleasure whatsoever, but ofttimes pass over many pleasures when a
greater annoyance ensues from them. And ofttimes we
consider pains superior to pleasures when submission to
the pains for a long time brings us as a consequence a
greater pleasure. While therefore all pleasure because
it is naturally akin to us is good, not all pleasure is
choiceworthy, just as all pain is an evil and yet not all
pain is to be shunned. It is, however, by measuring one
against another, and by looking at the conveniences and
inconveniences, that all these matters must be judged.
Sometimes we treat the good as an evil, and the evil, on
the contrary, as a good. Again, we regard independence
of outward things as a great good, not so as in all cases
to use little, but so as to be contented with little if we

have not much, being honestly persuaded that they have the sweetest enjoyment of luxury who stand least in need of it, and that whatever is natural is easily procured and only the vain and worthless hard to win. Plain fare gives as much pleasure as a costly diet, when once the pain of want has been removed, while bread and water confer the highest possible pleasure when they are brought to hungry lips. To habituate one's self, therefore, to simple and inexpensive diet supplies all that is needful for health, and enables a man to meet the necessary requirements of life without shrinking, and it places us in a better condition when we approach at intervals a costly fare and renders us fearless of fortune.

"When we say, then, that pleasure is the end and aim, we do not mean the pleasures of the prodigal or the pleasures of sensuality, as we are understood to do by some through ignorance, prejudice, or wilful misrepresentation. By pleasure we mean the absence of pain in the body and of trouble in the soul. It is not an unbroken succession of drinking-bouts and of revelry, not sexual love, not the enjoyment of the fish and other delicacies of a luxurious table, which produce a pleasant life; it is sober reasoning, searching out the grounds of every choice and avoidance, and banishing those beliefs through which the greatest tumults take possession of the soul. Of all this the beginning and the greatest good is prudence. Wherefore prudence is a more precious thing even than philosophy; from it spring all the other virtues, for it teaches that we cannot lead a life of pleasure which is not also a life of prudence, honour, and justice; nor lead a life of prudence, honour, and justice, which is not also a life of pleasure. For the virtues have grown into one with a pleasant life, and a pleasant life is inseparable from them.

"Who, then, is superior in thy judgment to such a man? He holds a holy belief concerning the gods, and is altogether free from the fear of death. He has diligently considered the end fixed by nature, and understands how easily the limit of good things can be reached and attained, and how either the duration or the intensity of evils is but slight. Destiny, which some introduce as sovereign over all things, he laughs to scorn, affirming rather that some things happen of necessity, others by chance, others through our own agency. For he sees that necessity destroys responsibility and that chance or fortune is inconstant; whereas our own actions are free, and it is to them that praise and blame naturally attach. It were better, indeed, to accept the legends of the gods than to bow beneath that yoke of destiny which the natural philosophers have imposed. The one holds out some faint hope that we may escape if we honour the gods, while the necessity of the naturalists is deaf to all entreaties. Nor does he hold chance to be a god, as the world in general does, for in the acts of a god there is no disorder; nor to be a cause, though an uncertain one, for he believes that no good or evil is dispensed by chance to men so as to make life blessed, though it supplies the starting-point of great good and great evil. He believes that the misfortune of the wise is better than the prosperity of the fool. It is better, in short, that what is well judged in action should not owe its successful issue to the aid of chance.

"Exercise thyself in these and kindred precepts day and night, both by thyself and with him who is like unto thee; then never, either in waking or in dream, wilt thou be disturbed, but wilt live as a god among men. For man loses all semblance of mortality by living in the midst of immortal blessings. . . ."

SOME MAXIMS OF EPICURUS

A[7] blessed and eternal being has no trouble himself and brings no trouble upon any other being; hence he is exempt from movements of anger and partiality, for every such movement implies weakness. . . .

Death is nothing to us; for the body, when it has been resolved into its elements, has no feeling, and that which has no feeling is nothing to us.

The magnitude of pleasure reaches its limit in the removal of all pain. When pleasure is present, so long as it is uninterrupted, there is no pain either of body or of mind or of both together. . . .

It is impossible to live a pleasant life without living wisely and well and justly, and it is impossible to live wisely and well and justly without living pleasantly. Whenever any one of these is lacking, when, for instance, the man is not able to live wisely, though he lives well and justly, it is impossible for him to live a pleasant life. . . .

No pleasure is in itself evil, but the things which produce certain pleasures entail annoyances many times greater than the pleasures themselves. . . .

It would be impossible to banish fear on matters of the highest importance, if a man did not know the nature of the whole universe, but lived in dread of what

[7] From Diogenes Laertius, Book X, 139; Hicks's translation, Vol. II, pp. 663 ff.

the legends tell us.   Hence without the study of nature there was no enjoyment of unmixed pleasures.

There would be no advantage in providing security against our fellow-men, so long as we were alarmed by occurrences over our heads or beneath the earth or in general by whatever happens in the boundless universe.

When tolerable security against our fellow-men is attained, then on a basis of power sufficient to afford support and of material prosperity arises in most geniune form the security of a quiet private life withdrawn from the multitude.

Nature's wealth at once has its bounds and is easy to procure; but the wealth of vain fancies recedes to an infinite distance.

Fortune but seldom interferes with the wise man; his greatest and highest interests have been, are, and will be, directed by reason throughout the course of his life.

The just man enjoys the greatest peace of mind, while the unjust is full of the utmost disquietude. . . .

He who understands the limits of life knows how easy it is to procure enough to remove the pain of want and make the whole of life complete and perfect.   Hence he has no longer any need of things which are not to be won save by labor and conflict. . . .

All such desires as lead to no pain when they remain ungratified are unnecessary, and the longing is easily got rid of, when the thing desired is difficult to procure or when the desires seem likely to produce harm.

Of all the means which are procured by wisdom to ensure happiness throughout the whole of life, by far the most important is the acquisition of friends. . . .

Those natural desires which entail no pain when not

gratified, though their objects are vehemently pursued, are also due to illusory opinion; and when they are not got rid of, it is not because of their own nature, but because of the man's illusory opinion.

Natural justice is a symbol or expression of expediency, to prevent one man from harming or being harmed by another. . . .

Taken generally, justice is the same for all, to wit, something found expedient in mutual intercourse; but in its application to particular cases of locality or conditions of whatever kind, it varies under different circumstances. . . .

Where without any change in circumstances the conventional laws, when judged by their consequences, were seen not to correspond with the notion of justice, such laws were not really just; but wherever the laws have ceased to be expedient in consequence of a change in circumstances, in that case the laws were for the time being just when they were expedient for the mutual intercourse of the citizens, and subsequently ceased to be just when they ceased to be expedient.

XIX

LUCRETIUS

[96–55 B.C.]

THE WAGES OF PHILOSOPHY

FOR [1] I will essay to discourse to you of the most high system of heaven and the gods and will open up the first-beginnings of things, out of which nature gives birth to all things and increase and nourishment, and into which nature likewise dissolves them back after their destruction. These we are accustomed in explaining their reason to call matter and begetting bodies of things and to name seeds of things and also to term first bodies, because from them as first elements all things are.

***

It [2] is sweet, when on the great sea the winds trouble its waters, to behold from land another's deep distress; not that it is a pleasure and delight that any should be afflicted, but because it is sweet to see from what evils you are yourself exempt. It is sweet also to look upon the mighty struggles of war arrayed along the plains without sharing yourself in the danger. But nothing is more welcome than to hold the lofty and serene positions well fortified by the learning of the wise, from which you may look down upon others and see them wandering all

[1] The extracts from Lucretius are given in Munro's translation, and the page references are to the translation. P. 2

[2] Ib., p. 28.

abroad and going astray in their search for the path of
life, see the contest among them of intellect, the rivalry
of birth, the striving night and day with surpassing
effort to struggle up to the summit of power and to be
masters of the world. O miserable minds of men! O
blinded breasts! in what darkness of life and in how great
dangers is passed this term of life whatever its duration!
not choose to see that nature craves for herself no more
than this, that pain hold aloof from the body, and that
she in mind enjoy a feeling of pleasure exempt from care
and fear! Therefore we see that for the body's nature
few things are needed at all, such and such only as take
away pain.

∗

For [3] even as children are flurried and dread all things
in the thick darkness, thus we in the daylight fear at
times things not a whit more to be dreaded than those
which children shudder at in the dark and fancy sure to
be. This terror therefore and darkness of mind must be
dispelled not by the rays of the sun and glittering shafts
of day, but by the aspect and law of nature.

Now mark and I will explain by what motion the
begetting bodies of matter do beget different things and
after they are begotten again break them up, and by
what force they are compelled so to do and what velocity
is given to them for travelling through the great void:
do you mind to give heed to my words. For verily
matter does not cohere inseparably massed together,
since we see that everything wanes and perceive that all
things ebb as it were by length of time and that age with-
draws them from our sight, though yet the sum is seen
to remain unimpaired by reason that the bodies which

[3] Munro's translation, pp. 29–30.

quit each thing, lessen the things from which they go, gift with increase those to which they have come, compel the former to grow old, the latter to come to their prime, and yet abide not with these. Thus the sum of things is ever renewed and mortals live by a reciprocal dependency. Some nations wax, others wane, and in a brief space the races of living things are changed and like runners hand over the lamp of life.

**
*

But [4] some in opposition to this, ignorant of matter, believe that nature cannot without the providence of the gods in such nice conformity to the ways of men vary the seasons of the year and bring forth crops, ay and all the other things, which divine pleasure the guide of life prompts men to approach, escorting them in person and enticing them by her fondlings to continue their races through the arts of Venus, that mankind may not come to an end. Now when they suppose that the gods designed all things for the sake of men, they seem to me in all respects to have strayed most widely from true reason. For even if I did not know what first-beginnings are, yet this, judging by the very arrangements of heaven I would venture to affirm, and led by many other circumstances to maintain, that the nature of the world has by no means been made for us by divine power: so great are the defects with which it stands encumbered.

THE COURSE OF THE ATOMS

This [5] point too herein we wish you to apprehend: when bodies are borne downward sheer through void by their own weights, at quite uncertain times and uncertain spots they push themselves a little from their course;

[4] Munro's translation, p. 32.

[5] Ib., pp. 33–4.

you just and only just can call it a change of inclination. If they were not used to swerve, they would all fall down, like drops of rain, through the deep void, and no clashing would have been begotten nor blow produced among the first-beginnings: thus nature never would have produced aught.

But if haply any one believes that heavier bodies, as they are carried more quickly sheer through space, can fall from above on the lighter and so beget blows able to produce begetting motions, he goes most widely astray from true reason. For whenever bodies fall through water and thin air, they must quicken their descents in proportion to their weights, because the body of water and subtle nature of air cannot retard everything in equal degree, but more readily give way, overpowered by the heavier: on the other hand empty void cannot offer resistance to anything in any direction at any time, but must, as its nature craves, continually give way; and for this reason all things must be moved and borne along with equal velocity though of unequal weights through the unresisting void. Therefore heavier things will never be able to fall from above on lighter nor of themselves to beget blows sufficient to produce the varied motions by which nature carries on things. Wherefore again and again I say bodies must swerve a little; and yet not more than the least possible; lest we be found to be imagining oblique motions and this the reality should refute. For this we see to be plain and evident, that weights, so far as in them is, cannot travel obliquely, when they fall from above, at least so far as you can perceive; but that nothing swerves in any case from the straight course, who is there that can perceive?

THE UNCONCERNED GODS

For [6] the nature of gods must ever in itself of necessity enjoy immortality together with supreme repose, far removed and withdrawn from our concerns; since exempt from every pain, exempt from all dangers, strong in its own resources, not wanting aught of us, it is neither gained by favors nor moved by anger.

***

If [7] you well apprehend and keep in mind these things, nature free at once and rid of her haughty lords is seen to do all things spontaneously of herself without the meddling of the gods.   For I appeal to the holy breasts of the gods who in tranquil peace pass a calm time and an unruffled existence.   Who can rule the sun, who hold in his hand with controlling force the strong reins of the immeasurable deep? Who can at once make all the different heavens to roll and warm with ethereal fires all the fruitful earths, or be present in all places at all times, to bring darkness with clouds and shake with noise the heaven's serene expanse, to hurl lightnings and often throw down his own temples, and withdrawing into the deserts there to spend his rage in practising his bolt which often passes the guilty by and strikes dead the innocent and unoffending?

THE NATURE OF MIND AND SOUL

And [8] now since I have shown what-like the beginnings of all things are and how diverse with varied shapes as they fly spontaneously driven on in everlasting motion, and how all things can be severally produced out of these, next after these questions the nature of the mind and

---

[6] Munro's translation, p. 43.
[7] Ib., p. 54.   [8] Ib., p. 58.

soul should methinks be cleared up by my verses and that dread of Acheron be driven headlong forth, troubling as it does the life of man from its inmost depths and overspreading all things with the blackness of death, allowing no pleasure to be pure and unalloyed.

***

Now [9] I assert that the mind and the soul are kept together in close union and make up a single nature, but that the directing principle which we call mind and understanding, is the head so to speak and reigns paramount in the whole body. It has a fixed seat in the middle region of the breast: here throb fear and apprehension, about these spots dwell soothing joys; therefore here is the understanding or mind. All the rest of the soul disseminated through the whole body obeys and moves at the will and inclination of the mind. It by itself alone knows for itself, rejoices for itself, at times when the impression does not move either soul or body together with it. And as when some part of us, the head or the eye, suffers from an attack of pain, we do not feel the anguish at the same time over the whole body, thus the mind sometimes suffers pain by itself or is inspirited with joy, when all the rest of the soul throughout the limbs and frame is stirred by no novel sensation. But when the mind is excited by some more vehement apprehension, we see the whole soul feel in unison through all the limbs, sweats and paleness spread over the whole body, the tongue falter, the voice die away, a mist cover the eyes, the ears ring, the limbs sink under one; in short we often see men drop down from terror of mind; so that anybody may easily perceive from this that the soul is closely united with the mind,

[9] Munro's translation, pp. 60–2.

and when it has been smitten by the influence of the mind, forthwith pushes and strikes the body.

This same principle teaches that the nature of the mind and soul is bodily; for when it is seen to push the limbs, rouse the body from sleep, and alter the countenance and guide and turn about the whole man, and when we see that none of these effects can take place without touch nor touch without body, must we not admit that the mind and the soul are of a bodily nature? Again you perceive that our mind in our body suffers together with the body and feels in unison with it. When a weapon with a shudder-causing force has been driven in and has laid bare bones and sinews within the body, if it does not take life, yet there ensues a faintness and a lazy sinking to the ground and on the ground the turmoil of mind which arises, and sometimes a kind of undecided inclination to get up. Therefore the nature of the mind must be bodily, since it suffers from bodily weapons and blows.

I will now go on to explain in my verses of what kind of body the mind consists and out of what it is formed. First of all I say that it is extremely fine and formed of exceedingly minute bodies. That this is so you may, if you please to attend, clearly perceive from what follows: nothing that is seen takes place with a velocity equal to that of the mind when it starts some suggestion and actually sets it agoing; the mind therefore is stirred with greater rapidity than any of the things whose nature stands out visible to sight. But that which is so passing nimble must consist of seeds exceedingly round and exceedingly minute, in order to be stirred and set in motion by a small moving power. Thus water is moved and heaves by ever so small a force, formed as it is of small particles apt to roll.   But on the other hand the nature of honey is more sticky, its liquid more sluggish and its movement more dilatory; for the whole mass of matter coheres more closely, because sure enough it is made of bodies not so smooth, fine, and round.   A breeze however gentle and light can force, as you may see, a high heap of poppy seed to be blown away from the top downward; but on the other hand Eurus itself cannot move a heap of stones.   Therefore bodies possess a power of moving in proportion to their smallness and smoothness; and on the other hand the greater weight and roughness bodies prove to have, the more stable they are.   Since then the nature of the mind has been found to be eminently easy to move, it must consist of bodies exceedingly small, smooth, and round.   The knowledge of which fact, my good friend, will on many accounts prove useful and be serviceable to you.   The following fact too likewise demonstrates how fine the texture is of which its nature is composed, and how small the room is in which it can be contained, could it only be collected into one mass: soon as the untroubled sleep of death has gotten hold of a man and the nature of the mind and soul has withdrawn, you can perceive then no diminution of the entire body either in appearance or weight: death makes all good save the vital sense and heat.   Therefore the whole soul must consist of very small seeds and be inwoven through the veins and flesh and sinews; inasmuch as, after it has all withdrawn from the whole body, the exterior contour of the limbs preserves itself entire and not a tittle of the weight is lost.   Just in the same way when the flavor of wine is gone or when the delicious aroma of a perfume has been dispersed into the air or when the savor has left some body, yet the thing itself does not therefore look smaller to the eye, nor does aught seem to have been taken from the weight, because sure enough many minute seeds make up the savors and the odor in the whole body of the several things. Therefore, again and again I say, you are to know that the nature of the mind and the soul has been formed of exceedingly minute seeds, since at its departure it takes away none of the weight.

DISPELLING THE DREAD OF DEATH

Death [10] therefore to us is nothing, concerns us not a jot, since the nature of the mind is proved to be mortal; and as in time gone by we felt no distress, when the Pœni from all sides came together to do battle, and all things shaken by war's troublous uproar shuddered and quaked beneath high heaven, and mortal men were in doubt which of the two peoples it should be to whose empire all must fall by sea and land alike, thus when we shall be no more, when there shall have been a separation of body and soul, out of both of which we are each formed into a single being, to us, you may be sure, who then shall be no more, nothing whatever can happen to excite sensation, not if earth shall be mingled with sea and sea with heaven. And even supposing the nature of the mind and power of the soul do feel, after they have been severed from our body, yet that is nothing to us who by the binding tie of marriage between body and soul are formed each into one single being. And if time should gather up our matter after our death and put it once more into the position in which it now is, and the light of life be given to us again, this result even would

[10] Munro's translation, pp. 77-8.

concern us not at all, when the chain of our self-consciousness has once been snapped asunder. So now we give ourselves no concern about any self which we have been before, nor do we feel any distress on the score of that self. For when you look back on the whole past course of immeasurable time and think how manifold are the shapes which the motions of matter take, you may easily credit this too, that these very same seeds of which we now are formed, have often before been placed in the same order in which they now are; and yet we cannot recover this in memory: a break in our existence has been interposed, and all the motions have wandered to and fro far astray from the sensations they produced. For he whom evil is to befall, must in his own person exist at the very time it comes, if the misery and suffering are haply to have any place at all; but since death precludes this, and forbids him to be, upon whom the ills can be brought, you may be sure that we have nothing to fear after death, and that he who exists not, cannot become miserable, and that it matters not a whit whether he has been born into life at any other time, when immortal death has taken away his mortal life.

Therefore when you see a man bemoaning his hard case, that after death he shall either rot with his body laid in the grave or be devoured by flames or the jaws of wild beasts, you may be sure that his ring betrays a flaw and that there lurks in his heart a secret goad, though he himself declare that he does not believe that any sense will remain to him after death. He does not, methinks, really grant the conclusion which he professes to grant nor the principle on which he so professes, nor does he take and force himself root and branch out of life, but all unconsciously imagines something of self to survive.

For when any one in life suggests to himself that birds
and beasts will rend his body after death, he makes moan
for himself, he does not separate himself from that self,
nor withdraw himself fully from the body so thrown out,
and fancies himself that other self and stands by and
impregnates it with his own sense. Hence he makes
much moan that he has been born mortal, and sees not
that after real death there will be no other self to remain
in life and lament to self that his own self has met death,
and there to stand and grieve that his own self there
lying is mangled or burnt. For if it is an evil after death
to be pulled about by the devouring jaws of wild beasts,
I cannot see why it should not be a cruel pain to be laid
on fires and burn in hot flames, or to be placed in honey
and stifled, or to stiffen with cold, stretched on the
smooth surface of an icy slab of stone, or to be pressed
down and crushed by a load of earth above.

**_*_

Then [11] there is Democritus who, when a ripe old age
had warned him that the memory-waking motions of his
mind were waning, by his own spontaneous act offered
up his head to death. Even Epicurus passed away,
when his light of life had run its course, he who surpassed
in intellect the race of man and quenched the light of all,
as the ethereal sun arisen quenches the stars. Wilt thou
then hesitate and think it a hardship to die? Thou for
whom life is well-nigh dead whilst yet thou livest and
seest the light, who spendest the greater part of thy
time in sleep and snorest wide awake and ceasest not to
see visions and hast a mind troubled with groundless
terror and canst not discover often what it is that ails
thee, when besotted man thou art sore pressed on all

[11] Munro's translation, p. 82.

sides with full many cares and goest astray tumbling about in the wayward wanderings of thy mind.

NO DESIGNER OF NATURE

But [12] in what ways yon concourse of matter founded earth and heaven and the deeps of the sea, the courses of the sun and moon, I will next in order describe. For verily not by design did the first-beginnings of things station themselves each in its right place by keen intelligence, nor did they bargain sooth to say what motions each should assume, but because the first-beginnings of things, many in number in many ways impelled by blows for infinite ages back and kept in motion by their own weights, have been wont to be carried along and to unite in all manner of ways and thoroughly to test every kind of production possible by their mutual combinations, therefore it is that, spread abroad through great time after trying unions and motions of every kind, they at length meet together in those masses which suddenly brought together become often the rudiments of great things, of earth, sea, and heaven and the race of living things.

**

No [13] act is it of piety to be often seen with veiled head to turn to a stone and approach every altar and fall prostrate on the ground and spread out the palms before the statues of the gods and sprinkle the altars with much blood of beasts and link vow on to vow, but rather to be able to look on all things with a mind at peace.

[12] Munro's translation, p. 126.
[13] Ib., p. 145.

XX

EPICTETUS

[Flourished about 90 A.D.]

THINGS WHICH ARE IN OUR POWER

SEEK [1] at once, therefore, to be able to say to every unpleasing semblance, "You are but a semblance and by no means the real thing." And then examine it by those rules which you have; and first and chiefly, by this: whether it concerns the things which are within our own power, or those which are not; and if it concerns anything beyond our power, be prepared to say that it is nothing to you.
*_**

Men [2] are disturbed not by things, but by the views which they take of things. Thus death is nothing terrible, else it would have appeared so to Socrates. But the terror consists in our notion of death, that it is terrible. When, therefore, we are hindered, or disturbed, or grieved let us never impute it to others, but to ourselves; that is, to our own views. It is the action of an uninstructed person to reproach others for his own misfortunes; of one entering upon instruction, to reproach himself; and of one perfectly instructed, to reproach neither others nor himself.

[1] *Ench.* I. Higginson, II. 216. The selections from Epictetus are given in T. W. Higginson's translation. I quote from the two-volume edition, published in 1890.

[2] Ib., V. Higginson II. 218.

Demand [3] not that events should happen as you wish; but wish them to happen as they do happen, and you will go on well.

**

Be [4] assured that the essence of piety toward the gods lies in this, to form right opinions concerning them, as existing; and as governing the universe justly and well. And fix yourself in this resolution, to obey them, and yield to them, and willingly follow them amidst all events, as being ruled by the most perfect wisdom. For thus you will never find fault with the gods, nor accuse them of neglecting you. And it is not possible for this to be effected in any other way than by withdrawing yourself from things which are not within our own power, and by making good or evil to consist only in those which are.

**

As [5] it was fit, then, this most excellent and superior faculty alone, a right use of the appearances of things, the gods have placed in our own power; but all other matters they have not placed in our power. What, was it because they would not? I rather think that, if they could, they had granted us these too; but they certainly could not. For, placed upon earth, and confined to such a body and to such companions, how was it possible that, in these respects, we should not be hindered by things outside of us?

But what says Zeus? "O Epictetus, if it had been possible, I had made this little body and property of thine free, and not liable to hindrance. But now do not mistake; it is not thy own, but only a finer mixture of clay.

[3] *Ench.* VIII. Higginson, II. 219.
[4] Ib., XXXI. Higginson, II. 229.
[5] Ib., XXXI. *Disc.* I. 1. Higginson, I. p. 4.

Since, then, I could not give thee this, I have given thee
a certain portion of myself; this faculty of exerting the
powers of pursuit and avoidance, of desire and aversion,
and, in a word, the use of the appearances of things.
Taking care of this point, and making what is thy own
to consist in this, thou wilt never be restrained, never
be hindered; thou wilt not groan, wilt not complain, wilt
not flatter any one. How, then? Do all these advantages seem small to thee? Heaven forbid! Let
them suffice thee, then, and thank the gods."

But now, when it is in our power to take care of one
thing, and to apply ourselves to one, we choose rather to
take care of many and to encumber ourselves with many
—body, property, brother, friend, child, and slave—and,
by this multiplicity of encumbrances, we are burdened
and weighed down. Thus, when the weather does not
happen to be fair for sailing, we sit in distress and gaze
out perpetually. Which way is the wind? North.
What good will that do us? When will the west blow?
When it pleases, friend, or when Æolus pleases; for Zeus
has not made you dispenser of the winds, but Æolus.

What, then, is to be done?

To make the best of what is in our power, and take
the rest as it occurs.

And how does it occur?

As it pleases God.

***

Do [6] you therefore likewise, being sensible of this,
consider the faculties you have, and after taking a view
of them say, "Bring on me now, O Zeus, what difficulty
thou wilt, for I have faculties granted me by thee, and
powers by which I may win honor from every event"?

[6] *Ench.* XXXI.   *Disc.* I. 6.   Higginson, I. 26.

THE ESSENCE OF GOOD

God [7] is beneficial. Good is also beneficial. It should seem, then, that where the essence of God is, there too is the essence of good. What then is the essence of God —flesh? By no means. An estate? Fame? By no means. Intelligence? Knowledge? Right reason? Certainly. Here, then, without more ado, seek the essence of good. For do you seek that quality in a plant? No. Or in a brute? No. If, then, you seek it only in a rational subject, why do you seek it anywhere but in what distinguishes that from things irrational? Plants make no voluntary use of things, and therefore you do not apply the term *good* to them. *Good*, then, implies such use. And nothing else? If so, you may say that good and happiness and unhappiness belong to mere animals. But this you do not say, and you are right; for, how much soever they have the use of things, they have not the intelligent use, and with good reason, for they are made to be subservient to others, and not of primary importance. Why was an ass made? Was it as being of primary importance? No; but because we had need of a back able to carry burdens. We had need too that he should be capable of locomotion; therefore he had the voluntary use of things added, otherwise he could not have moved. But here his endowments end; for, if an understanding of that use had been likewise added, he would not, in reason, have been subject to us, nor have done us these services, but would have been like and equal to ourselves. Why will you not, therefore, seek the essence of good in that without which you cannot say that there is good in anything?

Ench. XXXI. *Disc.* II. 8. Higginson, I. 132–4.

What then? Are not all these likewise the works of
the gods? They are; but not primary existences, nor
parts of the gods. But you are a primary existence.
You are a distinct portion of the essence of God, and
contain a certain part of him in yourself. Why then are
you ignorant of your noble birth? Why do not you
consider whence you came? Why do not you remember,
when you are eating, who you are who eat, and whom
you feed? When you are in the company of women,
when you are conversing, when you are exercising, when
you are disputing, do not you know that it is the Divine
you feed, the Divine you exercise? You carry a God
about with you, poor wretch, and know nothing of it.
Do you suppose I mean some god without you of gold or
silver? It is within yourself that you carry him; and you
do not observe that you profane him by impure thoughts
and unclean actions. If the mere external image of God
were present, you would not dare to act as you do; and
when God himself is within you, and hears and sees all,
are not you ashamed to think and act thus—insensible
of your own nature, and at enmity with God?

***

Does [8] any one fear things that seem evils indeed,
but which it is in his own power to prevent?

No, surely.

If, then, the things independent of our will are neither
good nor evil, and all things that do depend on will are
in our own power, and can neither be taken away from
us nor given to us unless we please, what room is there
left for anxiety? But we are anxious about this paltry
body or estate of ours, or about what Cæsar thinks, and
not at all about anything internal. Are we ever anxious

* *Ench.* XXXI. *Disc.* II. 13. Higginson, I. 153–4.

not to take up a false opinion? No; for this is within our own power. Or not to follow any pursuit contrary to nature? No, nor this. When, therefore, you see any one pale with anxiety, just as the physician pronounces from the complexion that such a patient is disordered in the spleen, and another in the liver, so do you likewise say, this man is disordered in his desires and aversions; he cannot walk steadily; he is in a fever. For nothing else changes the complexion, or causes trembling, or sets the teeth chattering.

AS SOCRATES WOULD HAVE DONE

When [9] you are going to confer with any one, and especially with one who seems your superior, represent to yourself how Socrates or Zeno would behave in such a case, and you will not be at a loss to meet properly whatever may occur. . . . When you do anything from a clear judgment that it ought to be done, never shrink from being seen to do it, even though the world should misunderstand it; for if you are not acting rightly, shun the action itself; if you are, why fear those who wrongly censure you?

**

Everything [10] has two handles: one by which it may be borne, another by which it cannot. If your brother acts unjustly, do not lay hold on the affair by the handle of his injustice, for by that it cannot be borne; but rather by the opposite, that he is your brother, that he was brought up with you; and thus you will lay hold on it as it is to be borne.

[9] *Ench.* XXXIII. and XXXV.   Higginson, II. 234–5.
[10] Ib., XLIII.   Higginson, II. 238.

Never [11] proclaim yourself a philosopher; nor make much talk among the ignorant about your principles, but show them by actions. Thus, at an entertainment do not discourse how people ought to eat; but eat as you ought. For remember that thus Socrates also universally avoided all ostentation. And when persons came to him, and desired to be introduced by him to philosophers, he took them and introduced them; so well did he bear being overlooked. So if ever there should be among the ignorant any discussion of principles, be for the most part silent. For there is great danger in hastily throwing out what is undigested. And if any one tells you that you know nothing, and you are not nettled at it, then you may be sure that you have really entered on your work. For sheep do not hastily throw up the grass, to show the shepherds how much they have eaten; but, inwardly digesting their food, they produce it outwardly in wool and milk. Thus, therefore, do you not make an exhibition before the ignorant of your principles; but of the actions to which their digestion gives rise.

**

Whatever [12] rules you have adopted, abide by them as laws, and as if you would be impious to transgress them; and do not regard what any one says of you, for this, after all, is no concern of yours. . . . Let whatever appears to be the best, be to you an inviolable law. And if any instance of pain or pleasure, glory or disgrace, be set before you, remember that now is the combat, now the Olympiad comes on, nor can it be put off; and that by one failure and defeat honor may be lost—or won. Thus Socrates became perfect, improving himself

[11] *Ench.* XLVI. Higginson, II. 239.
[12] Ib., L. Higginson, II. 241.

by everything, following reason alone. And though you are not yet a Socrates, you ought, however, to live as one seeking to be a Socrates.

IN HARMONY WITH GOD AND HIS UNIVERSE

All [13] things serve and obey the [laws of the] universe: the earth, the sea, the sun, the stars, and the plants and animals of the earth. Our body likewise obeys the same, in being sick and well, young and old, and passing through the other changes decreed. It is therefore reasonable that what depends on ourselves, that is, our own understanding, should not be the only rebel. For the universe is powerful and superior, and consults the best for us by governing us in conjunction with the whole. And further, opposition, besides that it is unreasonable, and produces nothing except a vain struggle, throws us into pain and sorrows.

**

Bring [14] whatever you please, and I will turn it into *good*. Bring sickness, death, want, reproach, trial for life. All these, by the rod of Hermes, shall turn to advantage. "What will you make of death?" Why, what but an ornament to you; what but a means of your showing, by action, what that man is who knows and follows the will of Nature? "What will you make of sickness?" I will show its nature. I will make a good figure in it; I will be composed and happy; I will not beseech my physician, nor yet will I pray to die. What need you ask further? Whatever you give me, I will make it happy, fortunate, respectable, and eligible.

No, but, "take care not to be sick—it is an evil."

[13] Fr. CXXXI. Higginson, II. 276.
[14] *Disc.* III. 20. Higginson, II. 59.

Just as if one should say, "Take care that the semblance
of three being four does not present itself to you. It is
an evil." How an evil, man? If I think as I ought
about it, what hurt will it any longer do me? Will it not
rather be even an advantage to me? If then I think as I
ought of poverty, of sickness, of political disorder, is not
that enough for me? Why then must I any longer seek
good or evil in externals?

***

For [15] all other pleasures substitute the consciousness
that you are obeying God, and performing not in word,
but in deed, the duty of a wise and good man. How
great a thing is it to be able to say to yourself: "What
others are now solemnly arguing in the schools, and can
state in paradoxes, this I put in practice. Those qualities which are there discoursed, disputed, celebrated, I
have made mine own. Zeus hath been pleased to let
me recognize this within myself, and himself to discern
whether he hath in me one fit for a soldier and a citizen,
and to employ me as a witness to other men, concerning
things uncontrollable by will. See that your fears were
vain, your appetites vain. Seek not good from without;
seek it within yourselves, or you will never find it. For
this reason he now brings me hither, now sends me thither;
sets me before mankind, poor, powerless, sick; banishes
me to Gyaros; leads me to prison; not that he hates me—
Heaven forbid! for who hates the most faithful of his
servants?—nor that he neglects me, for he neglects not
one of the smallest things; but to exercise me, and make
use of me as a witness to others. Appointed to such a
service, do I still care where I am, or with whom, or
what is said of me—instead of being wholly attentive to
God and to his orders and commands?"

[15] *Disc*. III. 24. Higginson, II. 107.

XXI

MARCUS AURELIUS

[120–180 A.D.]

FOLLOW NATURE

Do [1] thou therefore I say absolutely and freely make
choice of that which is best, and stick unto it. Now,
that they say is best which is most profitable. If they
mean profitable to man as he is a rational man, stand
thou to it and maintain it; but if they mean profitable
as he is a creature only, reject it; and from this thy
tenet and conclusion keep off carefully all plausible
shows and colors of external appearance, that thou
mayst be able to discern things rightly.

**

The end [2] and object of a rational constitution is, to
do nothing rashly, to be kindly affected toward men,
and in all things willingly to submit unto the gods.
Casting therefore all other things aside, keep thyself to
these few, and remember withal that no man properly
can be said to live more than that which is now present,
which is but a moment of time. Whatsoever is besides
either is already past, or is uncertain. The time therefore that any man doth live is but a little, and the place
where he liveth is but a very little corner of the earth, and

[1] Marcus Aurelius, *Meditations*, III. 7.   The extracts from Marcus
Aurelius are, save for a few unimportant changes, given in the
translation made by Casaubon early in the 17th century.

[2] Ib., III. 10.

the greatest fame that can remain of a man after his death, even that is but little, and that too, such as it is whilst it is, is by the succession of silly mortal men preserved, who likewise shall shortly die, and even while they live know not what in very deed they themselves are: and much less can know one who long before is dead and gone.

**

Whatsoever [3] is expedient unto thee, O World, is expedient unto me. Nothing can either be unseasonable unto me, or out of date, which unto thee is seasonable. Whatsoever thy seasons bear shall ever by me be esteemed as happy fruit and increase. O Nature! from thee are all things, in thee all things subsist, and to thee all tend. Could he say of Athens, Thou lovely City of Cecrops; and shalt not thou say of the World, Thou lovely City of God?

**

He [4] that seeth the things that are now hath seen all that either was ever or ever shall be, for all things are of one kind and all like one unto another. Meditate often upon the connection of all things in the world, and upon the mutual relation that they have one unto another. For all things are after a sort folded and involved one within another, and by these means all agree well together. For one thing is consequent unto another by local motion, by natural conspiration and agreement, and by substantial union or the reduction of all substances into One.

Fit and accommodate thyself to that estate and to those occurrences which by the destinies have been annexed unto thee; and love those men whom thy fate

[3] Marcus Aurelius, *Meditations*, IV. 19.
[4] Ib., VI. 34-5.

it is to live with; but love them truly.   An instrument,
a tool, an utensil, whatsoever it be, if it be fit for the
purpose it was made for it is as it should be, though he
perchance that made and fitted it be out of sight and
gone.   But in things natural, that power which hath
framed and fitted them is and abideth within them still.
For which reason she ought also the more to be respected,
and we are the more obliged (if we may live and pass our
time according to her purpose and intention) to think
that all is well with us and according to our own minds.
After this manner also . . . He that is all in all doth
enjoy his happiness.   *⃰*

We [5] all work to one effect, some willingly and with a
rational apprehension of what we do, others without any
such knowledge.   *⃰*

If [6] so be that the gods have deliberated in particular
of those things that should happen unto me, I must
stand to their deliberation, as discreet and wise.   For
that a god should be an imprudent god is a thing hard
even to conceive.   And why should they resolve to do
me hurt?   For what profit either unto them or the
universe (which they specially take care for) could arise
from it?   But if so be that they have not deliberated of
me in particular, certainly they have of the whole in
general, and those things which in consequence and
coherence of this general deliberation happen unto me
in particular I am bound to embrace and accept of.   But
if so be that . . . they have not indeed, either in
general or particular, deliberated of any of those things
that happen unto us in this world, yet God be thanked

[5] Marcus Aurelius, *Meditations*, VI. 37.
[6] Ib., VI. 39.

that of those things that concern myself it is lawful for
me to deliberate myself, and all my deliberation is but
concerning that which may be to me most profitable.
Now that unto every one is most profitable which is
according to his own constitution and nature. And my
nature is to be rational in all my actions and, as a
good and natural member of a city and commonwealth,
toward my fellow-members ever to be sociably and
kindly disposed and affected. My city and country as
I am Antoninus is Rome; as a man, the whole world.
Those things therefore that are expedient and profitable
to those cities are the only things that are good and
expedient for me.

***

Either [7] with Epicurus we must fondly imagine the
atoms to be the cause of all things, or we must needs
grant a nature. Let this then be thy first ground, that
thou art part of th.t universe which is governed by
nature. Then, secondly, that to those parts that are
of the same kind and nature as thou art thou hast
relation of kindred. For of these if I shall always be
mindful, first, as I am a part, I shall never be displeased
with anything that falls to my particular share of the
common chances of the world. For nothing that is
behooveful unto the whole can be truly hurtful to that
which is a part of it. For this being the common
privilege of all natures, that they contain nothing in
themselves that is hurtful unto them, it cannot be that
the nature of the universe (whose privilege beyond other
particular natures is that she cannot against her will
by any higher external cause be constrained) should
beget anything and cherish it in her bosom that should

---

[7] Marcus Aurelius, *Meditations*, X. 6.

tend to her own hurt and prejudice. As then I bear in mind that I am a part of such an universe I shall not be displeased with anything that happens. And as I have relation of kindred to those parts that are of the same kind and nature that I am, so I shall be careful to do nothing that is prejudicial to the community, but in all my deliberations shall they that are of my kind ever be; and the common good shall be that which all my intentions and resolutions shall drive unto, just as that which is contrary unto it I shall by all means endeavor to prevent and avoid. These things once so fixed and concluded, as thou wouldest think him an happy citizen whose constant study and practice were for the good and benefit of his fellow-citizens, and the carriage of the city such toward him that he were well pleased with it —so must it needs be with thee that thou shalt live a happy life.

***

Ever [8] consider and think upon the world as being but one living substance and having but one soul; and how all things in the world are terminated into one sensitive power, and are done by one general motion, as it were, and by the deliberation of that one soul; and how all things that are concur in the cause of one another's being, and by what manner of connection and con- catenation all things happen.

What art thou, that better and divine part excepted, but as Epictetus well said, a wretched soul appointed to carry a carcass up and down?

To suffer change can be no hurt; as no benefit it is by change to attain to being. The age and time of the world is as it were a flood and swift current, consisting

---

[8] Marcus Aurelius, *Meditations*, IV. 33–4.

of the things that are brought to pass in the world. For as soon as anything hath appeared and is passed away another succeeds, and that also will pass presently out of sight.

*_**

They [9] will say commonly, Meddle not with many things if thou wilt live cheerfully. Certainly there is nothing better than for a man to confine himself to necessary actions; to such and so many only as reason in a creature that knows itself born for society will command and enjoin. This will not only procure that cheerfulness, which from the goodness, but that also which from the paucity of actions doth usually proceed. For since it is so, that most of those things which we either speak or do are unnecessary, if a man shall cut them off, it must needs follow that he shall thereby gain much leisure and save much trouble; and therefore at every action a man must privately by way of admonition suggest unto himself, What? may not this that now I go about be of the number of unnecessary actions? Neither must he accustom himself to cut off actions only, but also thoughts and imaginations that are unnecessary; for so will unnecessary consequent actions the better be prevented and cut off.

THE HARMONY OF THE UNIVERSE

All [10] parts of the world (all things I mean that are contained within the whole world) must of necessity at some time or other come to corruption. Alteration I should say, to speak truly and properly; but that I may be the better understood I am content at this time to use that more common word. Now, say I, if so be that this

[9] Marcus Aurelius, *Meditations*, IV. 20.
[10] Ib., X. 7.

be both hurtful unto them and yet unavoidable, would not, thinkest thou, the whole itself be in a sweet case, all the parts of it being subject to alteration—yea and by their making the whole itself fitted for corruption as consisting of things different and contrary? And did nature then either of herself thus project and purpose the affliction and misery of her parts, and therefore of purpose so made them, not only that haply they might, but of necessity that they should fall into evil; or did not she know what she did when she made them? For to say either of these things is equally absurd. But to let pass nature in general, and to reason of things particular according to their own particular natures, how absurd and ridiculous is it, first to say that all parts of the whole are by their proper natural constitution subject to alteration, and then when any such thing doth happen as when one doth fall sick and dieth, to take on and wonder as though some strange thing had happened? Though this besides might move us not to take on so grievously when any such thing doth happen, that whatsoever is dissolved is dissolved into those things whereof it was compounded. For every dissolution is either a mere dispersion of the elements into those elements again whereof everything did consist, or a change of that which is more solid into earth, and of that which is pure and subtile or spiritual into air. So that by this means nothing is lost, but all is resumed again into those rational generative seeds of the universe, and this universe is either after a certain period of time to be consumed by fire or by continual changes to be renewed, and so forever to endure. Now, that solid and spiritual that we speak of, thou must not conceive it to be that very same which at first was when thou wert

born. For alas! all this that now thou art in either kind,
either for matter of substance or of life, hath but two
or three days ago, partly from meats eaten and partly
from air breathed in, received all its influx, being the
same then in no other respect than a running river,
maintained by the perpetual influx and new supply of
waters, is the same. That therefore which thou hast
since received, not that which came from thy mother,
is that which comes to change and corruption. But suppose that that for the general substance and more solid
part of it should still cleave unto thee never so close, yet
what is that to the proper qualities and affections of it
by which persons are distinguished, which certainly are
quite different?

***

Whatsoever [11] doth happen in the world is, in the
course of nature, as usual and ordinary as a rose in the
spring and fruit in summer. Of the same nature is
sickness and death, slander and lying in wait, and
whatsoever else ordinarily doth unto fools use to be
occasion either of joy or sorrow. That, whatsoever it
is that comes after, doth always very naturally, and as
it were familiarly, follow upon that which was before.
For thou must consider the things of the world not as a
loose independent number consisting merely of necessary events, but as a discreet connection of things orderly
and harmoniously disposed. There is then to be seen
in the things of the world, not a bare succession, but an
admirable correspondence and affinity.

***

As [12] we say commonly, the physician hath prescribed
unto this man riding; unto another, cold baths; unto a

[11] Marcus Aurelius, *Meditations*, IV. 36.
[12] Ib., V. 8.

third, to go barefoot: so it is alike to say, The nature of
the universe hath prescribed unto this man sickness or
blindness or some loss or damage or some such thing.
For as there, when we say of a physician that he hath
prescribed anything, our meaning is that he hath appointed this for that, as subordinate and conducing to
health; so here, whatsoever doth happen unto any is
ordained unto him as a thing subordinate unto the fates,
and therefore do we say of such things that they do
συμβαίνειν, that is, happen, or fall together; as of square
stones, when either in walls or pyramids in a certain
position they fit one another, and agree as it were in an
harmony, the masons say that they do συμβαίνειν; as
if thou shouldst say, fall together. So that in general
though the things be divers that make it, yet the consent
or harmony itself is but one. And as the whole world is
made up of all the particular bodies of the world, one
perfect and complete body of the same nature as particular bodies: so is the destiny of particular causes and
events one general one, of the same nature that particular
causes are. What I now say even they that are mere
idiots are not ignorant of, for they say commonly τοῦτο
ἔφερεν αὐτῷ, that is, This his Destiny hath brought upon
him. This therefore is by the Fates properly and particularly brought upon this, as that unto this in particular is by the physician prescribed. These therefore
let us accept of in like manner as we do those that are
prescribed unto us by our physicians. For them also
in themselves shall we find to contain many harsh things,
but we nevertheless, in hope of health and recovery,
accept of them. Let the fulfilling and accomplishment
of those things which the common nature hath determined be unto thee as thy health. Accept them,

and be pleased with whatsoever doth happen though otherwise harsh and unpleasing, as tending to that end, to the health and welfare of the universe, and to Jove's happiness and prosperity. For this, whatsoever it be, would not have been produced had it not conduced to the good of the universe. For neither doth any ordinary particular nature bring anything to pass that is not agreeable and subordinate to whatsoever is within the sphere of its own proper administration and government. For these two considerations then thou must be well pleased with anything that doth happen unto thee. First, because for thee properly it was brought to pass and unto thee it was prescribed, and from the very beginning, by the series and connection of the first causes, it hath ever had a reference unto thee. And secondly, because the good success and perfect welfare, and indeed the very continuance of Him that is the Administrator of the whole, doth in a manner depend on it. For the whole (because whole, therefore entire and perfect) is maimed and mutilated if thou shalt cut off anything at all whereby the coherence and contiguity (as of parts, so) of causes is maintained and preserved. Of which certain it is that thou dost (as much as lieth in thee) cut off, and in some sort violently take somewhat away, as often as thou art displeased with anything that happeneth.   *∗*

Thou [13] must comfort thyself in the expectation of thy natural dissolution and in the meantime not grieve at the delay, but rest contented in these two things: First, that nothing shall happen unto thee which is not according to the nature of the universe. Secondly, that it is in

[13] Marcus Aurelius, *Meditations*, V. 10.

thy power to refrain from doing anything contrary to thine own proper god and inward spirit. For it is not in any man's power to constrain thee to transgress against him.

MAN'S INSIGNIFICANCE AND HIS GRANDEUR

What [14] a small portion of vast and infinite eternity it is that is allowed unto every one of us, and how soon it vanisheth into the general age of the world. Of the common substance and of the common soul also, what a small portion is allotted unto us, and in what a little clod of the whole earth it is that thou dost crawl. After thou shalt rightly have considered these things with thyself fancy not anything else in the world any more to be of any weight and moment, but this: to do that only which thine own nature doth require, and to conform thyself to that which the common nature doth afford.

What is the present estate of my understanding? For herein lieth all indeed. As for all other things they are without the compass of mine own will, and if without the compass of my will then are they as dead things unto me and as it were mere smoke.

To stir up a man to the contempt of death this among other things is of good power and efficacy, that even they who esteemed pleasure to be happiness and pain misery did nevertheless many of them contemn death as much as any. And can death be terrible to him to whom that only seems good which in the ordinary course of nature is seasonable? to him to whom, whether his actions be many or few, so they be all good, is all one; and who, whether he behold the things of the world being always the same, either for many years or for few years only, is

[14] Marcus Aurelius, *Meditations*, XII. 25.

altogether indifferent? O man! as a citizen thou hast lived
and conversed in this great City the World. Whether
just for so many years or no, what is it unto thee? Thou
hast lived (thou mayst be sure) as long as the laws and
orders of the city required; which may be the common
comfort of all. Why then should it be grievous unto thee
if [not a tyrant nor an unjust judge, but] the same nature
that brought thee into the world doth now send thee out
of it? It is as if the prætor should fairly dismiss him from
the stage whom he had taken in to act a while. Oh,
but the play is not yet at an end, there are but three acts
yet acted of it? Thou hast well said, for in matter of life
three acts is the whole play. Now to set a certain time
to every man's acting belongs unto him only who as
first he was the cause of thy composition so now is he the
cause of thy dissolution. As for thyself, thou hast to
do with neither. Go thy ways then well pleased and
contented, for so is He that dismisseth thee.

*_**

To [15] live happily is an inward power of the soul when
she is affected with indifference toward those things
that are by their nature indifferent. To be thus affected
she must consider all worldly objects, both divided and
whole, remembering withal that no object can of itself
beget any opinion in us, neither can come to us, but
stands without, still and quiet; but that we ourselves
beget, and as it were print in ourselves, opinions concerning them. Now it is in our power not to print
them; and if they creep in and lurk in some corner, it
is in our power to wipe them off. Remembering, moreover, that this care and circumspection of thine is to
continue but for a while, and then thy life will be at an

<hr>

[15] Marcus Aurelius, *Meditations*, XI. 15.

end.   And what should hinder but that thou mayst do well with all these things? For if they be according to nature, rejoice in them and let them be pleasing and acceptable unto thee. But if they be against nature, seek thou that which is according to thine own nature, and whether it be for thy credit or no, use all possible speed for the attainment of it; for no man ought to be blamed for seeking his own good and happiness.

*_**

Cast [16] away from thee opinion and thou art safe. And what is it that hinders thee from casting it away? When thou art grieved at anything hast thou forgotten that all things happen according to the nature of the universe, and that him only it concerns who is in fault, and moreover that what is now done is that which from ever hath been done in the world and will ever be done, and is now done everywhere? Hast thou forgotten how closely all men are allied one to another by a kindred, not of blood nor of seed, but of the same mind? Thou hast also forgotten that every man's mind partakes of the Deity and issueth from thence, and that no man can properly call anything his own, no, not his son, nor his body, nor his life, for they all proceed from that One who is the giver of all things: that all things are but opinion; that no man lives properly but that very instant of time which is now present, and therefore that no man, whensoever he dieth, can properly be said to lose any more than an instant of time.

*_**

How [17] easy a thing it is for a man to put off from him all turbulent adventitious imaginations, and presently to be in perfect rest and tranquillity!

[16] Marcus Aurelius, *Meditations*, XII. 19.
[17] Ib., V. 2.

Think thyself fit and worthy to speak or to do anything that is according to nature, and let not the reproach or report of some that may ensue upon it ever
deter thee. If it be right and honest to be spoken or
done, undervalue not thyself so much as to be discouraged
from it.

***

The[18] time of a man's life is as a point; the substance of
it ever flowing, the sense obscure; and the whole composition of the body tending to corruption. His soul is
restless, fortune uncertain, and fame doubtful; to be
brief, as a stream so are all things belonging to the body;
as a dream, or as a smoke, so are all that belong unto
the soul. Our life is a warfare, and a mere pilgrimage.
Fame after life is no better than oblivion. What is it
then that will adhere and follow? Only one thing, philosophy. And philosophy doth consist in this, for a man
to preserve that spirit which is within him, from all
manner of contumelies and injuries, and above all pains
or pleasures; never to do anything either rashly, or
feignedly, or hypocritically: wholly to depend from himself, and his own proper actions: all things that happen
unto him to embrace contentedly, as coming from Him
from whom he himself also came; and above all things,
with all meekness and a calm cheerfulness, to expect
death, as being nothing else but the resolution of those
elements, of which every creature is composed.

[18] Marcus Aurelius, *Meditations*, II. 15.

XXII

THE SCEPTICS

PYRRHO AND THE PYRRHONISTS

PYRRHO [1] accompanied (Anaxarchus) on his travels everywhere so that he even forgathered with the Indian Gymnosophists and with the Magi. This led him to adopt a most noble philosophy, to quote Ascanius of Abdera, taking the form of agnosticism and suspension of judgment. He denied that anything was honorable or dishonorable, just or unjust. And so, universally, he held that there is nothing really existent, but custom and convention govern human action; for no single thing is in itself any more this than that.

He led a life consistent with this doctrine, going out of his way for nothing, taking no precaution, but facing all risks as they came, whether carts, precipices, dogs or what not, and, generally, leaving nothing to the arbitrament of the senses; but he was kept out of harm's way by his friends who, as Antigonus of Carystus tells us, used to follow close after him. But Ænesidemus says that it was only his philosophy that was based

---

[1] Pyrrho of Elis (circa 360–275 B.C.) "was the first to teach, as the basis of a distinct movement, doubt, unadulterated by positive statements" (Patrick, *The Greek Sceptics*, p. 46), but he left no writings. His devoted follower Timon, the sillographer, left many, but the surviving fragments of his writings are meagre. It would appear, however, that Pyrrho's interest in scepticism was chiefly practical, as a way of escape from the anxieties of life. The account given in this and the following section is from Diogenes Laertius, who wrote in the third century A.D. The translation is by Hicks.

upon suspension of judgment, and that he did not lack foresight in his everyday acts. . . .

Philo of Athens, a friend of his, used to say that he was most fond of Democritus, and then of Homer, admiring him and continually repeating the line

As leaves on trees, such is the life of man,

. . . and all the passages which dwell on the unstable purpose, vain pursuits, and childish folly of man. . . .

The Sceptics, then, were constantly engaged in overthrowing the dogmas of all schools, but enunciated none themselves; and though they would go so far as to bring forward and expound the dogmas of the others, they themselves laid down nothing definitely, not even the laying down of nothing. So much so that they even refuted their laying down of nothing, saying, for instance, "We determine nothing," since otherwise they would have been betrayed into determining; but we put forward, say they, all the theories for the purpose of indicating our unprecipitate attitude, precisely as we might have done if we had actually assented to them. Thus by the expression "We determine nothing" is indicated their state of even balance; which is similarly indicated by the other expressions, "Not more (one thing than another)," "Every saying has its corresponding opposite," and the like. But "Not more (one thing than another)" can also be taken positively, indicating that two things are alike; for example, "The pirate is no more wicked than the liar." But the Sceptics meant it not positively but negatively, as when, in refuting an argument, one says, "Neither had more existence, Scylla or the Chimæra." And "More so" itself is sometimes comparative, as when we say that "Honey is more sweet than grapes"; sometimes both positive and negative, as when we say, "Virtue profits more than it harms," for in this phrase we indicate that virtue profits and does not harm. But the Sceptics even refute the statement "Not more (one thing than another)." For, as forethought is no more existent than non-existent, so "Not more (one thing than another)" is no more existent than not. Thus, as Timon says in the *Pytho*, the statement means just absence of all determination and withholding of assent. The other statement, "Every saying (has its corresponding opposite)," equally compels suspension of judgment; when facts disagree, but the contradictory statements have exactly the same weight, ignorance of the truth is the necessary consequence. But even this statement has its corresponding antithesis, so that after destroying others it turns round and destroys itself, like a purge which drives the substance out and then in its turn is itself eliminated and destroyed. . . .

Thus the Pyrrhonean principle, as Ænesidemus says in the introduction to his *Pyrrhonics*, is but a report on phenomena or on any kind of judgment, a report in which all things are brought to bear on one another, and in the comparison are found to present much anomaly and confusion. As to the contradictions in their doubts, they would first show the ways in which things gain credence, and then by the same methods they would destroy belief in them; for they say those things gain credence which either the senses are agreed upon or which never or at least rarely change, as well as things which become habitual or are determined by law and those which please or excite wonder. They showed, then, on the basis of that which is contrary to what induces belief, that the probabilities on both sides are equal.

THE TEN MODES OF DOUBT [2]

I. BASED ON THE VARIETY IN ANIMALS

The *first* mode relates to the differences between living creatures in respect of those things which give them pleasure or pain, or are useful or harmful to them. By this it is inferred that they do not receive the same impressions from the same things, with the result that such a conflict necessarily leads to suspension of judgment. . . . Some are distinguished in one way, some in another, and for this reason they differ in their senses

---

[2] I have taken the Tropes of Pyrrhonism from Diogenes Laertius. Except for a slight difference in order of arrangement they are in substance identical with the list as given in Sextus Empiricus, but briefer. Sextus gives a superabundance of illustrations. I have, however, supplied the headings from Sextus's account. Ænesidemus (circ. 100–40 B.C.) was the first to collect and arrange them in ten groups. But he did not originate them. They represent, rather, the accumulated wisdom of Early Pyrrhonism which Later Pyrrhonism took over and adopted; and, I think, though this is in dispute, that they go back to Pyrrho himself. Pyrrhonism stands for "suspense of judgment" as a preparation for the life of tranquillity. Pyrrho's lectures were famous, and he lived to be nearly ninety. It seems incredible that he should not have brought forward some or all of these obstacles that stand in the way of achieving certainty, or of breaking through appearances to some underlying reality. After all, they are empirical and fairly obvious. The arguments against this interpretation are negative and far from convincing. The critics have not sufficiently taken into account the part played by the sense of humor in giving Pyrrhonism its start. Timon, Pyrrho's disciple, lampooned preceding philosophers, or, in dialogues, brought one philosopher forward to refute the work of the others. Is it not reasonable to suppose that he was to a large extent simply putting into writing what Pyrrho had given orally? Humor and ridicule would seem, indeed, to be the only consistent weapons of attack for a thorough-going sceptic and relativist.

also, hawks for instance being most keen-sighted, and dogs having a most acute sense of smell. It is natural that if the senses, *e.g.*, eyes, of animals differ, so also will the impressions produced upon them; . . .

II. BASED ON THE DIFFERENCES IN HUMAN BEINGS

The *second* mode has reference to the natures and idiosyncrasies of men; for instance, Demophon, Alexander's butler, used to get warm in the shade and shiver in the sun. Andron of Argos is reported by Aristotle to have travelled across the waterless deserts of Libya without drinking. Moreover, one man fancies the profession of medicine, another farming, and another commerce; and the same ways of life are injurious to one man but beneficial to another; from which it follows that judgment must be suspended.

III. BASED ON THE DIFFERENT STRUCTURES OF THE ORGANS OF SENSE

The *third* mode depends on the differences between the sense-channels in different cases, for an apple gives the impression of being pale yellow in color to the sight, sweet in taste and fragrant in smell. An object of the same shape is made to appear different by differences in the mirrors reflecting it. Thus it follows that what appears is no more such and such a thing than something different.

IV. BASED ON THE CIRCUMSTANTIAL CONDITIONS

The *fourth* mode is that due to differences of condition and to changes in general; for instance, health, illness, sleep, waking, joy, sorrow, youth, old age, courage, fear, want, fullness, hate, love, heat, cold, to say nothing of breathing freely and having the passages obstructed. The impressions received thus appear to vary according to the nature of the conditions. . . .

V. BASED ON THE DISCIPLINES AND CUSTOMS AND LAWS, THE LEGENDARY BELIEFS AND THE DOGMATIC CONVICTIONS

The *fifth* mode is derived from customs, laws, belief in myths, compacts between nations and dogmatic assumptions. This class includes considerations with regard to things beautiful and ugly, true and false, good and bad, with regard to the gods, and with regard to the coming into being and the passing away of the world of phenomena. Obviously the same thing is regarded by some as just and by others as unjust, or as good by some and bad by others. . . . Different people believe in different gods; some in providence, others not. In burying their dead, the Egyptians embalm them; the Romans burn them; the Pæonians throw them into lakes. As to what is true, then, let suspension of judgment be our practice.

VI. BASED ON INTERMIXTURES

The *sixth* mode relates to mixtures and participations, by virtue of which nothing appears pure in and by itself, but only in combination with air, light, moisture, solidity, heat, cold, movement, exhalations and other forces. For purple shows different tints in sunlight, moonlight, and lamplight; and our own complexion does not appear the same at noon and when the sun is low. Again, a rock which in air takes two men to lift is easily moved about in water, either because, being in reality heavy, it is lifted by the water or because, being light, it is made heavy by the air. Of its own inherent property we know nothing, any more than of the constituent oils in an ointment.

VII. BASED ON POSITIONS AND INTERVALS AND LOCATIONS

The *seventh* mode has reference to distances, positions, places and the occupants of the places. In this mode things which are thought to be large appear small, square things round; flat things appear to have projections, straight things to be bent, and colorless colored. So the sun, on account of its distance, appears small, mountains when far away appear misty and smooth, but when near at hand rugged. Furthermore, the sun at its rising has a certain appearance, but has a dissimilar appearance when in mid-heaven, and the same body one appearance in a wood and another in open country. The image again varies according to the position of the object, and a dove's neck according to the way it is turned. Since, then, it is not possible to observe these things apart from places and positions, their real nature is unknowable.

VIII. BASED ON THE QUANTITIES AND FORMATIONS OF THE
UNDERLYING OBJECTS

The *eighth* mode is concerned with quantities and qualities of things, say heat or cold, swiftness or slowness, colorlessness or variety of colors. Thus wine taken in moderation strengthens the body, but too much of it is weakening; and so with food and other things.

IX. BASED ON THE FREQUENCY OR RARITY OF OCCURRENCE

The *ninth* mode has to do with perpetuity, strangeness, or rarity. Thus earthquakes are no surprise to those among whom they constantly take place; nor is the sun, for it is seen every day.

X. BASED ON THE FACT OF RELATIVITY

The *tenth* mode rests on inter-relation, *e.g.*, between light and heavy, strong and weak, greater and less, up and down. Thus that which is on the right is not so by nature, but is so understood in virtue of its position with respect to something else; for, if that change its position, the thing is no longer on the right. Similarly father and brother are relative terms, day is relative to the sun, and all things relative to our mind. Thus relative terms are in and by themselves unknowable. These, then, are the ten modes of perplexity.

THE FIVE MODES OF DOUBT ACCORDING TO AGRIPPA

[Agrippa [3] and his school reduced the modes of doubt to five], resulting respectively from disagreement, extension *ad infinitum*, relativity, hypothesis and reciprocal inference. The mode arising from disagreement proves, with regard to any inquiry whether in philosophy or in everyday life, that it is full of the utmost contentiousness and confusion. The mode which involves extension *ad infinitum* refuses to admit that what is sought to be proved is firmly established, because one thing furnishes the ground for belief in another, and so on *ad infinitum*. The mode derived from relativity declares that a thing can never be appre-

---

[3] D. L. IX, 88. Hicks's tr., II, p. 501. Agrippa, one of the leading representatives of Later Pyrrhonism, belongs to the first century A.D. I include his five "Tropes" at this point for comparison with those of Earlier Pyrrhonism as arranged by Ænesidemus.

hended in and by itself, but only in connection with something else. Hence all things are unknowable. The mode resulting from hypothesis arises when people suppose that you must take the most elementary of things as of themselves entitled to credence, instead of postulating them: which is useless, because some one else will adopt the contrary hypothesis. The mode arising from reciprocal inference is found whenever that which should be confirmatory of the thing requiring to be proved itself has to borrow credit from the latter, as, for example, if any one seeking to establish the existence of pores on the ground that emanations take place should take this (the existence of pores) as proof that there are emanations.

*
* *

PYRRHONISM IN PRACTICE

The [4] dogmatic philosophers maintain that the Sceptics do away with life itself, in that they reject all that life consists in. The others say this is false, for they do not deny that we see; they only say that they do not know how we see. "We admit the apparent fact," say they, "without admitting that it really is what it appears to be." We also perceive that fire burns; as to whether it is its nature to burn, we suspend our judgment. We see that a man moves, and that he perishes; how it happens we do not know. We merely object to accepting the unknown substance behind phenomena.

*
* *

"We [5] confess to human weaknesses; for we recognize that it is day and that we are alive, and many other

[4] D. L. IX, 104. Hicks's tr., II, p. 103.
[5] D. L. IX, 103.

apparent facts in life; but with regard to the things about which our opponents argue so positively, claiming to have definitely apprehended them, we suspend our judgment because they are not certain, and confine knowledge to our impressions. For we admit that we see, and we recognize that we think this or that, but how we see or how we think we know not. And we say in conversation that a certain thing appears white, but we are not positive that it really is white. As to our 'We determine nothing' and the like, we use the expressions in an undogmatic sense, for they are not like the assertion that the world is spherical. Indeed the latter statement is not certain, but the others are mere admissions. Thus in saying 'We determine nothing,' we are *not* determining even that."

*_**

The [6] Sceptic, seeing so great a diversity of usages, suspends judgment as to the natural existence of anything good or bad or (in general) fit or unfit to be done, therein abstaining from the rashness of dogmatism; and he follows undogmatically the ordinary rules of life, and because of this he remains impassive in respect of matters of opinion, while in conditions that are necessitated his emotions are moderate; for though, as a human being, he suffers emotion through his senses, yet because he does not also opine that what he suffers is evil by nature, the emotion he suffers is moderate. For the added opinion that a thing is of such a kind is worse than the actual suffering itself, just as sometimes the patients themselves bear a surgical operation, while the by-

[6] Sext. Emp., *Outlines*, III, 235. Bury's tr., I, p. 483.

standers swoon away because of their opinion that it is a horrible experience.

∗

The [7] Sceptics, neither affirming nor denying anything rashly but subjecting all things to criticism, maintain that those who assume the existence of good and evil by nature have in consequence an unhappy life, whereas for those who refuse to define, and suspend judgment—

> Freest from care is the life they lead.

And this we may learn if we first go back a little.

Now every unhappy state occurs because of some perturbation. But every perturbation in men is a consequence due either to an eager pursuit of certain things or to an eager avoidance of certain things. And all men eagerly pursue what is believed by them to be good and avoid what is supposed to be evil. Therefore every case of unhappiness occurs owing to the pursuit of the good things as good, and the avoidance of the evil things as evil. . . .

But if a man should declare that nothing is by nature an object of desire any more than of avoidance, nor of avoidance more than of desire, each thing which occurs being relative, and, owing to differences of times and circumstances, being at one time desirable, at another to be avoided, he will live happily and unperturbed, being neither exalted at good, as good, nor depressed at evil, manfully accepting what befalls him of necessity, and being liberated from the distress due to the belief that something evil or good is present.

[7] *Against Eth.*, 111, 118. Bury's tr., pp. 439, 443.

SCEPTICISM IN THE ACADEMY

(a) ARCESILAUS [8]

Arcesilaus,[9] however, who was the president and founder of the Middle Academy, certainly seems to me to have shared the doctrines of Pyrrho, so that his Way of thought is almost identical with ours. For we do not find him making any assertion about the reality or unreality of anything, nor does he prefer any one thing to another in point of probability or improbability, but suspends judgment about all. He also says that the End is suspension—which is accompanied, as we have said, by "quietude." He declares, too, that suspension regarding particular objects is good, but assent regarding particulars bad. Only one might say that whereas we make these statements not positively but in accordance with what appears to us, he makes them as statements of real facts, so that he asserts that suspension in itself really is good and assent bad. . . .

[He] did not,[10] to begin with, lay down any definite criterion, and those who are thought to have laid one down produced it by way of counterblast to that of the Stoics. For the latter assert that there are three criteria—knowledge and opinion and, set midway between these two, apprehension; and of these knowledge is the unerring and firm apprehension which is unalterable by reason, and opinion is weak and false assent, and apprehension is intermediate between these, being assent to an apprehensive presentation; and an apprehensive presentation, according to them, is one which

---

[8] Circ. 315–241 B.C.
[9] Sext. Emp., *Outlines*, I, 232. Bury's tr., I, p. 143.
[10] Sext. Emp., *Against Log.*, I, 150 ff. Bury's tr., II, pp. 83 ff.

is true and of such a kind as to be incapable of becoming false. And they say that, of these, knowledge subsists only in the wise, and opinion only in the fools, but apprehension is shared alike by both, and it is the criterion of truth. It was these statements of the Stoics that Arcesilaus controverted by proving that apprehension is not a criterion intermediate between knowledge and opinion. For that which they call "apprehension" and "assent to an apprehensive presentation" occurs either in a wise man or in a fool. But if it occurs in a wise man, it is knowledge, and if in a fool, opinion, and nothing else is acquired besides these two save a mere name. And if apprehension is in fact assent to an apprehensive presentation, it is non-existent —firstly, because assent is not relative to presentation but to reason (for assents are given to judgments), and secondly, because no true presentation is found to be of such a kind as to be incapable of proving false, as is shown by many and various instances. . . . And if apprehension does not exist, all things will be non-apprehensible. And if all things are non-apprehensible, it will follow, even according to the Stoics, that the wise man suspends judgment. . . .

But inasmuch as it was necessary, in the next place, to investigate also the conduct of life, which cannot, naturally, be directed without a criterion, upon which happiness—that is the end of life—depends for its assurance, Arcesilaus asserts that he who suspends judgment about everything will regulate his inclinations and aversions and his actions in general by the rule of "the reasonable," and by proceeding in accordance with this criterion he will act rightly; for happiness is attained

by means of wisdom, and wisdom consists in right actions, and the right action is that which, when performed, possesses a reasonable justification. He, therefore, who attends to "the reasonable" will act rightly
and be happy.

(b) CARNEADES [11]—PROBABILISM

Carneades [12] arrayed his arguments concerning the
criterion not only against the Stoics but against all his
predecessors. In fact his first argument, aimed at all
alike, is that by which he establishes that there is absolutely no criterion of truth—neither reason, nor sense,
nor presentation, nor anything else that exists; for these
things, one and all, play us false. Second comes the
argument by which he shows that even if a criterion
exists, it does not subsist apart from the affection produced by the evidence of sense. For since the living
creature differs from lifeless things by its faculty of
sense, it will certainly become perceptive both of itself
and of external things by means of this faculty. But
when the sense is unmoved and unaffected and undis-
turbed, neither is it sense nor perceptive of anything;
but when it is disturbed and somehow affected owing
to the impact of things evident, then it indicates the
objects. . . . So then, once more, since there is no
true presentation of such a kind that it cannot be false,
but a false presentation is found to exist exactly resembling every apparently true presentation, the criterion will consist of a presentation which contains the
true and the false alike. But the presentation which

[11] Circ. 213-129 B.C.
[12] Sext. Emp., *Against Log.*, I, 159 ff. Bury's tr., II, pp. 87 ff.

contains them both is not apprehensive, and not being apprehensive, it will not be a criterion. And if no presentation capable of judging exists, neither will reason be a criterion; for it is derived from presentation. And naturally so; for that which is judged must first be presented, and nothing can be presented without sense which is irrational. Therefore neither irrational sense nor reason is the criterion.

These were the arguments which Carneades set forth in detail, in his controversy with the other philosophers, to prove the non-existence of the criterion; yet as he, too, himself requires a criterion for the conduct of life and for the attainment of happiness, he is practically compelled on his own account to frame a theory about it, and to adopt both the probable presentation and that which is at once probable and irreversible and tested. What the distinction is between these must be briefly indicated. The presentation, then, is a presentation of something—of that, for instance, from which it comes and of that in which it occurs; that from which it comes being, say, the externally existent sensible object, and that in which it occurs, say, a man. And, such being its nature, it will have two aspects, one in its relation to the object presented, the second in its relation to the subject experiencing the presentation. Now in regard to its aspect in relation to the object presented it is either true or false—true when it is in accord with the object presented, but false when it is not in accord. But in regard to its aspect in relation to the subject experiencing the presentation, the one kind of presentation is apparently true, the other apparently false; and of these the apparently true is termed by the Aca-

demics "emphasis" and probability and probable presentation, while the not apparently true is denominated
"ap-emphasis" and unconvincing and improbable presentation; for neither that which itself appears false,
nor that which though true does not appear so to us,
is naturally convincing to us. . . .

But that which appears true, and appears so vividly,
is the criterion of truth according to the School of Carneades. And being the criterion, it has a large extension, and when extended one presentation reveals itself
as more probable and more vivid than another. . . .
Hence the criterion will be the apparently true presentation, which the Academics called "probable." . . .

Such then is the first and general criterion according
to Carneades. But since no presentation is ever simple
in form but, like links in a chain, one hangs from another, we have to add, as a second criterion, the presentation which is at once both probable and "irreversible."
For example, he who receives the presentation of a man
necessarily receives the presentation both of his personal
qualities and of the external conditions—of his personal
qualities, such as color, size, shape, motion, speech,
dress, footgear; and of the external conditions, such as
air, light, day, heaven, earth, friends, and all the rest.
So whenever none of these presentations disturbs our
faith by appearing false, but all with one accord appear
true, our belief is the greater. . . . And that the "irreversible" presentation is a concurrence capable of im-
planting belief is plain from the case of Menelaus; for
when he had left behind him on the ship the wraith of
Helen—which he had brought with him from Troy,
thinking it to be the true Helen—and had landed on

the island of Pharos, he beheld the true Helen, but though he received from her a true presentation, yet he did not believe that presentation owing to his mind being warped by that other impression from which he derived the knowledge that he had left Helen behind in the ship. Such then is the "irreversible" presentation; and it too seems to possess extension inasmuch as one is found to be more irreversible than another.

Still more trustworthy than the irreversible presentation and supremely perfect is that which creates judgment; for it, in addition to being irreversible, is also "tested." What the distinctive feature of this presentation is we must next explain. Now in the case of the irreversible presentation it is merely required that none of the presentations in the concurrence should disturb us by a suspicion of its falsity but all should be apparently true and not improbable; but in the case of the concurrence which involves the "tested" presentation, we scrutinize attentively each of the presentations in the concurrence. . . .

For all these factors together form the criterion—namely, the probable presentation, and that which is at once both probable and irreversible, and besides these that which is at once probable and irreversible and tested. . . . For they declare that they attend to the immediately probable in cases where the circumstances do not afford time for an accurate consideration of the matter. A man, for example, is being pursued by enemies, and coming to a ditch he receives a presentation which suggests that there, too, enemies are lying in wait for him; then being carried away by this presentation, as a probability, he turns aside and avoids the ditch, being led by the probability of the presentation, before he has exactly ascertained whether or not there really is an ambush of the enemy at the spot. But they follow the probable and tested presentation in cases where time is afforded for using their judgment on the object presented with deliberation and thorough examination. For example, on seeing a coil of rope in an unlighted room a man jumps over it, conceiving it for the moment to be a snake, but turning back afterwards he inquires into the truth, and on finding it motionless he is already inclined to think that it is not a snake, but as he reckons, all the same, that snakes too are motionless at times when numbed by winter's frost, he prods at the coiled mass with a stick, and then, after thus testing the presentation received, he assents to the the fact that it is false to suppose that the body presented to him is a snake. And once again, as I said before, when we see a thing very plainly we assent to its being true when we have previously proved by testing that we have our senses in good order, and that we see it when wide awake, and not asleep, and that there exists at the same time a clear atmosphere and a moderate distance and immobility on the part of the object perceived, so that because of these conditions the presentation is trustworthy, we having had sufficient time for the scrutiny of the facts observed at the seat of the presentation. The same account is to be given of the irreversible presentation as well; for they accept it whenever there is nothing capable of controverting it, as was said above in the case of Menelaus.

LATER PYRRHONISM

They[13] would deny all demonstration, criterion, sign, cause, motion, the process of learning, coming into being, or that there is anything good or bad by nature. . . .

(a) The Criterion. Of those,[14] then, who have treated of the criterion some have declared that a criterion exists, by some its existence is denied, . . . while we have adopted suspension of judgment as to whether it does or does not exist. This dispute, then, they will declare to be either capable or incapable of decision; and if they shall say it is incapable of decision they will be granting on the spot the propriety of suspension of judgment, while if they say it admits of decision, let them tell us whereby it is to be decided, since we have no accepted criterion, and do not even know, but are still inquiring, whether any criterion exists. Besides, in order to decide the dispute which has arisen about the criterion, we must possess an accepted criterion by which we shall be able to judge the dispute; and in order to possess an accepted criterion, the dispute about the criterion must first be decided. And when the argument thus reduces itself to a form of circular reasoning the discovery of the criterion becomes impracticable. . . .

We suppose, then, that this is sufficient to expose the rashness of the Dogmatists in respect of their doctrine of the Criterion; . . .

(b) On Signs. And[15] since they [the non-apprehended objects] seem to be apprehended and

[13] D. L. IX, 90. Hicks's tr., II, p. 501. All these matters are discussed at great length by Sextus. I give abbreviated accounts of his discussion of four of them as illustrations of the dialectic of Later Pyrrhonism. Carneades, however, used similar arguments about the criterion.
[14] Sext. Emp., *Outlines*, II, 18 ff. Bury's tr., I, 163 ff.
[15] Sext. Emp., *Outlines*, II, 96 ff. Bury's tr., I, pp. 213 ff.

confirmed by means of sign and proof, we shall show briefly that it is proper to suspend judgment also about sign and proof. We will begin with sign; for indeed proof seems to be a kind of sign. . . .

Of the signs, then, according to them, some are suggestive, some indicative. They term a sign "suggestive" when, being mentally associated with the thing signified, it by its clearness at the time of its perception, though the thing signified remains non-evident, suggests to us the thing associated with it, which is not clearly perceived at the moment—as for instance in the case of smoke and fire. An "indicative" sign, they say, is that which is not clearly associated with the thing signified, but signifies that whereof it is a sign by its own particular nature and constitution, just as, for instance, the bodily motions are signs of the soul. Hence, too, they define this sign as follows: "An indicative sign is an antecedent judgment, in a sound hypothetical syllogism, which serves to reveal the consequent." Seeing, then, that there are, as we have said, two different kinds of sign, we do not argue against every sign but only against the indicative kind as it seems to be invented by the Dogmatists. For the suggestive sign is relied on by living experience, since when a man sees smoke fire is signified, and when he beholds a scar he says that there has been a wound. Hence, not only do we not fight against living experience, but we even lend it our support by assenting undogmatically to what it relies on, while opposing the private inventions of the Dogmatists. . . .

For in order to prove the judgment upon the hypothetical syllogism, the conclusion of the proof must follow logically from its premises, as we said above, and, in turn, in order to establish this, the hypothetical syllogism and its logical sequence must be tested; and this is absurd. So then the valid hypothetical syllogism is non-apprehensible.

But the "antecedent" also is unintelligible. For the antecedent, as they assert, is "the leading clause in a hypothetical syllogism of the kind which begins with a truth and ends in a truth." But if the sign serves to reveal the consequent, the consequent is either pre-evident or non-evident. If, then, it is pre-evident, it will not so much as need the thing which is to reveal it but will be apprehended along with it and will not be the object signified thereby and hence also the thing mentioned will not be a "sign" of the object. But if the consequent is non-evident, seeing that there exists an unsettled controversy about things non-evident, as to which of them are true, which false, and in general whether any of them is true, it will be non-evident whether the hypothetical syllogism ends in a true consequent. And this involves the further fact that it is non-evident whether the leading clause in the syllogism is the logical antecedent. But to pass over this objection also, the sign cannot serve to reveal the consequent, if the thing signified is relative to the sign and is, therefore, apprehended along with it. For relatives are apprehended along with each other . . . as is "left" with "right," "up" with "down," and the rest of the relative terms. Whereas, if it serves to reveal the thing signified, it certainly ought to be apprehended before it, in order that by being foreknown it may lead us to a conception of the object which comes to be known by means of it.

But it is impossible to form a conception of an object which cannot be known before the thing before which it must necessarily be apprehended; and so it is impossible to conceive of an object which is both relative and also really serves to reveal the thing in relation to which it is thought. But the sign is, as they affirm, both relative and serving to reveal the thing signified; wherefore it is impossible to conceive of the sign. . . . Next we shall set forth those [arguments] which go to suggest the existence of a sign, in order that we may exhibit the equipollence of the counterbalancing arguments.

Either, then, the phrases used in criticism of the sign signify something or they signify nothing. But if they are non-significant how could they affect the reality of the sign? While if they signify something, there exists a sign. Further, the arguments against the sign are either probative or non-probative; but if they are non-probative they do not prove the non-existence of a sign; while if they are probative, since proof, as serving to reveal the conclusion, belongs to the genus sign, sign will exist. . . .

In short, then, since such plausible arguments are adduced both for the existence and for the non-existence of sign, we must declare that sign is "no more" existent than non-existent.

(c) Proof. Proof [16] is a matter of controversy; for some declare that it does not even exist, as do those who assert that nothing at all exists, but others, including the majority of the Dogmatists, that it does exist; and we affirm that it is "no more" existent than

[16] Sext. Emp., *Outlines*, II, 180 ff. Bury's tr., I, pp. 267 ff.

non-existent. And besides, proof always contains a dogma, and they are in dispute about every dogma, so that there must necessarily be dispute about every proof. For if (for the sake of argument) when the proof for the existence of void is accepted the existence of void is likewise accepted, it is plain that those who dispute the existence of void dispute its proof also; and the same argument applies to all the other dogmas with which the proofs are concerned. Therefore every proof is questioned and is in dispute.

Since, then, proof is non-evident, owing to the controversy which exists concerning it . . . its existence is not self-evident but needs to be established for us by proof. The proof, then, by which proof is established will not be evident and agreed . . . and being thus in dispute and non-evident it will need another proof, and this again a third, and so on *ad infinitum*. But it is impossible to prove an infinite series; therefore it is impossible to show that proof exists.

But neither can it be revealed by means of a sign. For since it is a matter of inquiry whether sign exists, and since the sign needs proof to ensure its reality, we find ourselves involved in circular reasoning—the proof requiring a sign, and the sign in turn a proof; which is absurd. And for these reasons neither is it possible to decide the controversy regarding proof, seeing that the decision requires a criterion, but—because it is a matter of inquiry, as we have shown, whether a criterion exists, and consequently the criterion needs a proof showing the existence of a criterion—we are again involved in the perplexity of circular reasoning. If, then, neither by proof nor by sign nor by criterion it is possible to show that proof exists, and it is not evident of itself either, as we have shown, then it will be non-apprehensible whether proof exists. Consequently, proof will also be unreal; for it is conceived together with the act of proving, and were it not apprehended it would be unable to prove. Wherefore proof will not exist. . . .

The Dogmatists, however, maintaining the opposite view assert that the arguments propounded against proof are either probative or not probative; and if they are not probative, they are incapable of showing that proof does not exist; while if they are probative, they themselves involve the reality of proof by self-refutation. . . .

Now to this we may reply, for instance, that, because we do not believe that any argument is probative, we do not assert either that the arguments against proof are absolutely probative but that they appear to us plausible; but those that are plausible are not necessarily probative. . . . These arguments are capable of cancelling themselves along with the other arguments which are said to be probative. Nor is this preposterous, since in fact the saying "nothing is true" not only refutes every other saying but also nullifies itself as well.

(d) Induction. It [17] is also easy, I consider, to set aside the method of induction. For, when they propose to establish the universal from the particulars by means of induction, they will effect this by a review either of all or of some of the particular instances. But if they review some, the induction will be insecure, since some of the particulars omitted in the induction may contravene the universal; while if they are to review all,

[17] Sext. Emp., *Outlines*, II, 204. Bury's tr., I, p. 283.

they will be toiling at the impossible, since the particulars are infinite and indefinite. Thus on both grounds, as I think, the consequence is that induction is invalidated.[18]

ÆNESIDEMUS—ON CAUSE

Just [19] as we teach the traditional Modes leading to suspense of judgment, so likewise some Sceptics propound Modes by which we express doubt about the particular "ætiologies," or theories of causation, and thus pull up the Dogmatists because of the special pride they take in these theories. Thus Ænesidemus furnishes us with *Eight Modes* by which, as he thinks, he tests and exposes the unsoundness of every dogmatic theory of causation. Of these the First, he says, is that which shows that, since ætiology as a whole deals with the non-apparent, it is unconfirmed by any agreed evidence derived from appearances. The Second Mode shows how often, when there is ample scope for ascribing the object of investigation to a variety of causes, some of them account for it in one way only. The Third shows

[18] Sextus Empiricus (circ. 160–210 A.D.) brings to a close the movement of Pyrrhonic Scepticism. His extensive works give a very complete account of that movement, but he effaces himself so completely in his writing as to give the impression that he made no significant original contribution. The earliest Pyrrhonists cultivated scepticism and the consequent suspension of judgment as a preparation for the life of tranquility. The scepticism of the Academy and of Later Pyrrhonism was directed especially against the dogmatic teachings of the Stoics. However, there is a very definite positive constructive side of the work of Carneades. He squarely faced the problem of the possibility of knowledge of any kind, granted that certainty cannot be attained and that we cannot go beyond the direct presentations of experience. His answer is given in his theory of probabilism, which is a very striking anticipation of the attitude of modern science. Sextus directs his attacks, not only against the dogmatic philosophers, but against dogmatism in science as well. He was a physician and seems to have had as at least one motive the complete divorce of medicine from metaphysics.

[19] Sext. Emp., *Outlines*, I, 180 ff. Bury's tr., I, p. 103.

how to orderly events they assign causes which exhibit no order. The Fourth shows how, when they have grasped the way in which appearances occur, they assume that they have also apprehended how non-apparent things occur, whereas, though the non-apparent may possibly be realized in a similar way to the appearances, possibly they may not be realized in a similar way but in a peculiar way of their own. In the Fifth Mode it is shown how practically all these theorists assign causes according to their own particular hypotheses about the elements, and not according to any commonly agreed methods. In the Sixth it is shown how they frequently admit only such facts as can be explained by their own theories, and dismiss facts which conflict therewith though possessing equal probability. The Seventh shows how they often assign causes which conflict not only with appearances but also with their own hypotheses. The Eighth shows that often, when there is equal doubt about things seemingly apparent and things under investigation, they base their doctrine about things equally doubtful upon things equally doubtful. Nor is it impossible, he adds, that the overthrow of some of their theories of causation should be referred to certain mixed Modes which are dependent on the foregoing. . . .

Ænesidemus [20] has, in his treatment of them, made a more elaborate use of the difficulties concerning becoming. Body will not be the cause of body, since such a body is either ungenerated, like the atom of Epicurus, or generated, as is man, and either visible like iron and fire, or invisible like the atom. And whichever of these

[20] Sext. Emp., *Against Phys.*, I, 218 ff. Bury's tr., III, pp. 111 ff.

it is, it cannot effect anything. For it acts on another thing either while continuing by itself or after uniting with the other. But while it remains by itself it would not be able to effect anything more than itself and its own nature; and when united with another it would not be able to produce a third thing which was not previously in existence. . . . Body, then, is not the cause of body. Moreover, for the same reasons, the incorporeal is not the cause of the incorporeal. . . . And besides, the incorporeal being an intangible nature cannot be either active or passive. . . . And thus the converse is not possible either—that is to say, body creating the incorporeal or the incorporeal, body. For body does not contain within itself the nature of the incorporeal, and the incorporeal does not include the nature of body. . . .

And again: If there exists any cause of anything, either the unmoved is the cause of the unmoved, or the moved of the moved, or the moved of the unmoved, or the unmoved of the moved.

. . . Now the motionless will not be the cause to the motionless of its want of motion, nor the moved to the moved of its motion, because of their being indistinguishable. For when both are equally motionless, or both equally in motion, we shall no more say that this is the cause to that of its want of motion or its motion than that to this. For if the one, because it moves, is the cause of motion to the other, since the other also moves in like manner it will be said to be supplying motion to the first. Therefore, no cause exists. . . .

Furthermore, if anything is the cause of anything, either the simultaneous is the cause of the simultaneous, or the prior of the posterior, or the posterior of the

prior. . . . Now the simultaneous cannot be the cause
of the simultaneous owing to the coexistence of both
and the fact that this one is no more capable of gen-
erating that one than is that one of this one, since both
are equal in point of existence. Nor will the prior be
capable of producing that which comes into being later;
for if, when the cause exists, that whereof it is cause
is not yet existent, neither is the former any longer a
cause, as it has not that whereof it is the cause, nor is
the latter any longer an effect, since that whereof it is
the effect does not coexist with it. For each of these
is a relative thing, and relatives must necessarily coexist
with each other, instead of one preceding and the other
following. It only remains for us, then, to say that the
posterior is the cause of the prior; but this is a most
absurd notion, worthy of men who turn things topsy-
turvy. . . .

Moreover, if a cause exists it is the cause of something either wholly of itself and using only its own power,
or else it needs for the purpose the assistance of the
passive matter, so that the effect is conceived as due
to the combination of both jointly. . . . For just as the
cause cannot act without what is called the passive thing,
so also the so-called passive thing cannot be passive
without the presence of the cause. So it follows that
the power productive of the effect does not reside in
the cause any more than in the passive thing. Thus
(for our meaning will be made clear by an example) if
fire is the cause of burning, either it is productive of
burning by itself and using only its own power, or it
needs for this purpose the co-operation of the burning
material. And if it produces the burning by itself, being

sufficient of its own nature, then, since it always possesses its own nature, it ought to have been continually burning. But it does not burn always, but burns some things and does not burn others; therefore it does not burn by itself and by using its own nature. But if it does so in conjunction with the suitability of the burning wood, how can we assert that it, rather than the suitability of the wood, is the cause of the burning? . . .

Further, if the cause exists, it either has one efficient power or many; but it cannot have one, . . . since if it had one power it ought to affect all things alike and not in different ways. The sun, for instance, burns the regions about Ethiopia, but warms our regions, and only illumines the Hyperboreans; and it dries mud, but melts wax; and it whitens clothes, but blackens our complexion, and reddens certain fruits; and it is the cause of seeing to us, but of not seeing to the birds which feed by night, such as owls and bats. So that, if it had one power, it ought to produce the same effect in all cases; but it does not produce the same effect in all cases; therefore it has not one power. Nor yet has it many, since then it ought to operate with them all in every case—burn everything, for example, or fuse everything, or congeal everything. But if it neither has one power nor many, it will not be the cause of anything.

Yes, but the Dogmatists usually reply to this by saying that the effects produced by the same cause naturally vary owing to the materials affected and the distances, as in the case of the sun. . . .

Now those who make this reply grant us, almost without dispute, that what acts is not different from what is acted upon. For if the melting of the wax occurs not because of the sun but because of the property of the substance of the wax, it is plain that neither of them is the cause of the melting of the wax but the combination of both of them, the sun and the wax. . . . And thus it is absurd not to ascribe the effect produced by the conjunction of two things to those two, but to attribute it to one of them only.

Moreover, if there exists any cause of anything, either it is separate from the matter affected or it coexists with it. . . . Now when separated from its matter, obviously it is not a cause, since the matter with respect to which it is termed a cause is not present, nor is the matter affected, since that which affects it is not present with it. But if the one is coupled with the other, that one which is said to be the cause either acts only and is not acted upon, or both acts and is acted upon at once. And if it both acts and is acted upon, each of them will be both active and passive. . . . Therefore no cause of anything exists.

XXIII

PLOTINUS †

[205–270 A.D.]

THE SOUL

ARE [1] we all immortal? Or do we utterly perish?
Or, a third alternative, does part of us pass way into
dissolution and destruction while part—the real self—
is everlasting? These are questions which we might
naturally investigate and learn to answer, after the
following fashion.

Man, we might say, is not something simple, but has
within him a soul. He has also a body attached to him,
it may be as an instrument, it may be in some other
capacity. Let us then distinguish the soul from the
body and have a look at the nature and character of them
both. Evidently a body which is composite cannot in
reason be lasting. Moreover our senses perceive its
dissolution and disintegration and liability to corruption
of every sort, the reversion of its ingredients each to
its proper nature, the destruction of one part by another,
and their change and corruption into things other than

---

[1] Plotinus, *Enneads*, IV. 7, §1, 456 (C. p. 843; V. II. p. 120).
The chapters referred to are those of the Creuzer text. Where
it seemed advisable to do so page references to this text—abbreviated as C.—are added, and parallel references to the Volkmann
text in the Teubner series—abbreviated as V.

† Dr. B. A. G. Fuller has made the selection and the translation
the passages from Plotinus.

they were. This is particularly noticeable whenever the soul, which puts them in accord, is not present in a mass of matter. Then, too, though each thing in the process of generation becomes an individual, it is not an unit, since it can be resolved into form and matter. Hence even the simple bodies are compound. Again it is a fact that since whatever is corporeal has magnitude and can be divided and broken up into bits, it must for this reason also be subject to corruption.

It follows that if the body be a part of us, the whole of us is not immortal. And if it be an instrument, it must be given to us for a certain time as such. But the dominant part and the essential man himself would bear the same relation to the body as form to matter, or as a man to the instrument he uses.

In either case, however, the soul is the man's real self.

* * *

What [2] now is the nature of the soul? If the soul be corporeal, it can be wholly disintegrated, seeing that everything corporeal is, as we have said, composite. If it be not corporeal, but of another nature, we must investigate this, too, either after the old or after some other fashion. In the first place [if the soul be corporeal] we must inquire into what this body which they call the soul can be resolved. For since life is necessarily at hand in the soul, this body—which the soul is—must, if it consist of two or more bodies, have life innate in both or each, or one only, or none of these bodies. If life belongs to one of them this body would be the soul. But what kind of body would that be which was naturally animate? For fire, and water, and air, and earth are naturally inanimate, and whenever any one of

[2] Plotinus, *Enneads*, IV. 7, § 2.

them has soul present in it it has possessed itself of life
as of something imported from without. But, besides
fire, air, water, and earth there are no bodies. And
even such as believe that there are elements different
from those enumerated, call them bodies, not souls, and
ascribe no life to them.

If, however, no one of the bodies [which make up the
soul] is possessed of life, it is absurd to think that their
conjunction has created life. And if each of them is
animate, then one of them is sufficient for our purpose.
It is peculiarly impossible, however, that a combination of bodies should produce life or that intellect should
be produced by that which is without it. Moreover,
it is not maintained that life is produced by any random
commingling. There must be then a principle which is
directive and causes the mixture. But this would take
the place of the soul. In fine, there could be no composite, nor even any simple body in being were there not
soul in the universe, if indeed it be a seminal reason
entering into matter which makes a body, and a seminal
reason can come from nowhere except from soul. . . .

***

For [3] there could be no body were there no psychic
power existent, since the corporeal is in flux and its
nature in motion, and would be immediately destroyed
if there were nothing but the corporeal. This would be
true even if one gave the name "soul" to one of these
bodies, since this would fare like the others, seeing that
they would be of one matter. Or rather, there would
be no generation at all, but all things would remain mere
matter for the lack of anything to give them form.

[3] Plotinus, *Enneads*, IV. 7, § 3, 458 C (C. p. 847, l. 15 et seq.;
V. II. 122, l. 17 et seq.).

Perhaps, too, there would not be even any matter, and this world-all would be dissolved, if one trusted for its existence to the conjunction of the corporeal, and gave to this the place of soul, at any rate, so far as the name went, ascribing it to air and to spirits which are most dissoluble and without any unity of themselves. For, I ask you, in view of the divisibility of all corporeal things, will not the man who confides this universe to any one of them, thereby make it unintelligent and borne about at random? What ordering principle is there in animal spirits which owe their order to soul, or what reason or what intelligence? But if soul exists, then all these things are ministrant to her constitution of the world and of the individual living being, in that one power proceeding from another contributes to the whole. Were she, however, not present in things, they would have no being at all, let alone an orderly existence. . . .

∗

That [4] if the soul were corporeal there would be no sensation nor thought nor undertaking nor virtue nor anything beautiful is clear also from the following considerations: If one thing is to perceive another it must be one, and grasp everything in the same operation, even though the incoming perception be multiple and enter through several senses, or there be several qualities of one object, or through the oneness there appear a variety, as in the case of a face. For one operation does not perceive a nose, another the eyes, but the same operation perceives all things together. Moreover, if one sensation come through the eyes, another through the hearing,

---

[4] Plotinus, *Enneads,* IV. 7, § 6, 461 A (C. p. 353, l. 3 et seq.; V. II. 126, l. 11 et seq.).

there must be some one thing to which both come.
Otherwise, if they did not come both together to this
same something, how could one say that the perceptions
were different?   This something must be like a centre to
which the sensations from all sides penetrate like lines
converging from the circumference of a circle.   Such
then is the apperceptive faculty—a real unity. . . .

₊

We [5] may also see the same thing from the case of pain
and the sensation of pain.   Whenever a man says that
his finger hurts, the pain naturally has to do with his
finger, but the sensation of pain, it will of course be
agreed, has to do with the ruling faculty.   Although the
part hurt is different from it, the ruling faculty perceives the animal spirits and the whole soul suffers the
same pain.   Now how does this happen?   By transmission, it is said, in that first the animal spirits which
are connected with the finger suffer and hand on their
suffering to the next part in turn, and this to still
another, and so on till it reaches the ruling faculty.
Necessarily then, if the part hurt first feels, the sensation of the second part will be another sensation—in case,
I mean, sensation is by transmission,—and that of the
third still another.   In this way there will be many, indeed innumerable sensations of the one pain generated,
and finally the ruling faculty will feel them all, and its
own pain besides.   The truth is that on this theory each
one of these parts will not feel the pain in the finger, but
the part next the finger will feel that the palm of the
hand hurts, and the third that there is a pain somewhere
else higher up.

[5] Plotinus, *Enneads*, IV. 7, § 7, 462 A (C. p. 855, l. 9 et seq.;
V. II. 128, l. 3 et seq.).

So there will be many pains, and the ruling faculty will not perceive the pain in the finger but the pain in itself. Only of this last will it be conscious, and will pay no heed to the other pains, and will not understand that it is the finger which is hurting. A sensation then of pain in the finger cannot be generated by transmission, nor can any one part of the body—which is an extended mass—be aware of another's suffering, since in every extended object when one part is in one place the others are in other places. Hence, I say it is necessary to conceive the perceiving faculty as throughout identical with itself. But such a conception is not appropriate to body but to some other form of being.

***

That [6] thought also is impossible if the soul be a body of any sort is to be proved as follows. If sensation be the soul's perceiving sensible objects with the help of the body, then thought also cannot be comprehension through the instrumentality of the body, since in that case it will be the same as sensation. If then thought be comprehension of objects without the aid of the body, surely that which thinks has even a stronger claim to not being body. Again, if sensation be of sensible objects, thought is of intelligible objects. If our opponents will not grant this, they must at least grant that there are thoughts of some intelligible objects, and apprehensions of things which have no extension. But then how can that which has extension think that which has not, and with its divisible nature think the indivisible? Do you say, with some indivisible portion of itself? In that case, however, that which thinks will not be a body. For under these circumstances there

[6] Plotinus, *Enneads*, IV. 7, § 8.

will be no need of the whole for the contact of thought with its object, but a single part will suffice.

Moreover, if it be conceded that the most abstract thoughts are of things in every respect pure of the corporeal, what thinks, also, by virtue of being or becoming pure of the corporeal, attains knowledge of them. And if it be asserted that thoughts are of forms inhering in matter, then the thoughts of the forms are attained only by abstracting the bodies, and it is intellect which does the abstracting. There is, for instance, no residuum of flesh or of matter of any sort in the abstractions of a circle, a triangle, a line, or a point. The soul then, when at such work, must of necessity abstract herself from the body. It follows that she herself cannot be body. I think also that the beautiful and the right are not extended things, and that hence the thought of them cannot be extended. So, when these things meet her, she will receive them with the indivisible part of herself, and they will lie in her indivisible self. . . .

Again there is the question whether the soul grasp the maxims of virtue and other intelligible objects as things eternal, or virtue be generated and must needs perish again. But what destroys it, and whence does it spring? For this again would abide. Virtue then must belong to the eternal and abiding, as do geometrical entities. But if it belongs to the eternal and the abiding, it is not corporeal. And that in which it resides must also be incorporeal, and cannot be a body. For all corporeal nature abides not, but is in flux. . . . But if the soul be neither body nor any property of body but rather active and creative, and possessed of much, both in and of herself, she must be a separate essence from bodies. What kind of an essence then? Clearly she must be that which we call real essence. For the corporeal might all be called a *process*, but not an essence, seeing that it is in a process of generation and corruption and never for a moment really *is* anything, but by its participation in being is kept in existence to the degree that it does participate in it. . . .

$*^*_*$

There [7] is then another nature that of itself possesses all real being such as is neither generated nor destroyed. For all things else would pass away and never again come into existence, if this were destroyed, since this it is which preserves them and this universe, keeping them in existence and in order through the mediation of soul. . . .

$*^*_*$

That [8] the soul is akin to the diviner and eternal nature is made clear by the facts that she has been proven to be incorporeal, has neither form nor color, and is intangible. But there are other proofs as well. And since we are agreed that everything divine and possessed of real being enjoys a good and rational life, our next task is to start with our own soul and inquire what her nature is. Let us take then a soul—not one sunk in the body which has laid hold of irrational desires and emotions and received into herself other passions, but one which has sloughed these all off and has as little commerce as possible with the body. Such an one shows clearly that evil is a foreign accretion on the soul, and that in the purified soul everything that is best, wisdom and every other virtue, inheres and is native.

[7] Plotinus, *Enneads,* IV. 7, 463 A (C. p. 863, l. 13; V. II. 136, l. 12 et seq.).

[8] ID., § 14, 464 A (C. p. 865, l. 1; V. II. 137, l. 13 et seq.).

. . . But [9] in investigating the nature of anything one must regard it in its purity, since any accretion always stands in the way of knowing that to which it is super-added. Abstract then in investigating, or rather let him who abstracts look at himself, and he will be persuaded that he is immortal when he sees himself on the intelligible and pure plane. For he will see his intellect regarding not any sensible or mortal thing, but with its eternal self thinking the eternal, and all things which exist in the intelligible world. Nay, he will see his intellect itself become intelligible and luminous, resplendent with the truths proceeding from the good which illuminates intelligible objects with truth. . . .

**

Again [10] what sane man could raise a doubt as to the immortality of such a nature, possessed as it is of a self-originated life that cannot be destroyed? . . . For either its essence is life or else life is something super-added to matter. In the first case, this essence will be either self-animated—which is just what we are looking for and we agree is immortal—or may be analyzed as a compound and the process repeated till an imperishable self-moved element be reached which cannot be liable to death. In the second case, if our opponents say that life be a property superadded to matter, they will be forced to confess that the source of this property of life in matter must itself be immortal, since it cannot be subject to the opposite of what it imparts. There is then one nature whose characteristic activity is life.

[9] Plotinus, *Enneads*, IV. 7, 464 E.
[10] Ib., § 15, 465 (C. p. 867, l. 11 et seq.; V. II. 139, l. 10 et seq.).

Again,[11] if it be said that all soul is corruptible, then all things would have perished long ago. But if it be said that some soul perishes, other not, as for instance that the world-soul is immortal but our souls mortal, the reason for this distinction must be given. For both are principles of motion, both are self-animated, and both grasp the same objects with the same faculty, thinking both heavenly objects and those which transcend the heavens, and both seek all essential being and mount up to the first principle of all things. Also her ability to classify each thing of herself because of the notion innate within her—an ability produced by reminiscence of the intelligible—gives our soul an existence prior to the body, and since she is in enjoyment of eternal principles, shows that she herself is also eternal.

Finally, everything dissoluble has been produced by combination, and is dissolved after the same fashion in which it was combined. But the soul is single and simple, a nature whose characteristic activity consists in living. She cannot then be destroyed by dissolution. But, do you say, she might be destroyed by being divided and broken up? However, she has no mass or quantity, as has been shown. Or, do you say, by a process of alteration she might pass into corruption? Alteration, however, in destroying, though it takes away the form leaves the matter. It is a composite being then, which is liable to it. But if the soul cannot be destroyed after any of these fashions, she must necessarily be immortal. . . .

***

We [12] speak of the soul of each individual as one, because she is present in her entirety throughout the

[11] Plotinus, *Enneads*, IV. 7, § 16.
[12] Ib., IV. 9, § 1, 477 (C. p. 888; V. II. 153).

body, and is really one in that she does not have one part here, another there. In sensitive beings, too, the same is true of the sensitive soul, and in plants the whole soul is present throughout in every part. Now are my soul and your soul one, and all souls one in the same way? And in the universe is one soul present in all things, not divided as a thing which has mass is divided, but everywhere the same? For why should this soul of mine be one but the soul in the universe not one? There is no question there either of mass or body. Moreover, if your soul and mine proceed from the world-soul, and it is one, then ours should be one also. And if the world-soul and my soul are derived from one soul, then again they should be one. What sort of a soul would this one then be?

First, however, we must decide whether it be indeed correct to call all souls one, in the sense that the soul of a single individual is one. Now it involves a real absurdity if my soul and the soul of any other person are one. For in that case when I perceived, he too would have to perceive, and if I were good, would have to be good, and if I desired, would also have to desire. And in general we should share the same sensations with one another and with the universe, so that whenever I were affected in any wise, the universe would share in my sensation. Again, if all souls be one, how can the rational be different from the irrational soul, or the soul in animals different from that in plants? But on the other hand if we do not posit this unity, the universe will not be one, and no single source of souls will have been found.

**

In [13] the first place then, if my soul and the soul of another man be one, it will not follow that both are

[13] Plotinus, *Enneads*, IV. 9, § 2.

reciprocally identical. For although the same thing may
be present in both, it will not have the same properties
in the two cases. Thus humanity may be present in me
who am in motion, and in you who are not in motion.
In me humanity will be moved, in you at rest, and still
there is nothing absurd or paradoxical in the fact that
it is the same humanity which is in you and me. It is
not necessary, then, that when I perceive something,
another man should have exactly the same experience.
For that matter, too, given a single body, one hand does
not perceive what the other feels, but rather the soul
which resides in the whole body. And had you to know
my feelings our bodies would have to merge into one
another, and we two become a single individual. Thus
knitted together both souls would have identical perceptions.

We ought also to note the many things of which the
whole is unconscious, even in the case of one and the
same body. This is the more noticeable the bigger the
body is. For instance, there are huge sea-monsters in
which no perception whatever of anything experienced
by a part reaches the whole, because of the comparative
slightness of the motion excited. We may conclude that
no clearly defined experience need be received by the
whole organism when one particular part is affected.
But that it should be affected sympathetically, though
there is not necessarily any definite sensation, is not
absurd and cannot be denied. It will not be absurd then
that the same thing should be virtuous in me, vicious
in you, seeing that it can exist in one man in a state of
motion, in another at rest. For after all we do not call
the soul one in a sense which altogether excludes plurality.
Such unity is to be attributed to the nature which is

better than soul. Soul, on the contrary, we call one-
and-many, and say that it participates in the divisible
corporeal nature, and in the indivisible as well, so that
again it is one. And just as in my case, whatever is
generated by the ruling faculty communicates something
to the part, in spite of the fact that the affection of the
part does not prevail over the whole; so everything which
the universe communicates to the particular is quite
manifest because of our manifold sympathetic relations
with the universe, whereas we do not know for certain
whether our experiences are contributed to the world-
all or not. . . .

**

The [14] question now is, After what fashion is the one
essence in the many souls? For either the one essence
in them all is a sum total, or else the many are derived
from the whole and single essence without disturbing its
wholeness or unity. It, however, is one, and the many
souls are related to it as the one unity which gives itself
to the many, and at the same time does not give itself.
For it is able to give itself to all, and yet to remain one.
It can penetrate simultaneously all things, and not be
severed at all from any one of them. It is one and the
same thing in many.

There should be no difficulty about believing this. A
science exists as a whole, and is related to its parts
in such wise that its wholeness is not impaired by the
derivation of the parts from it. A seed also is a whole,
and the parts are derived from it into which it naturally
divides itself, and each of these is a whole, and remains
a whole.

But the whole is not diminished—it is matter which

[14] Plotinus, *Enneads*, IV. 9, § 5, 480 A (C. p. 894; V. II. 157).

divides it up—and all the parts are one. Perhaps, however, it will be said that in the case of a science the part is not the whole. It is true, to be sure, in this case, that the part which we are using is at hand and is emphasized. Still, the other parts also follow, latent and potential, and are all contained in the part in question. It is in this sense that one speaks of the whole science and of a part of it. But in the soul all the parts coexist in their actuality. In the case of a science, to revert, each part is ready to which you may wish to put your hand. The readiness for use lies in the part, but it gets its efficacy from its contiguity to the whole. One cannot regard it as empty of the other propositions. Were it, it would not hold either in practice or in theory, but would be mere child's prattle. If it holds theoretically, it is because it contains all the parts potentially. A thinker in thinking, I say, deduces the other parts by implication. A geometer in his analysis makes clear how the one part or proposition contains all the other propositions through which the analysis has proceeded, and also all the consequent propositions which follow from it. These things, however, gain no credence because of our weakness and because they are obscured by the body. But in the intelligible world each and every thing is plain.

THE INTELLECT

Why [15] now must we use the soul as a stepping-stone to something higher and not posit her as the first principle? In the first place because intellect is different from and better than soul, and what is better by nature comes first. Intellect is better, because soul does not as

[15] Plotinus, *Enneads*, V. 9, § 4, 557 E (C. p. 1030, l. 16; V. II. 251, l. 9)

some think generate the intellect of her perfection. For how can the possible become actual, unless there be a cause which makes it actual? Were the process of actualization a matter of chance, perhaps the possible might not become actual. Hence we must regard our first principle as in actual existence, wanting nothing, and perfect. And the imperfect we must regard as coming later and as perfected by what has produced it, just as parents bring to maturity offspring which they generated in the beginning imperfect. Soul, moreover, is matter in comparison with her first cause, and then is formed and perfected by it. Again since soul is passible, there must be some impassible principle—or else all things in time would be destroyed—and something, too, prior to soul. Finally, since soul is in the world, there must be some principle outside the world, and this, too, must be prior to soul. For if what exists in the world exists in the corporeal and material, nothing there will preserve its identity. Hence the idea of man and all the forms will be neither eternal nor self-identical. From these considerations as well as from many others, it may be seen that intellect must exist prior to soul. . . . *_**

Although [16] then the soul is the kind of thing which our discussion has shown her to be, still she is merely a sort of image of the intellect. In fact, just as a thought expressed in words is an image of the thought in the soul, so she is both the thought of the intellect and the entirety of its activity and the life which it sends forth to constitute a new form of being. An illustration of

[16] Plotinus, *Enneads*, V. 1, § 3, 484 B (C. p. 900, l. 4; V. II. 164, l. 19).

what I mean is fire which has both an inherent heat,
and a heat which it radiates. . . .

***

It [17] is the intellect then which makes the soul ever
more divine by its fatherhood and companionship. Nor
does anything separate them save the fact that they are
different, inasmuch as the soul is one lower in rank and
is the receptive principle, whereas the intellect is, as it
were, the form. Still even the matter of the intellect is
beautiful since it is intelligible and simple. And the
excellence of the intellect can be clearly estimated by
this superiority to soul, which is such as we have described.

***

We [18] should also see the excellence of the intellect, if
first admiring the phenomenal universe with an eye to its
grandeur and beauty, the orderliness of its eternal motion,
its gods both visible and invisible, its spirits, and all
its animals and plants, we should then rise to its far
truer and more real archetype, and should see how all
things there are intelligible and eternal of themselves
and dwell in native reason and live with uncorrupted
intellect at their head, and unspeakable wisdom and the
true life of Chronos which is the offspring of God and
the intellect. For the intellect comprehends everything
that is immortal, every intellect, every god, every soul,
in its eternal peace. Its peace, I say, for why should it
in its felicity seek change? And into what could it
change, seeing that it has all things of its own self. Nor
will the intellect seek to develop itself, since it is absolutely perfect. Hence everything that shares its

[17] Plotinus, *Enneads,* V. 1, § 3, 484 D (C. p. 901, l. 16; V. II.
165, l. 3).

[18] Ib., § 4.

existence is perfect, to the end that it may be perfect in every respect, possessed of nothing imperfect and nothing which is not the object of its thought.

Its thought, however, is not a search but a possession. Its felicity, too, is not acquired from without. Rather is it eternally all things, and is the true eternity of which time encircling the soul is an image—time which leaves the old things behind and lays hold of new. For, to speak still of time, now one thing now another revolves about the soul, now Socrates, and now a horse, and always some single thing. The intellect, on the other hand, is all things. It contains all things in itself at rest within itself. Only the present exists for it, and is present eternally, and for it there is nothing future, since the future is already present to it, and nothing past. Nothing, I say, is past, but all realities have remained at rest there from eternity, as though content with themselves as they are. Each of them is intellect and real existence, and the sum of them is all intellect and all real existence.

The intellect in the act of thought produces existence, and existence by being thought gives thought and existence to the intellect. Of both existence and thought, however, there is yet another cause. For they exist simultaneously and never desert one another. But though two, they together constitute that unity which is at once intellect and existence, thinking and the object thought. Intellect this unity is *qua* thinking, existence *qua* the object thought, for thinking could not arise were there not identity and difference. The first principles then are intellect, existence, difference, identity. The categories of motion and rest, however, must also be included, motion if there is to be thinking,

rest for the sake of identity. Difference must exist
that there may be thinking and an object of thought.
Take away the category of difference, and the unity
which arises from thinking and the object of thought
will be given its quietus. The ideas must also differ
from one another, and yet be the same in that each is self-
identical and all have a common element. Their difference is otherness. These principles by virtue of their
plurality generate number and quantity. Quality is
generated by the fact that each one of these principles
from which all else proceeds has its peculiar and proper
character. . . .

***

It [19] is necessary to understand then by intellect, if
we are to attach any true significance to the name, not
the potential intellect, or the intellectual knowledge
developed out of ignorance. Did we, we should have
to seek for yet another intellect prior to this. By
intellect we are to understand that which is intellect
in actu, and eternally. But if its thought be not imported from without, when it thinks anything it must
itself be the occasion of its thought, and when it is
possessed of any object be the occasion of that possession.
But if it be the occasion and source of its thought, it
will itself be the object of its thought. For were its
essence one thing, and the object of its thought another,
its essence would not be an intelligible object, and
would exist potentially, not actually. The one then is
not separable from the other, though it is our custom
drawn from our own experience to think of them as
separate.

[19] Plotinus, *Enneads*, V. 9, § 5, 558 C (C. p. 1031, l. 14; V. II.
251, l. 32).

What then is the object of the activity and thought of the intellect like, that we should regard the intellect as itself the object of its thought? Clearly the intellect, being real existence, must think and support the world of real existences (the ideas). It *is* then the real existences. It must think of these as existing either elsewhere than in itself, or in itself as its own nature. To think them as elsewhere than in itself is impossible. For where could they exist? It thinks them as constituting its own nature and existing in itself.

We come to this conclusion because the seat of the form is not the sensible object as some think. For in no case is the primary and fundamental the phenomenal. The form in sensible objects imposed upon matter is an image of real existence, and every form in objects comes from something without, refers thither, and is an image thereof.

Again, if there must needs be a maker of this universe, he will not think of what does not as yet exist, in order to create it. The forms of things then must exist prior to the world, not indeed as impressions struck from other things, but as archetypes and originals and the very essence of the intellect. If, however, some people talk of seminal reasons as sufficient, evidently they must be talking of the eternal reasons. But if the reasons are eternal and impassible, they must exist in an intellect, and in an intellect such that it is prior to conditioned existence, nature, and soul, seeing that these have a potential existence.

The intellect then is all real existences thought as not external to itself. They are neither prior nor subsequent to it, but it is, as it were, the primal lawgiver, or rather the law itself of existence. The saying then is correct

that thinking and existing are one and the same thing,
and that the knowledge of immaterial entities is the same
as the things themselves—also the saying "I sought myself" [as] one of the real existences; and the doctrine of
reminiscence is true too. For no real existence is outside
the intellect, or in space. Rather do they exist eternally
in themselves, subject neither to change nor destruction,
and for this reason are real existences. On the other
hand what is generated and destroyed enjoys existence
as something superadded. Not they, then, but what is
superadded, is real existence. Phenomena exist as defin-
able objects through participation, in that their substratum gets its form from without. Thus bronze receives its form from the art of casting statues, and
wood from that of carpentry, through the entrance into
them of images of the arts in question. At the same
time the arts themselves remain outside of matter in
their self-identity, and contain the true statue and the
true bed. This is also true of corporeal things. The
difference between images and real existences is shown
likewise by this universe which participates in images.
For in the intelligible world real existences are im-
mutable (whereas the things of this world are mutable),
and being without extension reside in themselves without
need of space, and have an intellectual and self-sufficient
kind of existence. But the nature of corporeal things
wants preservation by something outside itself, while the
intellect, which with its wonderful nature supports what
naturally tends to fall, itself seeks no support.

**

We [20] grant then that the intellect is real existence
and contains all the real existences in itself, not after a

[20] Plotinus, *Enneads*, V. 9, § 6.

spatial fashion, but as though they were its own self, and it were one with them. All things exist together there, and nevertheless are distinguished from one another. For the soul also is possessed of many notions at the same time, without confusing them. Each does its proper work at the proper time without involving the others. So, too, each thought has a pure activity drawn from the thoughts which lie within it. After this fashion, and to a far greater extent, the intelligible universe is all things together and yet not together inasmuch as each real existence is an individual and peculiar power. But the whole intellect includes them as a genus contains its species, or as a whole its parts. . . .

**

Whatever [21] appears in the phenomenal world as form is contained in the intelligible world, but what does not so appear has no place there. Hence there is nothing contrary to nature there, just as there is nothing contrary to art in the arts, nor for that matter lameness in the seed, seeing that lameness arises during growth from the failure of the seminal reason to overcome matter, and is a chance mutilation of form. In the intelligible world also are all harmonious qualities and quantities, numbers and magnitudes, conditions, actions and natural properties, motions and rests, both in whole and in part. In place of time there is eternity, and space there is represented by logical implication. . . . [22] Are then only phenomena represented in the intelligible world, or are still more things? First we must inquire about artificial objects. . . .

[21] Plotinus, *Enneads*, V. 9, § 10, 562 (C. p. 1038, l. 10 et seq.; V. II. 256, l. 21).
[22] Ib., 562 E.

As [23] regards then art and artificial objects. Such arts as are imitative like painting and sculpture, dancing and gesticulation, which take their rise in the phenomenal world, and make use of a sensible model and imitate forms and motions, and repeat the symmetries which they behold, could not properly be referred to the intelligible world except as included in the idea of man. But if from the symmetry in animals we be led to reflect upon some condition of living beings in general, our reflection would be part of the power of considering the intelligible world, and beholding the symmetry of all things therein. Every sort of music, too, which is occupied with the concepts of harmony and rhythm, would be in the same class as an art occupied with intelligible rhythm. Also such arts as fashion sensible objects like architecture and carpentry get their principles and some of their skill from the intelligible world. But inasmuch as they have mixed their principles up with the phenomenal, they do not reside wholly in the intelligible, but rather in man. Agriculture, however, which deals with sensible things like plants does not come from the intelligible, nor medicine which looks to earthly health, and busies itself with keeping people strong and in good condition. For in the intelligible world there is another kind of strength and health by virtue of which all living things are not subject to disturbance and are self-sufficient. Rhetoric and generalship, political economy and statesmanship, if they join beauty to their deeds and have the vision of it, get a portion of their wisdom from the wisdom on high. Geometry which deals with intelligible entities must be placed there, and also the highest wisdom which is occupied with real

[23] Plotinus, *Enneads*, V. 9, § 11, 563 A.

existence.   So much must suffice for the arts and artificial objects.

$*^*_*$

Are [24] there then also ideas of particular objects?
Let us see.   If I and every man can trace ourselves back
to the intelligible world, then each man has his separate
origin there.   And if Socrates and the soul of Socrates
are eternal, there will exist in the intelligible world a
Socrates in himself as it is called, in so far as the souls
of individuals are there.   But if what was formerly
Socrates becomes at another time another individual like
Pythagoras or some one else, then the particular idea
of Socrates no longer exists in the intelligible world.   Still
if the soul of the individual contain the seminal reasons
of all those through whom it passes, all will be represented
in the intelligible world.   For we say also that each soul
possesses all the seminal reasons that are in the world.
If now the world contains the seminal reasons not only
of man, but of particular animals, the soul will possess
them too.   There will then be an infinite number of
seminal reasons, unless indeed they be periodically
repeated in world-cycles, and in this way a limit set to
their infinity, as often as they are reëxemplified.

However, if generally speaking there are more particulars produced than there are patterns, why need there
be seminal reasons and patterns for everything produced
within a single world-cycle?   One archetypal man is
enough for many men, just as a definite number of souls
produce [in their reincarnations] an indefinite number of
human beings.   Still, different things have not the same
seminal reason, nor is a single man sufficient as a pattern
for men who differ from one another not only in point

[24] Plotinus, *Enneads*, V. 7, 1. 539 A (C. p. 995; V. II. 228).

of matter, but in countless specific points. For such men are not related as the pictures of Socrates are related to the original, but their differences have to be regarded as due to different reasons or ideas. A world-cycle, however, in its entirety contains all the seminal reasons. And then [in the next world-cycle] the same world is repeated after the same ideas. Infinity in the intelligible world is not to be feared. For its infinity is all contained in the indivisible, and proceeds from it, as it were, when the intelligible world exercises its proper activity. . . .

THE ONE

Everything [25] which exists, both primary existences and whatsoever is in any way spoken of as being, exists by virtue of its unity. For what would a thing be were it not one thing? Take away its unity and it is no longer what we define it to be. There is for instance no army except it be a unity, and no chorus or flock which is not one. Nor is there any house or ship which has not unity, since the house is a single thing, and likewise the ship. If this unity be lost, the house is no longer a house nor the ship a ship. Compound and extended bodies then could not exist, unless unity were present in them. And if cut up, so far as they lose their unity they change their existence. So too, the bodies of plants and animals which are each a unit, if in being broken up they escape from unity into plurality, destroy the essence which they had and are no longer what they were, but become something else, and this indeed only in so far as they are still units. Health also exists when the body is organized as a unit, and beauty when the nature of the one holds the parts together, and virtue in the

[25] Plotinus, *Enneads*, VI. 9, § 1, 757 A (C. p. 1385; V. II. 518).

soul when she is made a unit and unified in a single harmony. . . .

We must now see whether the unity and the being of the individual be the same, and existence in general identical with the One. But if the being of each individual is a plurality, and the one cannot be many, then they must be different. Now man is both an animal and a rational being, and has many parts which in their multiplicity are bound together in unity. Man then is one thing, unity another. Man is divisible, unity indivisible. Also existence in general, since it comprises within itself all the real existences, is multiple in nature, and different from unity, and by participation possesses and shares in unity. Real existence has both life and intellect—since it is no lifeless corpse. Hence it is multiple. And if the intellect be real existence, it must be multiple, and still more so, if it comprise the ideas. For the idea is not one but is rather a number of things— each individual idea as well as their sum total. They are one in the same sense as the universe is one. Generally speaking, too, unity is fundamental and primal, but the intellect, and the ideas, and real existence are not primal. Each idea is made up of many parts, is composite, and a consequent, inasmuch as what a thing is composed of is prior to it.

That intellect cannot be primal is also plain from the following considerations: The intellect necessarily is in thought, and since it regards what is both supremely good and at the same time not external to itself, the object of its thought is prior to itself. For in reverting to itself it reverts to its origin. Moreover, if it be both the thinking and the object of thought, it is dual, not simple, and is not the One. But if it regard another than itself, it will regard what is in every respect better than and prior to itself. If, however, it regard itself, it regards [*qua* thinking] what is better [*qua* object of its thought] than itself, and so is a secondary entity.

Now we must consider the intellect such that it communes with the good and the first of all things, and regards it, and also communes with itself and thinks itself, and thinks itself as the whole world of real existences. Its variety then falls far short of being unity. The One cannot be all things, since in that case it would be no longer One, nor can it be intellect since it would then be all things because the intellect is all things. Nor can it be existence, for existence is all things.

What now is the One? What is its nature? It is no wonder that we cannot easily say, in view of the fact that neither existence nor form is easily described. Yet our knowledge is based upon forms and concepts. But the more the soul proceeds into the formless, the more she becomes unable to comprehend it, because it is indefinable and lacks the impress of variety. Hence she wavers and begins to fear that she has laid hold of blank nothing, and tires at such a height and is glad to descend frequently and to fall back from everything till she has reached the phenomenal world. There she rests from her labors as if on firm ground once more. In the same way our sight when wearied with tiny things gladly falls upon large objects. On the other hand when the soul desires vision absolutely of and by itself, in this vision which comes through communion and union she does not believe that she has attained the object of her search through union with it, just because the object of her thought is not a different thing from herself.

We, however, who are going to make the One the

object of our philosophic meditation must needs do as follows. Since it is the One which we are searching for, and the source of all things, the good and the primal, which we are beholding, we must not depart from the neighborhood of things primal, nor sink to those which come last, but must strive rather to betake ourselves from them and their show of sense to the primal things. We must free ourselves from all vice, too, if we be eager for the good, and must rise to the principle hidden within ourselves, and throwing off our multiplicity become one, and be made that principle and a beholder of the One. We must become then intellect, and intrust our souls to our intellect, and establish them there, so that we may be conscious of what the intellect beholds, and through it enjoy the vision of the One. We must not add thereto any sense-experience, nor receive into our thought anything that comes from sense, but with the pure intellect, and the primal part of the intellect behold the Most Pure.

If now, when so prepared, we attribute in our imagination either extension or form or mass to this nature, it will not be intellect which guides our vision, because these properties are not naturally objects of intellectual vision, but rather of the activity of sense, and opinion which follows sense. We must rather get from the intellect views of what lies within its power. Now the intellect can behold either what is prior to itself, or its own nature, or what comes after it. Pure is its own nature, but still purer and simpler what are or rather is prior to it. This is not intellect but prior to intellect. For intellect is something which exists. But this other nature is not something, but is prior to everything. It is not an existence, for what exists has the form of existence, and it is formless, even without intelligible form. I say this, because the nature of the One being the creator of all things is itself no one of them. So it is not a thing, nor quality, nor quantity, nor intellect, nor soul, nor in motion, nor at rest, nor in space, nor in time, but is the absolutely "monoform," or rather formless, prior to all form, prior to motion, prior to rest. For these things pertain to existence, and it creates them in their multiplicity.

Why now, if it be not in motion is it not at rest? Because either or both of these properties pertain to being, and what is at rest is so by virtue of stability, and is not the same as stability. Hence stability is an attribute of it, and it is no longer simple. Also if we call the One a cause, we are not predicating something of it, but rather something of ourselves, inasmuch as we are receiving something from it while it exists in itself. Again, strictly speaking we cannot talk of the One as a "this," or a "that," but looking at it from without, may only wish to interpret the ways in which it affects us. Now we get nearer to it, now we fall farther short of it, because of the difficulties that hedge it about.

The greatest of these difficulties is that our apprehension of the One does not partake of the nature of either understanding or abstract thought as does our knowledge of other intelligible objects, but has the character of presentation higher than understanding. For understanding proceeds by concepts, and the concept is a multiple affair, and the soul misses the One when she falls into number and plurality. She must then pass beyond understanding, and nowhere emerge from her unity. She must, I say, withdraw from understanding and its objects and from every other thing, even the vision of beauty. For everything beautiful comes after it and is derived from it, as all daylight from the sun. It is for this reason that Plato says that the One is ineffable in spoken or written word. We speak and write of it, however, that we may despatch our spirits toward it, and rouse them from the contemplation of mere concepts to the vision of it, pointing out the way, as it were, to one eager for some sight. Instruction goes as far as showing the road and the way. But the vision is the work of him who has already willed to behold it. . . .

**

In [26] what sense now is the One one? And how is it to be grasped by our thought? I reply, it must be regarded as more one than monad or point. For with these latter entities the soul subtracts magnitude and numerical quantity and stops and rests at the smallest possible remainder—which is indivisible in truth, yet was contained in the divisible and is found in other things. The One, however, is found neither in other things, nor in the divisible, nor is it indivisible in the sense in which the smallest possible remainder is indivisible. It is the greatest of all things not in extension, but in power, and hence space and extension have nothing to do with its power. The real existences which come next to it in rank, are also indivisible and undivided in a dynamic not a spatial sense. We are to understand, too, that it is infinite not by virtue of being immeasurable in extension or number, but because its power cannot be comprehended or circumscribed. When you think of it as intellect or God, it is more. And when you unify

[26] Plotinus, *Enneads*, VI. 9, § 6, 763 E (C. p. 1397, l. 17; V. II. 515, l. 20).

it in your thought it is more—more even than you could imagine God himself to be, if you imagined him to be more one than your thought. For it exists in itself and has no attributes.

One would not be wrong perhaps in representing God's unity through the concept of self-sufficiency. For he must be the sufficient and self-sufficing, and free from wants of all things, whereas everything which is multiple and not one wants, since it has been made of many things, and its essence stands in need of unity. But the One does not stand in need of itself, since it is itself. Moreover, a thing which is multiple needs as many things as it is composed of. And all such things are subsequent to their components, and not self-existent, but need other things, and display this need both in their parts and as wholes.

If then there must be something which is absolutely self-sufficient, this must be the One, and must be so in this respect alone, namely, that it wants nothing in relation either to itself or to other things. The One seeks nothing in order that it may exist or be happy, nor yet anything to support it. Since it is the cause of all else, it owes its own existence to nothing else. For the same reason why should its happiness be an object external to itself? It follows that happiness is not an attribute of the One. The One is happiness. Furthermore, it is not to be found in space, seeing that it needs no space as if it were not able to support itself. What has spatial position is inanimate and is a falling mass if it be not placed in position. Things have position for the same reasons that they coexist, and each has the place to which it has been assigned. What needs, however, a place in space wants something.

Then too the source does not need the things which follow after it, and the source of all things has no need of any. For what wants, wants in the sense that it strives after its source. Again if the One needs anything, it is clearly seeking not to be One, and hence needs its own destruction *qua* One. Everything which wants, however, stands in need of well-being and preservation. It follows that for the One, nothing can be good, nor can it wish anything. It is rather super-good, a good not for itself but for other things, if any of them be able to attain it. Nor can the One be thinking, lest there be difference and motion in it. It is prior to motion and to thinking. For what shall it think? Itself? In that case before it thinks it will be ignorant, and what is self-sufficient will need thought in order to know itself. But it does not follow that because it does not know or think itself, it will be ignorant of itself. For ignorance has to do with an external object, as when one thing is ignorant of another. But the Only One will neither know anything, nor have anything to be ignorant of. Being One and united with itself it does not need to think of itself. You cannot even catch a glimpse of it by ascribing to it union with itself. Rather must you take away thinking and the act of being united, and thought of itself and of anything else. It must not be conceived as the thinker, but more after the fashion of mere thought, which does not think but is the cause of thinking in something else. The cause, however, is not the same as the caused, and the cause of all things is no one of them. It must not then be called the good which it gives to other things, but in some other sense the good above all other goods.

The [27] One is all things and yet no one of them. For
the origin of all things is itself, not they, yet all things are
in their origin inasmuch as they may all be traced back to
their source. It is better, perhaps, to say that in their
origin they exist not as present but as future things.
How then can they proceed from the One in its simplicity,
in whose self-identity there is no appearance of variety
or duality whatsoever? I reply, for the very reason that
none of them was in the One, are all of them derived
from it. Furthermore, in order that they may be real
existences, the One is not an existence, but the father of
existences. And the generation of existence is as it were
the first act of generation. Being perfect by reason of
neither seeking nor possessing nor needing anything,
the One overflows as it were, and what overflows forms
another hypostasis. . . . For [28] whenever anything else
comes to perfection we see that it procreates and, unwilling to remain in itself, creates another being. This is
true not only of beings which possess conscious purpose,
but also of things which develop without conscious
purpose. Indeed, even inanimate objects share themselves as far as may be. Thus fire heats and cold chills
and drugs have their appropriate effects upon other
things, and all things imitate their origins as they are
able with a view to their everlasting self-perpetuation
and goodness. How then should the most perfect and
primal good stay shut up in itself as if it were envious or
impotent? And it the power of all things! How could
it be the origin of anything? Something then must be
begotten of it, if any of the other hypostases which are

[27] Plotinus, *Enneads*, V. § 2, 493 (C. p. 918; V. II. 176).
[28] Ib., V. § 4, 517 (C. p. 958, l. 17; V. II. 203, 19).

derived from it are to exist. Necessarily, then, something comes from it. Also what begets all that comes after it must be most worthy of worship, and the hypostasis second to it better than any other created thing. . . .

***

If [29] now there be an hypostasis second to it, and it be unmoved itself, the second hypostasis must come into being without any inclination or will or motion of any sort on the part of the One. How is this accomplished and how are we to think of this second hypostasis that surrounds the abiding and changeless essence of the One? We are to think of it as a radiance proceeding from the One, and from the One abiding in its changelessness, just as the light about and surrounding the sun is eternally generated from it, without any change or motion in the solar substance. Indeed all things while they last necessarily give of their own power an hypostasis proceeding from their own essence, outside of and surrounding them, and attached to them—an image as it were of the archetypes which have brought it forth. Fire dispenses heat from itself, and snow does not keep its cold only within itself. But the best witnesses of this fact are sweet-smelling substances. For as long as they exist there goes forth something from them which surrounds them and is enjoyed by any one who happens to stand near. And everything on attaining perfection generates, and what is eternally perfect eternally generates the eternal; but what is generated is less than the generator. What now are we to say of the most perfect? Nothing comes from it but what is greatest after it. And the greatest after it and second in rank is the intellect. . . .

[29] Plotinus, *Enneads*, V. § 1, 487 (C. p. 906, l. 16; V. II. 168, l. 15).

We [30] say that the intellect is an image of the One.
But we must speak with more precision. In the first
place we call it an image because it is begotten of the
One, and preserves much of the nature of the One, and
is very like the One, as light is like the sun. But it is not
the One. How then does the One generate the intellect?
In this wise—through what is generated by it turning
back to behold it. This vision is the intellect. . . .
That [31] world of which the One is the possibility, the
intellect perceives, separating it as it were from its
possibility. Else it would not be intellect, since the
essence of intellect consists in a kind of awareness of its
possibilities and powers. It defines then through itself
its own being by virtue of the possibilities got from the
One. It is as it were a part of what comes from the One,
and gets its essence thence and is established by the One,
and perfected in essence from and of it. It sees that to
itself as to the divisible from the indivisible have come
life and thought and all things, and that the One is none
of them. . . . This [32] intellect so begotten is worthy
of being the purest intellect, and has no other source
than the first principle [the One]. In being begotten, it
generates everything else with it, all the beauty of the
ideas, all the intelligible goods. And it is filled with
everything it generates, and swallows them again, so to
speak, and contains them within itself lest they fall into
matter. . . .

*_**

Now [33] the intellect being like the One follows the
example of the One and pours forth a mighty power.
This power is a particular form of itself, as was the case

[30] Plotinus, *Enneads*, V. § 1 488 A. [31] Ib., 488 B. [32] Ib., 489 A.
[33] Ib., V. § 2, 494 (C. p. 919, l. 9; V. II. 176, l. 18).

with that which the principle prior to intellect poured forth. And this activity proceeding from essence is soul, begotten without change or motion in the intellect—for intellect was begotten without change or motion in the principle prior to it. But the soul does not create, abiding in her changelessness, but in change and motion she generates an image. Looking to the source of her existence, she is filled with intellect, but when she proceeds to other and opposite motions then she generates an image of herself, sensation and the nature in plants. But none of these things is removed or cut off from what is prior to it. . . . **

There [34] is then a procession from the origin of all things to the last and least of them, and each is left in its appropriate position. What is begotten holds another and lower place than what begets, yet each thing remains identified with that which it follows, as long as it seeks after it.

[34] Plotinus, *Enneads*, V. § 2, 494 A.

XXIV

PLOTINUS—*Continued*

MATTER

IF [1] now the world of real existences and what transcends real existence is such as we have described, no
evil can inhere either in real existence or in the transcendent One. For they are good. If then evil exist,
there remains for it the sphere of not-being, and it is as it
were a certain form of not-being, and is concerned with
things mixed with not-being or having some commerce
with it. By not-being I do not mean absolute non-
existence, but only what is different from real existence.
Nor do I mean not-being in the sense that motion and
rest which are attributes of being are not being, but
rather in the sense of an image of real existence, or of
something which has even less existence than an image.

What I am alluding to is the phenomenal universe and
all the affections of the sensible world. Or it may be it
is either something which follows upon the phenomenal,
and is as it were a property thereof, or else is its origin
or some one of the things which go to make up the sensible world, such as it is. And one might come to think
of it as lack of measure with respect to measure, and
as infinity with respect to finitude, and formless with
respect to the formative, and eternally wanting with
respect to the self-sufficient, as indeterminate, never

[1] Plotinus, *Enneads*, I. 8, § 3, 73 D (C. p. 139; V. I 101).

at rest, subject to every affection, insatiate, poverty absolute. These characteristics are not properties of it but its essence, and whatever part of evil you may see you will find has them all.

Now whatever else participates in it and is assimilated to it becomes bad, yet is not the principle of evil. What then is the hypostasis in which evil is present not as something extraneous but as the hypostasis itself? For were evil an attribute of something else, there must needs be something prior to it, even if it be not an essence of some sort. Just as there is good the principle, and good the predicate, so there is also evil which exists as a principle, and evil predicated according to this principle of some other subject. But, do you say, what is measuredness if it does not consist in being measured, what measure if it does not lie in the measured? I reply that just as there is measure beside what is measured, so there is unmeasuredness which is not merely in the thing unmeasured. For did it exist in some other subject, it must exist either in the unmeasured—which is impossible since it has no need of unmeasuredness, being itself unmeasured—or in the measured, which is impossible since the measured cannot possess unmeasuredness in so far as it is measured. Hence there must be something infinite in itself, and formless in itself and everything else aforesaid which characterized the nature of evil. And if anything else be evil, it either has evil by admixture, or by regarding it, or by performing it. That, then, which underlies figures and forms and structures and measures and bounds, and is adorned with an orderliness foreign to it, having nothing good of itself, and being a mere phantom as compared with the soul, the very essence of evil, if evil can have an essence—that, I say, is discovered by our discourse to be the primal and the absolute evil. . . .

*_**

We [2] must now consider the meaning of the saying that evil cannot be destroyed but exists of necessity, and that it does not exist among the gods, but ever hovers about this mortal nature of "this place." The meaning is that the heaven is pure of evil, and goes with a regular and orderly motion, and that there is no unrighteousness there, nor other vice, nor injury of one part by another in their appointed courses; whereas on earth there is unrighteousness and disorder. This is what Plato means by mortal nature, and the phrase "this place." And the duty of fleeing hence is not to be taken locally as referring to earthly places. Our flight, he says, does not lie in going away from the earth, but in living on earth in righteousness and holiness and sweet reasonableness, which is as much as to say that we must flee from vice. It is vice then and its consequences that he means by evil.

But when Theodorus in the dialogue answers that evil could be removed if only men could be persuaded of the truth of this opinion, Socrates answers that this could not possibly happen, since evil exists of necessity, seeing that there must be some opposite to the good. . . . But [3] in what sense does it follow that if good exists evil also will exist? In this, I say, that there has to be matter in the universe. For this universe is necessarily composed of opposites, and could not exist were there no matter. The nature of the universe is mixed, as Plato says, of reason and necessity. And whatever comes to it from

[2] Plotinus, *Enneads*, I. 8, 75 G (C. p. 144, l. 6; V. I. 104, l. 29).
[3] Ib., § 7, 77 B (C. p. 147, l. 6; V. I. 106, l. 31).

God is good, but the evil comes from the primeval nature, by which he means the underlying matter as yet unbeautified by form. . . . From [4] what has been said then we can now understand the necessity of evil. Since the good is not solitary, there must necessarily result from the emanation or, if one prefer, from the degeneration and departure from the good, something ultimate and last, beyond and after which nothing more can be generated. This ultimate and last thing is evil. That something should follow from the first principle is necessary, hence this last thing is necessary. And this is matter which has no remainder of the good and the first in it. Hence the necessity of evil.

***

That [5] there must be some substratum in bodies different from the bodies themselves is evidenced by the conversion of the elements into one another. For the destruction of what is converted is not complete since, if it were, a substance would be put out of existence. Nor does what is generated come into being from absolute not-being. There is rather a change of form from one form to another. In change that remains changeless which receives the form of what it becomes, and puts off the form of what it previously was. Destruction shows this plainly, for it pertains to compound objects. If this be true, everything is composed of matter and form. Induction bears witness also, in showing that what is destroyed is compound, also analysis. For example if a cup can be dissolved into gold, and gold into water, analogy demands also that the water be dissoluble. The elements then must be either form or primitive mat-

[4] Plotinus, *Enneads*, I. § 7, 77 E.
[5] Ib., II. 4, § 6, 162 C (C. 288, l. 3; V. I. 154, l. 30).

ter or a composite of matter and form. It is impossible,
however, that they should be form, for how could they
have magnitude and extension without having matter?
But they cannot be primitive matter, seeing that they
are destroyed. They are then a composite of matter
and form, form in respect to quality and structure,
matter in respect to a substratum which is indeterminate
because it has no form.

What then is this substratum which we say is one and
continuous and without quality like? That it cannot be
corporeal if it is without quality is plain enough. If we
say that it is the matter of all sensible objects—I don't
mean the matter of some, and form in relation to others
as clay is matter for the potter yet absolutely speaking
not matter, but I do mean matter in relation to everything—we ought not to attach to its nature any property
perceived in sensible objects. In that case, in addition
to qualities like colors and heat and cold, we ought not
to attribute to it lightness or heaviness or density or
rarity or structure and hence not even extension. For
extension is one thing, that which is given extension
another, structure one thing, that which is given structure
another. It must also not be compound but simple and
one in nature. For in this wise is it empty of all attributes.

And what gives it form will give it a form which is
different from and independent of matter, bringing extension and everything else to it from the realm of real
existences. Otherwise the formative principle would be
conditioned by the extent of matter on hand, and would
do not as it wishes but as matter wishes. That its will
should coincide with the extent of matter is an absurd
supposition. But if the formative principle be prior to

matter then matter will be entirely such as the principle wishes and will be easily cast into all sorts of forms, and hence into extension. But if it had extension it would also possess a structure, and hence would be more intractable. Form then enters into it and brings everything to it. The form possesses everything, even extension and everything else which is contained in the seminal reason and exists through its agency. It follows from this that in the case of particular kinds of things their quantity is determined along with their form. For the quantity of a man is different from that of birds, and of this or that bird. It is no more remarkable that quantity should bring a new property to matter than that quality should. Nor could quality be a seminal reason, and quantity, which is measure and number, not a form. . . .

***

If,[6] however, the substratum were some quality which all the elements had in common, we should have in the first place to say what that quality was, and then to show how a quality could be a substratum, and how quality could be seen in the unextended with neither matter nor extension to it; and yet again, how if quality be determinate it can be matter. On the other hand were it something indeterminate it would not be quality but substratum and the matter which we are looking for. But one may object at this point—granted that matter has no qualities in that its nature is to partake of none, what is still to prevent its being qualified by just this fact, that it partakes of none, and to hinder it from possessing a property in all respects peculiar to itself, and

• Plotinus, *Enneads*, II. 4, § 13, 167 B (C. p. 298, l. 14; V. I. 162, l. 8).

from differing from all other qualities in this very point
of being an absence or privation of every quality? One
who has been deprived of any quality is qualified by his
privation, as for example a blind man. If then an
absence or privation of qualities be attributed to matter why is it not qualified thereby? And if absolute
privation be ascribed to it why is it not even more
qualified? That is, of course, if privation be a kind of
quality.

If, however, a man argue thus, what is he doing but
turning everything into qualifications and qualities?
Quantity then would be a quality, and essence. But if
a thing be qualified, quality is added to it. It is, however, absurd to make a qualified thing of what is different
from the qualified and is not qualified. Or do you say
that it is qualified by the fact of this difference? But if
you mean that matter is sheer absolute difference then it
cannot be qualified, since simple quality is not itself a
qualified thing. If you mean, on the contrary, that
matter is merely different from other things, then it is
merely different, not of its own nature but by virtue of
difference, and the same by virtue of sameness. Privation then is not quality or a qualified thing, but is a want
of quality or of anything else, just as silence is a want of
sound or of anything else you please. For privation is
negation, and the qualified is found in the sphere of the
positive. The peculiar property of matter is not form,
but rather not being qualified and not having any form.
It is absurd to say that what is not qualified is qualified.
That is like saying that a thing has not extension for
the very reason that it has.

Moreover this peculiar property of matter is not something different from the essence of matter and is not

added to it, but lies rather in the relation matter bears to other things, to wit, that it is something different from them. Other things, however, are not merely "other," but each has an individual form. Matter, on the contrary, ought properly to be called merely "an other," or perhaps "other" in the plural, so that you may not determine it by using the singular, but by the use of the plural indicate its indeterminate character. . . .

***

But [7] if matter be without quality how can it be evil? I reply that it is defined as without quality in the sense that it possesses itself none of those qualities of which it is receptive and which inhere in it as a substratum, but not in the sense that it has no nature. If, however, it have a certain nature, what prevents this nature's being evil? I do not mean evil, as qualified thereby. For quality is that by predication of which something else is qualified. It is then an attribute and is located in a subject other than itself. But matter is not located in a subject different from itself, but is the substratum of which all attributes are predicated. Since then every quality is by nature a predicate, and matter happens to have no predicates, matter is said to be without quality. Again if quality is itself unqualified, how could matter which has received no qualities be called qualified?

It is correct then to speak of matter both as having no qualities, and as being evil. For it is not called evil because it has qualities but rather because it has not, lest otherwise it were evil from being form, and not from being the nature opposite to form.

[7] Plotinus, *Enneads*, I. 8, § 10, 79 C (C. p. 152; V. I. 110, l. 8).

Finally [8] how are we to have knowledge of the unextended in matter? And how are we to know anything that has no qualities? And what must be the concept thereof, and the starting-point for our reflection? I say, indeterminateness. For if like is known by like, then the indeterminate is known by the indeterminate. There might indeed be a definite concept of the indeterminate, but the point from which we must start toward it is indeterminate. And if each thing be known by means of conception and thought, and here the concept tells what it ought to tell about matter, and still the thought which we desire is not a thought but rather the absence thereof, then our representation of matter would be rather a bastard and illegitimate concept, born of the untrue principle of the Other, and mixed with it. Perhaps it is with this in his mind's eye that Plato talks of matter as apprehended by a bastard concept.

What, however, is the indeterminateness of the soul? Is it a complete ignorance like an absence of all knowledge? No, the indeterminate has a kind of positiveness, and just as for the eye darkness is the matter of all invisible colors, so the soul when she takes away everything from sensible objects as one might take away light, and is left with something which it is no longer possible to define, becomes like the eye in the dark, and finally is in a sense identified with what she sees. What then does she see? Something like formlessness and want of color and absence of light, and also lack of extension. Otherwise this something will present itself in some form or other. But when she sees nothing is she not affected in

[8] Plotinus, *Enneads*, II. 4, § 10, 164 D (C. p. 292, l. 14; V. I. 158, l. 4).

the same way?   Not at all.   For when she sees nothing,
she reports nothing, or rather she is not affected at all.
But when she sees matter she is affected as it were by an
impression of the formless.   And when she thinks of
what has form and extension, she thinks of something
compound, as colored and as concretely determined.
She thinks of the whole, and thinks of it as all belonging
together, and her thought or perception of its properties
is clear.   But her thought of the formless substratum
underlying them is obscure, and obscure is the nature of
the formless substratum underlying them, for it is without form.   There is then a residuum in the whole and
compound object which is comprehended along with the
properties, and is left by reason in its analysis and abstraction of the properties.   And this the soul thinks
obscurely as an obscure thing, and darkly as a dark
thing, and thinks it by not thinking.   But since matter
itself does not remain formless but has been given form
in concrete things, the soul also immediately adds the
form of concrete things to it, being pained by the indeterminate as if afraid of being beyond the pale of real existence, and not suffering herself to stop long in the realm
of not-being.

SIN AND SALVATION

The [9] soul is not essentially vicious, and again every
soul is not vicious.   What then is a vicious soul?   She,
says Plato, who has become the slave of a man whose
nature engenders evil in her through the reception of
evil and lack of measure and superfluity and deficiency on
the part of her irrational form.   From these characteristics wantonness and cowardice and the rest of the soul's

[9] Plotinus, *Enneads*, I. 8, § 4, 740 (C. p. 141, l. 3; V. I. 102, l. 22).

vices arise, as involuntary affections provocative of false opinions and estimations of the good and evil which she shuns and pursues. What, however, is it that is responsible for this viciousness, and after what fashion are we to refer vice to an origin and cause?

I reply that in the first place the vicious soul is not outside of matter and is not wholly herself. She is mixed with disproportion, and is without part in the form which brings order and induces proportion. For she is mingled with the body which is material. In the second place, if her reasoning faculty be damaged, her vision is hindered both by her affections, and by being darkened by matter and inclined toward matter, and in general by her looking not toward existence but toward generation. And of transition and generation the nature of matter is the source, a nature so evil that the soul which even looks toward it, though it be not yet in it, is filled with evil. For since matter is wholly without part in the good and is the privation thereof, and pure lack, it makes like to itself everything whatsoever which touches it.

The soul, however, which is perfect and ever inclined to the intellect is ever pure and turned from matter, and neither sees nor approaches anything which is indeterminate, or without measure, or evil. She remains then pure, absolutely determined as she is by the intellect. But if she does not remain so, but goes forth from herself, then she is on an imperfect and secondary plane of existence, and is a mere shadow of her former self because of her failure in so far as she has failed, and is filled with disproportionateness and sees darkness. At this point she already has hold of matter, seeing what she does not see, just as we talk about "seeing the dark."

Now [10] often I am roused from the body to my true self, and emerge from all else and enter myself, and behold a marvellous beauty, and am particularly persuaded at the time that I belong to a better sphere, and live a supremely good life, and become identical with the godhead, and fast fixed therein attain its divine activity, having reached a plane above the whole intelligible realm; and then after this sojourn in the godhead I descend from the intelligible world to the plane of discursive thought. And after I have descended I am at a loss to know how it is that I have done so, and how my soul has entered into my body, in view of the fact that she really is as her inmost nature was revealed, and yet is in the body. . . .

**

In [11] seeking to learn Plato's teaching concerning our souls, we are forced to inquire in addition into the question of soul in general, and ask how it comes in the nature of things to have commerce with the body. Also we ought to consider the nature of the universe in which the soul lives. . . . The [12] body of the world, we find, is complete and sufficient and self-sufficing, and has nothing in it contrary to nature. Hence it needs but slight ordering, and its soul is eternally as she wishes herself to be, and is without desires or affections. Nothing is absent from her, and nothing is added to her. So it is that Plato says that our soul when in the companionship of that perfect world-soul becomes perfect herself, lives on high and directs the whole universe. Did she not separate herself therefrom and enter into bodies and become the

[10] Plotinus, *Enneads,* IV. 8, § 1, 468 (C. p. 872; V. II. l. 142).
[11] Ib., § 2, 470.
[12] Ib., 470 C.

soul of some particular body, she herself like and with the world-soul would easily govern the universe. It is not then under all circumstances an evil thing for the soul to provide the possibility of existence and well-being to a body. For not all providential care of things inferior deprives him who exercises it of living on the best and highest level. . . .

***

There [13] are two ways in which the commerce of the soul with bodies may cause trouble. In the first place it may be a hindrance to thought, and secondly it may fill the soul full of pleasures and desires and griefs. Still neither of these contingencies should occur in the case of a soul that has not sunk into the interior of the body, nor is the soul of a particular body nor has come to belong to one—a case where rather the body belongs to the soul, and is such as to have no want or deficiency, and hence as not to fill the soul with desires or fears. For nothing to fear occurs to her in connection with such a body, nor does any want of leisure make her incline downward and lead her away from the better and beatific vision. On the contrary the soul of such a body is ever in the higher regions ordering the world with a power free from all care.

***

Now,[14] individual souls which are endowed on the one hand with inclination toward the intellect, turning as they do to that which generates them, and on the other possess a power which reaches even to this terrestrial sphere, just as light both depends on the sun above and yet does not grudge giving itself to the world

[13] Plotinus, *Enneads*, IV. 8, § 2, 471 A.
[14] Ib., 472 A, § 4.

below; individual souls, I say, are without sin so long as they remain with the world-soul in the intelligible world, and in heaven rule things in her company. Like kings associated with the ruler of all things they reign jointly with her without descending from their royal thrones. And they are co-regents with her because they are conjoined with her in the same royal state. But if they alter their mode of existence and change from the whole to the part, and take to existing independently and of themselves, and find, so to speak, their association with the world-soul irksome, they revert each to an independent existence. When they have done this for some time, and have deserted the world-soul and estranged themselves from her through their separation, and no longer regard the intelligible universe, then each becomes a part and is isolated and weakened and busied with many things, and regards the part instead of the whole. And then when each through her separation from the whole has lighted upon some one particular part, and has deserted everything else, and turned to and entered into that one part which is subject to the impact and influence of other things, her apostasy from the whole is accomplished, and she directs the individual surrounded as he is by an environment, and is already in contact and concerned with external things, and lives in their presence and has sunk deep into them. Then it is that she is aptly said to have lost her wings and to lie in the bonds of the body—erring as she is from her life of innocence passed in governing the higher world at the side of the world-soul. This prior state is altogether better if she will but return thither, but as it is, she is fallen and fettered, and inasmuch as she exercises her activities through the medium of sense, because prevented in the beginning from exercising them through the intellect, Plato talks of her as buried and in a dark cave.

But her return to pure thought when through her recollection of her former state she gets a point of departure toward the vision of real existence is called a loosening of her bonds and an ascent to the upper world. For despite her fall the soul has always a higher part.

***

The [15] soul then has naturally a love of God and desires to be united with him with the love which a virgin bears to a noble father. But when she has betaken herself to creation, deceived as it were in her nuptials, she exchanges her former love for mortal love, and is bereft of her father and becomes wanton. Still if she begin again to hate the wantonness of earth, she is purified and turns once more to her father and all is well with her. Those to whom this heavenly love is unknown may get some conception of it from earthly love, and what joy it is to obtain possession of what one loves most. Let him then reflect that these objects of his love are mortal and perishable, mere shadows for his love to feed upon, and soon turned to loathly things, because they are not the true beloved, nor our good, nor what we seek; whereas in the higher world we find the true beloved with whom it is possible for us to unite ourselves when we have seized and held it, because it is not clothed with flesh and blood.

He who has beheld this beloved knows the truth of what I say, how the soul then receives a new life when she has gone forth to it, and come to it and participated in it, so that in her new condition she knows that the

[15] Plotinus, *Enneads*, VI. 9, 768 C (C. p. 1406, l. 10: V. II. 521, l. 20).

giver of true life is beside her, and that she needs nothing else. Such an one knows also, however, that we must put all else away, and abide in the beloved alone, and become only it, stripping off all else that wraps us about; and hence that we must hasten to come forth from the things of this world, and be wroth at the bonds which bind us to them, to the end that we may embrace the beloved with all our soul, and have no part of us left with which we do not touch God. It is possible for us even while here in the body to behold both him and ourselves in such wise as it is lawful for us to see. Ourselves we see illumined, full of the light of the intelligible, or rather as that very light itself, pure, without heaviness, upward rising. Verily we see ourselves as made, nay, as being God himself. Then it is that we are kindled. But when we again sink to earth, we are, as it were, put out.

⁎

But [16] why then do we not remain in the vision? I reply, because we have never wholly come forth from our earthly selves. But there shall come a time for us when the vision will be unbroken, and we are no longer disturbed by any unrest of the body. It is not the faculty of vision which is disturbed but some other, when the seer leaves the vision unaccomplished, but deserts not the knowledge which lies in demonstration and belief and the dialectical operation of the soul. The seer and his seeing, however, are no longer reason and reasoning, but superior to reason and prior to reason and extraneous to reason, even as is the object of the vision.

Now whosoever beholds himself, when he beholds his real self will see it as such a being, or rather he will be

16 Plotinus, *Enneads*, VI. 9, § 10.

united with such a being, and feel himself to have become such as is wholly simple. Indeed we ought perhaps hardly to say "he will see himself." Nor should we speak of an object of his vision, if we have to mean thereby a duality of the seer and the seen and do not identify the two as one. It is a bold thing to say, but in the vision a man neither sees, nor if he sees, distinguishes what he sees from himself nor fancies that there are two—the seer and the seen. On the contrary it is by becoming as it were another than himself, and by neither being himself nor belonging to himself that he attains the vision. And having surrendered himself to it he is one with it, as the centre of two circles might coincide. For these centres when they coincide become one, and when the circles are separated there are two centres again. And it is in this sense that we too speak of a difference. It follows that the vision is hard to describe. For how could a man report as something different from himself, what at the time of his vision he did not see as different but as one with himself?

This is clearly the intent of that injunction of the mysteries which forbids communication of their secret to the uninitiated. Since it was not communicable it was forbidden to explain the divine secret to any one to whom it had not been vouchsafed to see it of himself. Now since in the vision there were not two, but the seer was made one with the seen, not as with something seen, but as with something made one with himself, he who had been united with it might, if he remembered, have by him some faint image of the divine. He himself was one, with no distinctions within himself either as regarded himself or outer things. There was no movement of any sort in him, nor was emotion or desire of any outer thing present in him after his ascent, no, not any reason or any thought, nor was he himself present to himself, if I may so express it; but as rapt and inspired he rested isolated in his unmoved and untroubled essence, inclining nowhere and not even reflecting upon himself, at rest in all respects, yea, as if he had become rest itself. Nor did he concern himself with the beautiful, but had passed beyond beauty and had transcended the series of virtues as one might penetrate into the interior of the holy of holies, leaving behind in the temple the statues of the gods. And these he would not see again till he came out after having had the vision of what lay within and communion there with what was no statue or image but the divine itself—of which the statues were but secondary images. And perhaps his experience was not a vision but some other kind of seeing, ecstasy and simplification and self-surrender, a yearning to touch and a rest and a thought centred upon being merged in the divine. Perhaps this was his experience if he beheld anything in the holy of holies. Did he look elsewhere, there was nothing there.

These are mere figures and only hint to the wise among the prophets of the manner in which that God of whom we spoke is beheld. But the wise priest who reads the riddle aright may when he has entered the sanctuary enjoy the vision there; and even if he has not entered, yet because he has believed the sanctuary to be something invisible and has regarded it as a fountain and a source, he will yet know it as the source of all things, and behold it as such, and be merged with it, by like perceiving like, and will miss no divine thing which the soul is capable of attaining. And before the vision comes, he begs for the remnant and remainder of the vision. But for him who has transcended all things there remains that which is prior to all things.

All that I have said is true, for the nature of the soul never reaches absolute non-existence, but in her descent reaches evil, and in this sense non-existence, but not complete non-existence. And in pursuing the opposite course she reaches no outer object, but herself, and hence she does not dwell in nothing because she is in no outer object, but in herself. But to be in herself and not in existence is to be in God. For a man himself becomes not an essence, but superessential in so far as he clings fast to God. When now he sees that he has transcended essence he is himself an image of God. And when he proceeds out of himself turning from a copy into the original he has reached the goal of his journey. Does he at time fall from the vision, then virtue is aroused within him, and beholding himself adorned in every way, he is again lifted up by the help of virtue to the intelligible world, and thence proceeds through the aid of wisdom back to God. So it is that the life of the gods and of godlike and blessed men is a liberation from the things of earth, a life that takes no joy in them, a flight of the soul isolated from all that exists to the isolation of God.

INDEX OF NAMES

INDEX OF NAMES

Ænesidemus, 340, 342, 343, 347, 364, 365.
Agrippa, 347.
Alcmæon, 37.
Anaxagoras, 4, 48, **49,** 97, 118, 229, 244.
Anaximander, **3.**
Anaximenes, **7.**
Antigonus of Carystus, 340.
Antipater of Tarsus, 272.
Antipho, 95.
Antisthenes, **145.**
Apollodorus, 272, 275.
Arcesilaus, 351, 352.
Archedemus, 274.
Aristippus, 91, **142.**
Aristotle, 4, 86, **217–268.**
Ascanius of Abdera, 340.

Boëthus, 272.

Carneades, 353–357.
Chrysippus, 269, 271, 272, 274, 275, 276, 277, **278.**
Cleanthes, 269, 273, 274, 276, **277.**

Democritus, 48, 58, **59,** 315, 341.
Diogenes, 143, **147,** 274.

Empedocles, **43,** 48, 229, 247.
Epictetus, **317,** 330.
Epicurus, 143, 144, 281, **290–305,** 315, 329.
Euthydemus, 94.
Evenus, 108.

Gorgias, **67,** 85, 108.

Hecatæus, 30.
Hecaton, 273.
Heraclitus, **28–35.**
Hippias, 74, 75, 108.

Leucippus, **57,** 65, 228, 229.
Lucretius, **305–316.**

Marcus Aurelius, **326–339.**
Melissus, 21.
Meno, 85, 101.

Parmenides, **11,** 21, 57, 170 *et seq.*
Persæus, 275.
Phædrus, 149.
Philo of Athens, 341.
Plato, 129, 135, **148–216,** 228, 229, 398, 407, 413, 414, 416, 419.
Plotinus, **370–424.**
Plutarch, 278.
Posidonius, 273.
Prodicus, 74, 76, 108.
Protagoras, **67,** 68, 78.
Pyrrho, 340 *et seq.*
Pythagoras, 30, 35, 36, 149, 284, 362.

Sextus Empiricus, 343.
Socrates, 1, **86–141,** 284, 317, 322, 323, 324, 386, 392, 393.
Speusippus, 284.

Thales, **1.**
Theætetus, **78.**
Theognis, 267.
Timæus, 160.
Timon, 340, 342.

Xenocrates, 284.
Xenophanes, **8,** 20, 21, 30, 57.
Xenophon, 86.

Zeno of Citium, 269, 273, 275, 284, 322.
Zeno of Elea, **22,** 168.